EQUAL TREATMENT OF RELIGION
IN A PLURALISTIC SOCIETY

Equal Treatment of Religion in a Pluralistic Society

Edited by

Stephen V. Monsma
and
J. Christopher Soper

WILLIAM B. EERDMANS PUBLISHING COMPANY
GRAND RAPIDS, MICHIGAN / CAMBRIDGE, U.K.

© 1998 Wm. B. Eerdmans Publishing Co.

255 Jefferson Ave. S.E., Grand Rapids, Michigan 49503 /

P.O. Box 163, Cambridge CB3 9PU U.K.

Printed in the United States of America

03 02 01 00 99 98   7 6 5 4 3 2 1

Library of Congress Cataloging-in-Publication Data

Equal treatment of religion in a pluralistic society / edited by
Stephen V. Monsma and J. Christopher Soper.
p.   cm.
Includes bibliographical references.
ISBN 0-8028-4296-8 (pbk.: alk. paper)
1. Church and state — United States.
2. Equality before the law — United States.
I. Monsma, Stephen V., 1936-
II. Soper, J. Christopher.
KF4865.E68 1998

342.730852 — dc2   97-45848
                                          CIP

Contents

Introduction:
Equal Treatment and Societal Pluralism   1

1. Equal Treatment: Its Constitutional Status   9
   CARL H. ESBECK

2. Equal Treatment and Religious Discrimination   30
   MICHAEL W. MCCONNELL

3. The Theoretical Roots of Equal Treatment   55
   JAMES W. SKILLEN

4. What Would Equal Treatment Mean for Public
   Education?   75
   CHARLES L. GLENN

5. Equal Treatment: Implications for Nonprofit
   Organizations   101
   ROBERT A. DESTRO

6. Equal Treatment: A Christian Separationist
   Perspective   136
   DEREK H. DAVIS

v

7. American Jews and the Equal Treatment Principle   158
   GREGG IVERS

8. "Equal" Treatment? A Liberal Separationist View   179
   ROGERS M. SMITH

Conclusion:
The Implications of Equal Treatment   200

Equal Treatment
and Societal Pluralism

Three end-of-the-twentieth-century facts converge to form the seedbed for the topic of this book: the increasing religious pluralism of the United States, the rise of the comprehensive administrative state, and continuing widespread dissatisfaction with Supreme Court church-state jurisprudence. In this introduction, we begin by delineating the topic of this book. Next we develop more fully the three facts mentioned in the previous sentence; and in the final section we briefly describe the logic underlying the flow of the chapters.

Equal Treatment

The basic concept of equal treatment says that the establishment clause of the First Amendment (Congress shall make no law respecting an establishment of religion) is not violated, even if government grants aid, recognition, or support to religion or religious groups, as long as government gives equal aid, recognition, or support to *all* religions and parallel or similar secularly based systems of belief and their organized groups. Equal treatment, says the First Amendment, does not mandate an artificial, perhaps impossible-to-attain strict separation between government and all of religion in its various manifestations. Instead, it argues that the establishment clause mandates governmental neutrality on

1

matters of religion, a neutrality that is more fully attained by the equal treatment of persons and groups of all faiths — religious and secular — than by an attempt strictly to separate religion and government, which leads to a rejection of all governmental aid, support, and recognition for religious groups.

Although recently the equal treatment principle has received a measure of acceptance by the U.S. Supreme Court — as Carl Esbeck demonstrates in the following chapter — it still is largely eclipsed in Supreme Court jurisprudence and American legal circles by strict separationism. But in other Western democracies, equal treatment has been embraced in a much more thoroughgoing way. For example, Gerhard Robbers, a leading German legal scholar, has written, "Many churches receive allocations from the State for activities in the same way as other publicly funded events; it is a part of the idea of State neutrality that Church activities are not to be put in a worse position than that of State funded local athletic clubs."[1] Similarly, Sophie van Bijsterveld, who is probably the foremost legal scholar on church-state relations in the Netherlands today, has written that the Dutch Constitution "guarantees equal treatment in equal circumstances to all persons. . . . It is clear that under the Constitution public authorities in the Netherlands shall be neutral with respect to the various religious and non-religious denominations. . . . It is clear that once authorities subsidize or support certain activities, religious counterparts cannot be excluded for that reason."[2] Both of these scholars emphasize the crucial point that equal treatment of all religious groups and nonreligious groups is the key to attaining governmental religious neutrality.

According to legal scholar Douglas Laycock, the ideal of governmental religious neutrality is reached when government minimizes "the extent to which [it] either encourages or discourages religious belief or disbelief, practice or nonpractice, observance or nonobservance."[3] Per-

1. Robbers, "State and Church in Germany," in *State and Church in the European Union,* ed. Gerhard Robers (Baden-Baden: Nomos Verlagsgesellschaft, 1996), pp. 69-70.

2. Van Bijsterveld, "The Constitutional Status of Religion in the Kingdom of the Netherlands," in *The Constitutional Status of Churches in the European Union Countries* (European Consortium for Church-State Research, proceedings of the 1994 meeting, University of Paris), pp. 207, 211.

3. Laycock, "Formal, Substantive, and Disaggregated Neutrality Toward Religion," *DePaul Law Review* 39 (1990): 1001.

sons whose consciences have been shaped by a particular faith tradition ought not to have the practices their consciences dictate either burdened or favored by government policies. Similarly, persons whose consciences have been shaped either by a secular worldview or by what Martin Marty has called "religion in general"[4] should be neither burdened nor favored in the living out of their beliefs. That is governmental neutrality.

Strict separationists tend to believe that this sort of neutrality is attained when government gives no aid to religion, for when government aids religion, it must choose which religions to aid and what levels of aid to provide. And even if it aids all religions, it is showing preference to religion over secular belief structures. Equal treatment advocates like Robbers and Van Bijsterveld argue that neutrality is violated if government grants support to a variety of secularly based programs — social, educational, health, welfare, and even sports programs — but systematically excludes all of their religiously based counterparts. It is these contrasting perspectives that this book explores.

Why Consider Equal Treatment Now?

At the start of this introduction, we suggested that now is a particularly appropriate time for a wide-ranging, thoughtful consideration of equal treatment as an approach to establishment-clause interpretation for three reasons: the increasing religious pluralism of the United States, the rise of the comprehensive administrative state, and the continuing dissatisfaction with Supreme Court church-state jurisprudence. The first two of these factors are important to an understanding of how the goal of religious freedom for all based on governmental neutrality can best be reached in the context of the establishment clause.

First, the United States is characterized by increasing religious pluralism. Throughout most of the nineteenth century, the United States was an overwhelmingly Protestant country, dominated by several mainline Protestant groups, including the Methodists, the Presbyterians, the Lutherans, and the Episcopalians. During the latter decades of the nineteenth century and the earlier decades of the twentieth, changing

---

4. See Marty, *The New Shape of American Religion* (New York: Harper & Row, 1958), p. 2.

tides of immigration increased the religious pluralism of the United States by bringing in large numbers of Catholics and Jews. The twentieth century also saw the mainline Protestant denominations lose numbers and social influence, a trend that continues today. They are being challenged by rapidly growing, typically conservative groups such as the Mormons, the Assemblies of God, the Southern Baptists, and evangelical megachurches. Meanwhile, immigration patterns have again shifted, bringing in more persons of non-Christian faiths such as Islam, Hinduism, and Buddhism.

Further increasing the religious pluralism of the United States is the growth in the proportion of the population adhering — explicitly or implicitly — to thoroughly secular systems of belief. Sociologist James Davison Hunter has concluded that "the secularists . . . represent the fastest growing community of 'moral conviction' in America."[5] He goes on to note that the proportion of the population without any religious commitment has increased from a mere 2 percent in the 1950s to about 11 percent at the start of the 1990s. If one looks behind individuals' simple identification with a particular religious tradition (or the absence of any religious identification) and asks about more specific religious beliefs and practices, one finds that as much as 30 percent of the population can, for all intents and purposes, be considered secular.[6]

These changes notwithstanding, religion continues to be a strong, vital force among the general American public. George Gallup, Jr., and Jim Castelli, in summarizing fifty years of data collected by the Gallup organization, referred to "the enduring popularity of religion" in the United States, and went on to note, "There have been several periods of heightened interest in religion, but the baseline of religious belief is remarkably high — certainly, the highest of any developed nation in the world."[7]

The great religious pluralism of today, combined with the rise of secularism as a "community of moral conviction," poses a new situation that establishment clause interpretations need to take into account. Policies that avoid all government funding of religion but still

---

5. See Hunter, *Culture Wars: The Struggle to Define America* (New York: Basic Books, 1991), p. 76.

6. See "The Rites of Americans," *Newsweek*, 29 November 1993, pp. 80-82.

7. Gallup and Castelli, *The People's Religion* (New York: Macmillan, 1989), p. 20.

4

fund secular programs and services may be neutral toward all religions, but are they maintaining neutrality toward both religious and secular belief systems? Given the religious pluralism of American society, can an equal treatment approach create a level playing field in which the government is genuinely neutral, or does it pose the danger of increasing the religious divisions in society to the point where overall societal unity is threatened?

A second basic change that has taken place in American society is the rise of the comprehensive administrative state. As the twentieth century draws to a close, government is involved in running programs, providing services, and enforcing regulations undreamed of at the start of the century. Government today reaches into education, health care, prevention of unwanted pregnancies, treatment for drug dependency, innumerable social welfare services, international aid and disaster relief, domestic disaster relief, civil rights protection, neighborhood renewal, spouse-abuse programs, and protection of children from abuse and neglect. In all these and many more areas, government now reaches out to assist, fund, and regulate services that have historically been organized within religious communities.

Therefore, the rise of the comprehensive administrative state means that government, secularly based organizations, and religiously based organizations are now all actively involved in similar or parallel activities: educating the youth, feeding the hungry, sheltering the homeless, counseling the drug dependent, and much, much more. Any conception of church-state relations must take into account the fact that all three now provide many of the same services. On the surface it would seem a violation of neutrality for the government itself to provide services in a "secular" manner and to aid private secular agencies that are providing those services, but to refuse aid to religious agencies that are providing the same services.

At the very least, we believe that the increasing pluralism of American society and the rise of the comprehensive administrative state call for a re-examination of the strict separationist principle and raise the question whether an approach rooted in equal treatment may bring us closer to genuine governmental neutrality.

The importance of answering this question is increased by the widespread dissatisfaction with current Supreme Court church-state jurisprudence. Scholars have used terms such as "incoherent," "tangled," and "eccentric" to describe current church-state law.[8] No one seems to be happy with the status quo. Law professor Steven Smith made a telling point when he wrote that "in a rare and remarkable way, the Supreme Court's establishment clause jurisprudence has unified critical opinion: people who disagree about nearly everything else in the law agree that establishment clause doctrine is seriously, perhaps distinctively, defective."[9] The Supreme Court justices themselves issue closely divided rulings on church-state questions, at times with vitriolic opinions and often with the majority and the dissenting justices unable to agree on why they have reached their conclusions. This unhappiness with Supreme Court church-state jurisprudence suggests that perhaps a paradigm shift may be in order. Equal treatment, or neutrality, is one candidate for a paradigm to replace strict separationism. We believe it should receive consideration, discussion, and debate. We hope this book will assist in that process.

A key reason why we believe that now is a good time for a wider discussion of equal treatment is that it is already receiving wider consideration before the Supreme Court and Congress. In Chapter 1, Carl Esbeck details the extent to which equal treatment is being relied upon in cases that involve the freedom of religious expression. Esbeck identifies four justices who seem to be relying primarily on equal treatment reasoning in cases involving private religious speech. Clearly there is support on today's Supreme Court for an equal treatment approach in certain areas.

In addition, Congress followed an equal treatment approach when it added the "Charitable Choice" amendment, proposed by Senator John Ashcroft of Missouri, to the welfare reform act of 1996. This amendment encourages states to make use of nonprofit agencies to deliver welfare services and stipulates that if they make use of secularly based agencies, they may not exclude religiously based agencies.[10] Secular and religious

---

8. See Michael A. Paulsen, "Religion, Equality, and the Constitution: An Equal Protection Approach to Establishment Clause Adjudication," *Notre Dame Law Review* 61 (1986): 317; A. James Reichley, *Religion in American Public Life* (Washington: Brookings Institution, 1985), p. 117; and Phillip E. Johnson, "Concepts and Compromise in First Amendment Religious Doctrine," *California Law Review* 72 (1984): 817.

9. Smith, "Separation and the 'Secular': Reconstructing the Disestablishment Decision," *Texas Law Review* 67 (1989): 955-56.

10. See Public Law 104-93, section 104. For an excellent description and explication of that section of the law, see *A Guide to Charitable Choice: The Rules of Section 104 of*

agencies are to be treated equally. The new law also seeks to protect the religious-freedom rights of religious agencies that receive government funds. It explicitly stipulates that agencies receiving such funds shall maintain the right to develop and express their religious orientation, may keep religious pictures and symbols in their facilities, and may favor members of their own religious faith in hiring decisions.

In 1996, Congress also gave active consideration to a "religious equality" constitutional amendment that is based on equal treatment principles. House Joint Resolution 184 was proposed by Representative Dick Armey, the Republican floor leader; it reads, in part, "Neither the United States nor any State shall deny any person equal access to a benefit, or otherwise discriminate against any person, on account of religious belief, expression, or exercise."[11] This amendment to the Constitution, as well as several other similar proposed amendments, seeks to assure that the establishment clause would no longer be interpreted in a strict separationist, no-aid-to-religion fashion. It requires "equal access" to government benefits, and thereby is based on equal treatment principles.

The topic of this book is timely. The old approach to establishment clause interpretation, rooted in strict separation and no aid to religion, has drawn increasing fire because of the increasing pluralism of the United States — especially the rise of secular belief systems — and the rise of the comprehensive administrative state. As a result, many commentators believe that Supreme Court church-state law is in disarray, the Court itself is exploring equal treatment as an alternate approach, and Congress has adopted or is considering measures based on equal treatment thinking.

The Plan of This Book

This book systematically explores these issues. Following this introduction is a chapter by Carl Esbeck in which he carefully sets out the extent to which the Supreme Court has embraced the equal treatment ap-

the 1996 Federal Welfare Law Governing State Cooperation with Faith-based Social-service Providers (Washington: Center for Public Justice, and Annandale, Va.: Center for Law and Religious Freedom of the Christian Legal Society, 1997).

11. House Joint Resolution 184, 104th Congress, 2nd Session.

proach. In Chapter 2, Michael McConnell makes the case that current judicial interpretations are not religiously neutral, documenting the lack of religious equality he sees in the United States today. In Chapter 3, James Skillen critiques the theoretical roots of separationism and contrasts them with the theoretical roots of a neutrality approach to questions of religious establishment. These three chapters lay the basic foundation for equal treatment. In the next two chapters, some of the potential effects of equal treatment are explored. Charles Glenn applies the equal treatment concept to education (Chapter 4), and Robert Destro applies the concept to nonprofit service organizations (Chapter 5). All these chapters are written by individuals who, on the whole, favor equal treatment.

The next three chapters are written by three critics of equal treatment. In Chapter 6, Derek Davis argues that equal treatment would harm religion by removing the special constitutional status that it currently enjoys. In Chapter 7, Gregg Ivers analyzes the negative effects he believes equal treatment would have on religious minorities, particularly the Jewish community. And in Chapter 8, Rogers Smith provides a liberal evaluation that highlights the theoretical implications of the equal treatment principle. In the conclusion, we as editors make some observations and seek to reach some conclusions based on the foregoing discussions.

CHAPTER 1

Equal Treatment:
Its Constitutional Status

CARL H. ESBECK

*In this chapter, Carl Esbeck analyzes what is meant by equal treatment
as a theory for interpreting the establishment clause of the First Amendment, and contrasts that with the strict separation theory. He also
clarifies the settings in which and the extent to which the Supreme
Court has used these two contrasting theories to interpret the meaning
of the First Amendment. Esbeck is the Isabelle Wade and Paul C. Lyda
Professor of Law at the University of Missouri–Columbia. Significant
portions of this chapter were taken from an article by Esbeck that
appeared in the Winter 1997 issue of the* Emery Law Journal.

Since 1947, when the United States Supreme Court handed down its
decision in *Everson v. Board of Education*,[1] all competing theories of
church-state relations have had to define themselves over against the
strict separation interpretation of the establishment clause embraced in
that decision. Accordingly, an analysis of equal treatment theory and
the Supreme Court can best begin with a consideration of strict separationism and its continued pull on a majority of the sitting justices of
the Court, as well as its considerable grip upon the allegiance of many
Americans, both religious and nonreligious.

1. 330 U.S. 1 (1947).

The Continuing Vitality of Strict Separation

Strict separationism has two quite distinct lines of argumentation employed on its behalf. The first of these is the perceived need for protection of the body politic from certain forms of religion that would co-opt the offices of government and seize the levers of sovereign power. As Chief Justice Warren stated the matter in *McGowan v. Maryland*, Western civilization records arrangements between organized religion and the offices of state which are still "feared because of [their] tendencies to political tyranny and subversion of civil authority."[2] Religion is viewed as a potentially divisive force within civil society. A formally established church is instinctively understood as harmful to individual religious minorities, but history has shown that certain combinations of church and state can cause structural harm to the body politic as well. Separationism reaches beyond just the protection of individuals and their liberty of conscience and goes further by distancing government from certain religious practices lest they should inflame political passions and disrupt civic unity. For separationists, the dangers of sectarian division are neither exaggerated nor a matter of ancient history. Rather, as America has become more pluralistic, that moral consensus thought to be so essential to a continual legitimation of the nation's vision is seen as becoming an increasingly thinned-out social contract.

The other line of argument undergirding strict separation theory is voluntarism. The term "voluntarism" derives from the separationist insistence that a truly authentic church must be a "free" and hence voluntary church. It means that a religious society is most genuine when its devotees are brought into the fold as a result of minds willingly and hearts enthusiastically won over, rather than by the allure of government's approval or endorsement. The use of "voluntarism" in the context of the establishment clause can be confusing, for it is not used narrowly in the sense of uncoerced belief — an abuse already guarded against by other clauses in the First Amendment. Rather, voluntarism here refers to freedom from active governmental involvement in religious affairs, a circumstance that separationists believe redounds to the benefit of a multiplicity of heartfelt and vibrant faiths.

2. 366 U.S. 420, 430 (1961).

For separationists, the government's intervention in religious concerns can corrupt religion in multiple ways. Respect for a religion is properly grounded in the appeal of its doctrine rather than in any desire for the privileges that accompany a close identification with the government. Professing a religion out of civic convention confounds the social traditions of the nation with the sacred, and confuses religious symbols and holy days with the patriotic. Separationists argue that such uncritical mixing of the sacred with the secular soon degenerates into the corruption known as civil religion, where culture and nationalism go hand in hand with spiritual identity. Finally, for the church to accept government's financial aid implies that it has yielded to the state some authority over its own affairs. Churches unduly involved with the agencies of government risk becoming subverted because their schools and charities are soon busied with regulatory compliance and the meeting of goals set by legislators. Having contracted away their independence and allied with the government, these churches are soon compromised in their efforts to define and follow their own calling. Lost in the bargain is the ability to speak critically of the state, to which church officials have become beholden. Civil religion is a religion of civility, its sharp edges rounded off, its prophetic voice dulled.

Chief Justice Burger struck close to the heart of these twin arguments for separationism when in *Tilton v. Richardson* he wrote that the "main concerns against which the Establishment Clause sought to protect [were] sponsorship, financial support, and active involvement of the sovereign in religious activity."[3]

Despite the Court's long association with strict separation theory, the outer boundary of the establishment clause is difficult to fix in place. The reason is that the two harms which the theory seeks to prevent from occurring — political divisiveness along sectarian lines and the negation of voluntarism — are so amorphous. Such broadly conceived harms are inherently matters of degree not amenable to the adjudicatory process; hence there is untoward inconsistency in the Supreme Court's establishment clause cases. But the centering postulates of separationism are not in doubt: peace within the civil polity follows government's disengagement from religious observance, and religion flourishes best when it is free from the adulterating patronage of government. The foregoing

---

3. 403 U.S. 672, 677 (1971) (internal quotation omitted).

means that separationists would have religious organizations barred from state funding and the receipt of other benefits because, paradoxically, state aid is harmful to religion's continued vitality among the people as well as its independence from government.

Is Strict Separation No Longer Plausible?

Because a strict separation interpretation of the establishment clause requires government to avoid granting direct benefits to faith-based schools and social-service organizations in virtually all circumstances, it is at odds with equal treatment theory. While agreeing that government must be "neutral" concerning religion, separationists reject the characterization that it is discriminatory for government to exclude religious organizations from participation in financial-assistance programs. Rather, the baseline from which they measure deviations from "neutrality" is the insistence that church and state each remain free of any dependence on the other.

Equal treatment theory approaches the debate over the establishment clause from an altogether different point of entry. It asserts that when government provides benefits to encourage activities that serve the public good — such as education, health care, and social services — there should be no discrimination or other exclusionary criteria based on religion.[4] Nor should religious schools and charities be required to engage in self-censorship or otherwise have to water down their religious character as a condition of program eligibility. Equal treatment theory would allow religious individuals and groups to participate fully and equally with their fellow citizens in America's public life, without being forced to either shed or disguise their religious convictions or character. Importantly, the theory is not a call for preferential treatment for religion in the administration of publicly funded programs. Equal treatment theory is thereby distinguishable from nonpref-

4. Both theories, strict separationism and equal treatment, maintain that the establishment clause prohibits the state from purposefully discriminating among religious groups. Hence, intentional discrimination among religions is not a point that divides these two theories. Prohibiting such inequality is also the rule followed by the Supreme Court. *Larson v. Valente*, 456 U.S. 228 (1982).

erentialism: the position that the establishment clause, although prohibiting the establishment of a single national religion, was intended to allow Congress to support all religious denominations on a nonpreferential basis.[5] Rather, the theory of equal treatment merely claims for persons of faith the same opportunities enjoyed by all others.

When government was small and much of society was in the private sector, strict separation of church and state was quite workable. The schools and social-service ministries of religious organizations were deeply involved in community life and at the same time largely avoided becoming entangled with government. However, with the arrival of the New Deal and explosive growth in the regulatory/welfare state, enforcing strict separation confined religious education and charitable ministries to ever smaller and smaller enclaves. If the two were not to mix, religion had to recede as the state grew larger. Thus, if social-service ministries and schools were to participate in government's largess, the theory demanded that religious social services and schools must first become secular. These secularizing demands ran the gamut from the superficial (insistence that religious symbols be stripped from a charity's walls) to the core (jettisoning the confessional content of a school's curriculum). To increasing numbers of Americans, strict separation presents a cruel choice between suffering funding discrimination or forced secularization.[6]

The separationist's rejoinder is that the way to safeguard the religious character of schools and charities is to fund them privately. This assumes that the modern affirmative state — like smaller governments of decades past — continues to have only limited control over the resources a society can divert to education and social welfare. Because the size

---

5. The Supreme Court rejected nonpreferentialism in *Wallace v. Jaffree,* 472 U.S. 38 (1985).

6. The insistence that strict separation is "neutral" with regard to religion has thereby become less plausible. All models of church-state relations embody substantive choices. Strict separation is a value-laden judgment that certain areas of the human condition best lie within the province of religion, while other areas of life properly lie within the authority of civil government. Strict separation is in no sense the inevitable product of "pure" reason unadulterated by ideological commitment to some higher point of reference. It cannot stand outside the political and religious milieu from which it emerged and claim to be "neutral." The same, of course, must be said for equal treatment theory. Indeed, to demand that any theory of church-state relations transcend either its pedigree or its presuppositional thinking and be substantively "neutral" concerning the nature of religion and the purposes of modern government is to ask the impossible.

and role of government has changed, those arguing for equal treatment believe this assumption is now false. Consider the matter from the perspective of a family whose educational and charitable dollars are first withheld as taxes. If this family desires to commit resources to a religious school or charity, it must pay the tuition or donation again — this time out of after-tax income. So, those who want to make religious choices pay twice. Limited finances, of course, will discourage some families from choosing a religious education or charity. For low-income families, the choice is all but dictated.

Is the government's influence over religious choices in education and social welfare — as strict separation requires — itself a violation of religious liberty and the First Amendment? An affirmative answer would make equal treatment a constitutional right. Or, if not a right guaranteed by the First Amendment, may Congress or a state legislature nonetheless elect to provide, in response to the majority's will, for the equal participation of religious organizations in tax-funded education, health care, and social-service programs? It is to these questions that I now turn, beginning with the origin of equal-treatment theory — not in the law of religious freedom, as would be expected, but in the law of free speech.

A New Paradigm via Equal Access for Religious Speech?

Should strict separation, no-aid-to-religion eventually lose its place as the controlling paradigm, we will be able to say that it began in 1981 with the Supreme Court's decision in *Widmar v. Vincent*.[7] In *Widmar*, a state university permitted secular student organizations to hold their meetings in campus buildings when the facilities were not being used for other purposes. However, religious student organizations were specifically denied access. The university maintained that the denial was required because it could not support religion by providing meeting space for worship, prayer, and Bible study, a denial consistent with a no-aid interpretation of the establishment clause. A group of students brought suit, first pointing out that the university had voluntarily established a limited public forum generally open to student expression. Once having created the forum, the students argued, the university could not single out expres-

7. 454 U.S. 263 (1981).

sion of religious content for discrimination. A near unanimous Supreme Court agreed. More importantly, the Court went on to hold that the establishment clause did not override the free speech clause so long as the creation of the forum had a secular purpose, religious groups were just one of many student organizations permitted into the forum, and the circumstances were such that the university did not appear to be placing its power or prestige behind the religious message.

The *Widmar* approach was soon dubbed "equal access," and in 1984 Congress extended the same equality-based right to students enrolled in public secondary schools.[8] Following the triad of recent free-speech victories in *Lamb's Chapel v. Center Moriches Union Free School District,*[9] *Capitol Square Review Board v. Pinette,*[10] and *Rosenberger v. Rector,*[11] equal treatment theory has indeed become the normative rule of law concerning private speech of religious content or viewpoint.

It should be noted that when the expression is not private speech but speech by government, then the controlling norm remains a separationist model. Government may neither confess inherently religious beliefs nor advocate that individuals profess such beliefs or observe such practices.[12]

Notwithstanding the unbroken line of victories for the equal treatment of religion, it must be emphasized that in each case from *Widmar* to *Rosenberger* it was the free speech clause that required nondiscrimination, thereby supplying the victory. It remains to be explored below whether equal treatment theory can make the transition from an equality right in free speech to a right of equal participation in programs of financial aid.

8. Equal Access Act, 20 U.S.C. §§4071-74. The constitutionality of the act was upheld in the face of an establishment clause challenge in *Board of Education v. Mergens,* 496 U.S. 226 (1990).

9. 508 U.S. 384 (1993). This decision disallowed viewpoint discrimination against a church that had sought to show a film about family life in a forum otherwise open to that subject.

10. 515 U.S. 753 (1995). This decision found content-based discrimination in the refusal to permit a controversial group to sponsor a religious display in a civic park.

11. 515 U.S. 819 (1995). This decision found viewpoint discrimination in a public university's refusal to pay printing costs for a student publication presenting religious perspectives on current issues.

12. See, for example, *Stone v. Graham,* 449 U.S. 39 (1980), which struck down a state law requiring the posting of the Ten Commandments in public school classrooms; and *School District v. Schempp,* 374 U.S. 203 (1963), which disallowed devotional Bible reading and recitation of prayer by public school officials.

15

On Distinguishing between Burdens and Benefits

If one's thesis is that the Supreme Court is moving from a strict separation model to one of equal treatment, then the line of cases involving religious exemptions from regulatory or tax burdens must be set apart from this analysis — which are about equal treatment as far as governmental benefits are concerned.[13] For when the establishment clause challenge is to laws that exempt religious organizations from legislative burdens, the normative rule of law continues to follow a separationist model.

The Supreme Court has repeatedly held that the establishment clause is not violated when government refrains from imposing a burden on religion, even though that burden is imposed on the nonreligious who are otherwise similarly situated. *Corporation of the Presiding Bishop v. Amos*[14] is the leading case. *Amos* upheld an exemption for religious organizations in federal civil-rights legislation. The exemption permits religious organizations to discriminate on a religious basis in matters of employment. Finding that the exemption did not violate the establishment clause, the Court explained that "it is a permissible legislative purpose to alleviate significant governmental interference with the ability of religious organizations to define and carry out their missions."[15]

The rationale for the burden/benefit distinction is twofold. First, to establish a religion connotes that a government must take some affirmative step to seek to achieve the prohibited result. Conversely, for government to passively "leave religion where it found it" logically cannot be the establishing of a religion.[16] The words of the First Amendment, "Congress shall make no law," imply some action by government,

---

13. In this context, a "burden" is taken to mean a government-imposed regulation, tax, or criminal prohibition. A "benefit" is taken to mean direct or indirect government-granted financial assistance for a secular public purpose.

14. 483 U.S. 327 (1987).

15. 483 U.S. at 335.

16. *Amos* is most explicit in making the salient distinction between benefits and burdens. Pointing out that it had previously upheld laws that helped religious groups advance their purposes, the Court explained, "A law is not unconstitutional simply because it allows churches to advance religion, which is their very purpose. . . . It must be fair to say that the government itself has advanced religion through its own activities and influence. . . . The Court . . . has never indicated that statutes that give special consideration to religious groups are per se invalid." 483 U.S. at 337, 338.

16

not inaction. Stating the practical sense of the matter, Professor Douglas Laycock observed that "the state does not support or establish religion by leaving it alone."[17] Second, unlike benefit programs, religious exemptions reduce civic-religious tensions and minimize church-state interactions, both matters that enhance the nonentanglement so desired by the establishment clause.[18]

The distinction in the Court's approach between declining to impose regulatory burdens on religion (controlled by separationist theory) and conferring financial benefits on religion (examined here in relation to equal treatment theory) has a common thread that ties the two together. In equal treatment theory, equality is not an end in itself but a means to a deeper purpose. The purpose at work is the minimization of the government's influence over religious belief and practice. Thus, whether pondering the constitutionality of exemptions from regulatory burdens or equal treatment in benefit programs, the integrating principle is to reduce the impact of governmental action on religious choices.[19] The goal is to avoid having the government to either spur or discourage religious choices by its actions. From that common axis, it makes sense to fully align with the position of the Court that religious exemptions from legislative burdens

17. Laycock, "Towards a General Theory of the Religion Clauses," *Columbia Law Review* 81 (1981): 1416.

18. *Walz v. Tax Commission*, 397 U.S. 664, 676 (1970), held that it is desirable for government to refrain from imposing a burden on religion so as "to complement and reinforce the desired separation insulating each from the other."

19. Religious choice as the core value of the establishment clause is not being elevated here as good theology, just good jurisprudence. I say "good jurisprudence" because religious choice as a judicial value allows each religion to flourish or die in accord with its own appeal. Choice as the controlling legal standard is individualistic and maximizes liberty, while minimizing the impact of governmental action on religious life. In these respects, it is admittedly biased toward a Western view of human rights and a limited state. Good theology is another matter, for in Christian tradition, religious liberty consists not in doing what we choose, but in the freedom to do what we ought. In Christian orthodoxy, religious belief and practice are understood in terms of one's motivation to do God's will, not choice. In the views of Luther, Calvin, and Saint Augustine, we do not choose God; he chooses us. Even theologians such as Arminius, Wesley, and Aquinas, who believed that the human will is free and must cooperate in the process of salvation, did not view salvation as a purely autonomous choice. My point here is that it should not be troubling to Christians that religious choice is the core legal value when interpreting the establishment clause. There is no reason that law and theology must converge on this point.

are rightly upheld as consistent with the establishment clause, and on the other hand, to maintain that the establishment clause permits the equal treatment of religion when it comes to financial benefits.

Direct vs. Indirect Aid to Religion

The Supreme Court has consistently held that government may confer a public benefit on individuals, who in turn have freedom in the choice of institutions to which they take their benefit and "spend" it, whether that institution is public or private, nonsectarian or religious. Any resulting aid to religion having its origin in such a program only indirectly reaches — and thereby advances — a religious school or charity. In these instances of indirect aid to religion, the equal treatment of religion — not separationism — is the Court's operative model for interpreting the establishment clause.

The leading cases are *Mueller v. Allen*,[20] *Witters v. Washington Department of Services for the Blind*,[21] *Zobrest v. Catalina Foothills School District*,[22] and most recently *Agastini v. Felton*.[23] Even the more liberal justices on the Court appear to have acquiesced in the direct/indirect distinction.[24]

20. 463 U.S. 388 (1983). This decision upheld a state income-tax deduction given to parents to assist in their children's tuition and other educational expenses.

21. 474 U.S. 481 (1986). This decision upheld a state vocational grant program to pay for postsecondary education of blind students. An otherwise qualified blind student sought to use the grant at a Christian school to obtain a degree to enter a religious vocation. The state's refusal to allow the use of the grant in this manner because it violated the establishment clause was overturned by the Supreme Court.

22. 509 U.S. 1 (1993). This decision upheld the provision of an interpreter to a deaf student attending a parochial high school as not violative of the establishment clause. Even *Everson v. Board of Education*, 330 U.S. 1 (1947), which upheld a state law allowing local governments to provide reimbursement to parents for the expense of transporting their children by bus to school, including to parochial schools, can be read as subscribing to the direct/indirect distinction.

23. 117 S. Ct. 1997 (1997). This decision upheld a federal educational program to provide primary and secondary school students with remedial assistance. The assistance was provided by public school teachers on the campuses of the religious schools.

24. See *Rosenberger v. Rector*, 515 U.S. 819, 879-80 (1995). Justice Souter, in his dissent (in which Justices Stevens, Ginsburg, and Breyer joined), acknowledged that the direct/indirect distinction was applied in *Mueller, Witters,* and *Zobrest*.

The rationale for this distinction is twofold. First, the constitutionally salient cause of any consequential aid to religion is the determination of numerous independent actors, not the decision of the government. Merely enabling private decisions — where individuals freely choose or do not choose religion — cannot logically be a governmental establishment of religion. The government is essentially passive about the relevant decision, and hence not the agent of any resulting religious use. Second, the indirect nature of the aid, channeled as it is through countless individuals, reduces church-state interaction and regulatory oversight. This enhances the nonentanglement that is desirable from the perspective of the establishment clause.

There are numerous familiar programs that operate pursuant to this rule: individual income-tax deductions for contributions to charitable organizations, including those that are religious; the GI Bill and other federal aid to students attending the college or university of their choice, including those affiliated with a church; and federal child-care certificates for low-income parents of preschool-age children, including church-based centers.[25] Pursuant to this rule of law, educational vouchers for parents that are redeemable at any accredited school, whether public or private, religious or nonreligious, are constitutional.

It bears emphasizing that the programs of aid upheld in *Mueller, Witters, Zobrest,* and *Agastini* were adopted as a matter of legislative judgment. These cases do not hold that there is a constitutional right to equal treatment between public and private institutions. Government may decide to provide that these indirect benefits are redeemable at its agencies alone, thereby excluding all similarly situated private organizations. Accordingly, should a state decide to provide indirect support only to government-operated schools, it can do so without violating the First Amendment.[26]

25. The Child Care and Development Block Grant Act of 1990, 42 U.S.C. §§9858-9858q. The act allows parents receiving child-care certificates from the government to obtain child care at a center operated by a church or other religious organization, including a pervasively sectarian center. 42 U.S.C. at §§9858n(2), 9858k(a), 9858c(c)(2)(A)(i)(I).

26. The only caveat here is that a state cannot adopt a program-of-aid that funds all schools, public and private, but explicitly disqualifies participation of schools that are religious. The free exercise clause prohibits intentional discrimination on the basis of religion. See *Church of the Lukumi Babalu Aye v. City of Hialeah,* 508 U.S. 520

Equal Treatment Theory and
Programs of Direct Financial Aid

When a government's general program-of-aid flows directly to all organizations, including religious institutions, then strict separation remains the Supreme Court's framework for its analysis. As a general proposition, the Court has said that direct support can be provided for the "secular" services offered by a religious organization but not for those services constituting "religious" beliefs or practices. The Court presumes that this secular/religious dichotomy accurately describes reality, an assumption vigorously challenged by equal treatment theorists. Under this presumption, when an organization's religious and secular functions are reliably separable, direct aid can be provided for the secular functions alone. But if they are not separable, then the Court disallows the benefit altogether, with the explanation that the establishment clause will not risk the aid furthering the transmission of religious beliefs or practices.

The juridical criterion that the Court utilizes to determine if the program-of-aid risks advancing religion is whether the recipient is "pervasively sectarian." Should the recipient fit the profile of a pervasively sectarian organization, then separationist theory prohibits any aid that is not by its nature usable for secular purposes only. The meaning of "pervasively sectarian" can be gleaned from the cases. In *Roemer v. Board of Public Works,* the Court turned back a challenge to a state program awarding noncategorical grants to colleges, including religious institutions that offered more than just seminarian degrees. In discussion focused on the fostering of religion, Justice Blackmun wrote, "The primary-effect question is the substantive one of what private educational activities, by whatever procedure, may be supported by state funds. *Hunt* requires (1) that no state aid at all go to institutions that are so 'pervasively sectarian' that secular activities cannot be separated from sectarian

---

(1993). Should such a case ever arise, separationists will argue that there is a compelling interest in overriding the free exercise clause, namely the no-aid rule of the establishment clause. There are no Supreme Court cases on this precise point. However, one recent case did uphold direct aid to a publication with an overtly religious viewpoint. See *Rosenberger v. Rector,* 515 U.S. 819 (1995). The establishment clause was held not to bar the direct funding.

ones, and (2) that if secular activities *can* be separated out, they alone may be funded."[27] The Roman Catholic colleges were held not to be pervasively sectarian. Justice Blackmun noted the relevance of findings that the institutions employed chaplains who held worship services on campus, had mandatory religious classes, and started some classes with prayer. Their lack of a pervasively sectarian nature was nevertheless indicated by their high degree of autonomy from the Roman Catholic Church, by their faculty not being hired on a religious basis and having complete academic freedom except in religious classes, and by students being chosen without regard to their religion.[28]

All of the Supreme Court's cases striking down direct programs-of-aid have involved primary and secondary church-related schools.[29] Contrariwise, in each of the three instances that have come before the Court involving direct aid to colleges and universities, including those that are faith-related, the Court has upheld the financial aid.[30] Only twice has the Court passed on the constitutionality of a direct state-aid program for social services, sustaining both programs. *Bowen v. Kendrick*[31] is the leading case. *Kendrick* upheld "on its face" a program of federal grants for counseling on teenage sexuality, including counseling done by religious centers. However, the Court remanded *Kendrick* to the trial court

27. *Roemer v. Board of Public Works,* 426 U.S. 734, 755 (1976). The internal reference is to *Hunt v. McNair,* 413 U.S. 734 (1973).

28. A comparison of the colleges in *Roemer* with the elementary and secondary schools in *Committee for Public Education v. Nyquist,* 413 U.S. 756, 767-68 (1973), clarifies the term "pervasively sectarian." The schools in *Nyquist,* found to be pervasively sectarian, placed religious restrictions on student admissions and faculty appointments, enforced obedience to religious dogma, required attendance at religious services, required religious or doctrinal study, and imposed religious restrictions on how and what the faculty could teach. In addition, the schools were an integral part of the mission of the sponsoring church, and had religious indoctrination as a primary purpose.

29. For cases disallowing all or some direct aid to primary and secondary parochial schools, see, for example, *Aguilar v. Felton,* 473 U.S. 402 (1985); *Grand Rapids v. Ball,* 473 U.S. 373 (1985); *Meek v. Pittenger,* 421 U.S. 349 (1975); *Committee for Public Education v. Nyquist,* 413 U.S. 756 (1973); *Lemon v. Kurtzman,* 403 U.S. 602 (1971). *Aguilar* and *Grand Rapids* were recently overruled in *Agostini v. Felton,* 117 S. Ct. 1997 (1997).

30. See *Roemer v. Maryland Public Works Board,* 426 U.S. 736 (1976); *Hunt v. McNair,* 413 U.S. 734 (1973); *Tilton v. Richardson,* 403 U.S. 672 (1971).

31. 487 U.S. 589 (1988). See also *Bradfield v. Roberts,* 175 U.S. 291 (1899). *Bradfield* held that a church-affiliated hospital may receive a capital improvement grant.

for a case-by-case or "as applied" review in order that teenage counseling centers found to be pervasively sectarian would have their grants discontinued.[32]

Previously mentioned were two cases handed down by the Court in late June of 1995: *Capitol Square Review Board v. Pinette*,[33] and *Rosenberger v. Rector*.[34] They represent the Court's most recent pronouncements on · the establishment clause, and the two newest appointees to the Court, Justices Ginsburg and Breyer, were sitting. The *prima facie* claim in both of these cases was that private religious speech was denied equal access to a public forum, a violation of the free speech clause. The Court agreed. Further, in both cases the government sought to justify its discriminatory treatment of religious speech as being compelled by the establishment clause. A majority of the justices rejected this defense. Hence, both cases followed an equal treatment model rather than a separationist one.

In *Pinette*, the Ku Klux Klan in Ohio sought a permit to place a display consisting of a Latin cross in the Capitol Square, a public area surrounding the statehouse. The square was otherwise open for private displays sponsored by a variety of citizen groups. The state denied the permit, claiming that the cross would be viewed as an endorsement of religion in violation of church-state separation. By a vote of seven to two, the Court sided with the Klan. All of the justices in the majority were of the opinion that placement of the cross by a private group was not barred by the establishment clause. However, these seven justices generated four opinions, none of which commanded a five-vote majority concerning the application of the establishment clause to these facts.

Justice Scalia, joined by Chief Justice Rehnquist and Justices Kennedy and Thomas, believed that the exclusion of a private religious symbol

---

32. In a concurring opinion joined by Justice Scalia, Justice Kennedy stated that he doubted whether "the term 'pervasively sectarian' is a well-founded juridical category." He went on to adopt an equal treatment model: a public assistance program was facially constitutional so long as its purpose was "neutral as to religion" and a diverse array of organizations were eligible to participate. Upon remand of the case, for Justice Kennedy the "question in an as-applied challenge is not whether the entity is of a religious character, but how it spends its grant." In his view, there would be no violation of the establishment clause so long as the grant is spent for the designated public purpose — not to advance inherently religious beliefs or practices. 487 U.S. at 624-25.

33. 515 U.S. 753 (1995).

34. 515 U.S. 819 (1995).

from a public forum could never be justified by the establishment clause. General free-speech doctrine required that there be no discrimination as to content, and religious speech was not to be singled out for special scrutiny. Merely because onlookers might view a religious display and mistake it for the message of the state was no reason to suppress private speech. Rather, the solution to the problem of the mistaken observer is to correct the erroneous conclusion about the source of the message. So long as the government treated all speakers equally and did nothing to intentionally foster the onlooker's mistake, the government did all that the establishment clause required.[35]

Justice O'Connor wrote separately on the mistaken-observer point. Applying an endorsement test, Justice O'Connor said that in some instances the establishment clause imposed a duty on the state to take steps to disclaim sponsorship of a private religious message. In her view, government's formal equality toward religion may not always be enough. In circumstances where, for example, private religious messages "so dominate a public forum that a formal policy of equal access is transformed into a demonstration of approval" in the eyes of the reasonable observer, the establishment clause requires the state to take affirmative measures to see that religion is not advanced.[36]

Justice Souter, joined by Justices O'Connor and Breyer, wrote separately on the inadequacy of formal equality. Justice Souter agreed that equal treatment of religion should prevail on these facts. However, he agreed because, as he saw it, the appearance of state endorsement of religion could be remedied by requiring the affixing of a sign to the cross disclaiming state sponsorship. Such a disclaimer, of course, would be required only when the speech is religious. In Justice Souter's view, an access rule that is nondiscriminatory in purpose is required, but alone it is not sufficient. "Effects matter to the Establishment Clause," he wrote.[37] The tone and content of Justice Souter's opinion left little doubt that in his view church-state separation rather than equal treatment was the dominant concern of the First Amendment.

---

35. 515 U.S. at 765-70. Justice Thomas also wrote separately, stating his view that the content of the Klan's message was political rather than religious. 515 U.S. at 770-71.

36. 515 U.S. at 774-78. Justice O'Connor's opinion was joined by Justices Souter and Breyer.

37. 515 U.S. at 786-92.

Justices Stevens and Ginsburg dissented in separate opinions. Justice Stevens believed that the establishment clause created "a strong presumption against the installation of unattended religious symbols on public property." Thus, in his view separationism subordinates the free speech clause and its rule of equal access.[38] Justice Ginsburg was even more extreme, articulating not a presumption but an absolute rule of religious censorship. She was of the opinion that "if the aim of the Establishment Clause is genuinely to uncouple government from church," then "a State may not permit, and a court may not order, a display of this character."[39] As authority for this absolutist separationism, Justice Ginsburg cited a law review article.[40] The article is openly hostile to the contributions of traditional religion and urges that it be driven out of the public square. It is deeply disturbing that Justice Ginsburg, sitting on her first religion case as a Supreme Court justice, would cite with approval this article, with its brutish regard for religion and religious expression.

In *Rosenberger*, a university-recognized student organization published a newspaper called *Wide Awake*. The newspaper ran a number of stories on contemporary matters of interest to students such as racism, homosexuality, eating disorders, and music reviews, all written from an unabashedly Christian perspective. As a rule, the university provided such organizations with work space and paid for the expense of printing student publications. The printing costs were paid from a fund generated by student activity fees. But the university refused to reimburse the cost of printing *Wide Awake*. The refusal was pursuant to a policy disqualifying printing costs for groups promoting "a particular belief in or about a deity or ultimate reality." The student organization sued, claiming that this was yet another instance of discrimination against private religious speech in violation of the free speech clause. The university sought to justify its discriminatory treatment as required by a no-aid interpretation of the establishment clause.

By a vote of five to four, the Court ruled in favor of the students and directed the university to treat *Wide Awake* as equal to other student

38. 515 U.S. at 807-15.
39. 515 U.S. at 817.
40. See Kathleen M. Sullivan, "Religion and Liberal Democracy," *University of Chicago Law Review* 59 (1992): 195, 197-214, 222.

publications, without regard to religion. Justice Kennedy, joined by Chief Justice Rehnquist and Justices O'Connor, Scalia, and Thomas, wrote the majority opinion. Justice Kennedy determined that the university had created a limited public forum for student expression on a wide array of topics. Further, the denial of student activity funds to pay for the cost of printing *Wide Awake* was discrimination on the basis of the newspaper's Christian viewpoint on topics otherwise permitted in the forum. The university's policy denied funding not because the group that produced *Wide Awake* was a religious organization, but because of the publication's religious perspective. Justice Kennedy also rejected the argument that providing a scarce resource such as money differed from providing abundant resources such as classroom meeting space. The university could not dispense its resources, whether in abundant or limited supply, on a basis that discriminated against certain viewpoints.[41]

Justice Kennedy went on to reject the university's argument that providing direct funding for a religious newspaper was prohibited by the establishment clause. In so doing, Justice Kennedy stated a rule of law consistent with equal treatment theory, although he added that compliance with an equality-based rule was a significant factor — but not itself sufficient — in finding that the establishment clause was not violated:

A central lesson of our decisions is that a significant factor in upholding governmental programs in the face of Establishment Clause attack is their neutrality towards religion. . . . In enforcing the prohibition against laws respecting establishment of religion, we must be sure that we do not inadvertently prohibit the government from extending its general state law benefits to all its citizens without regard to their religious belief. . . . We have held that the guarantee of neutrality is respected, not offended, when the government, following neutral criteria and evenhanded policies, extends benefits to recipients whose ideologies and viewpoints, including religious ones, are broad and diverse.[42]

41. 515 U.S. at 830-35.
42. 515 U.S. at 839 (citations and internal quotations omitted). Although Justice Kennedy uses the language of neutrality, he is clearly using it in the sense of equal treatment.

Continuing, Justice Kennedy assessed both the purpose and the "practical details" of the university's program. The university's purpose was clearly not the advancement of religion. The university collected the activity fee to promote a wide variety of speech of interest to students. Hence, the fee was not like an earmarked tax for the support of religion.[43] As to the "practical details" that augured in favor of constitutionality, Justice Kennedy noted that state funds did not flow directly into the coffers of *Wide Awake;* rather, the newspaper's outside printer was paid by the university upon submission of an invoice.[44] Finally, Justice Kennedy noted that *Wide Awake* was a student publication, "not a religious institution, at least in the usual sense of that term as used in our case law, and it is not a religious organization as used in the University's own regulations."[45]

Although joining the majority opinion, Justice O'Connor had greater difficulty concluding that the establishment clause was not violated. In the choice between strict separation and equal treatment theories, she declared that *Rosenberger* did not elevate equal treatment as the new paradigm favored by the Court: "The Court's decision today therefore neither trumpets the supremacy of the neutrality principle nor signals the demise of the funding prohibition in Establishment Clause jurisprudence."[46] Accordingly, separationism appears to be Justice O'Connor's starting point in cases involving direct funding of religious organizations. However, she found several mitigating details which on balance satisfied her that providing assistance in this case did not carry the danger of state funds endorsing a religious message. First, university policies made it clear that the ideas expressed by student organizations, including religious groups, were not those of the university. Second, the funds were disbursed in a manner which ensured that monies would be used only for the university's purpose of maintaining a robust marketplace of ideas. Finally, Justice O'Connor noted the possibility that students objecting to their fees going toward ideas they opposed might not be compelled to pay the entire fee.[47]

Also joining the majority opinion, Justice Thomas wrote separately

43. 515 U.S. at 840.
44. 515 U.S. at 841.
45. 515 U.S. at 844.
46. 515 U.S. at 852.
47. 515 U.S. at 849-52.

to criticize the historical account in Justice Souter's dissent. Justice Thomas noted that history indeed indicates that the founders intended the establishment clause to prevent earmarked taxes for the support of religion. However, the equal participation of religious and nonreligious groups in a direct program-of-aid funded by general tax revenues was never an issue faced by the founding generation, and thus, in Justice Thomas's view, is not prohibited by the establishment clause.[48]

Justice Souter dissented, joined by Justices Stevens, Ginsburg, and Breyer. Concerning a program of direct aid funded by state monies, Justice Souter was of the opinion that any such program that supplied funds to support religion was unconstitutional. Hence, the four dissenting justices followed the strict separation model.[49]

Justice Souter severely criticized Justice Kennedy's opinion insofar as it made distinctions based on the funds going to the printer, not *Wide Awake;* on the funds coming from student fees, not taxes; and on *Wide Awake* not being a religious organization, although it was a newspaper of overtly religious perspective. The "practical details" part of Justice Kennedy's opinion does appear dazed and confused. These are indeed chimerical distinctions on which the establishment clause is seemingly made to turn. In fairness to Justice Kennedy, however, he may have been forced into these rationalizations in order to keep Justice O'Connor on the opinion. She supplied the crucial fifth vote. But if keeping Justice O'Connor from separately concurring is what explains Justice Kennedy's attention to "practical details," it came at a high price, *to wit:* officials and judges who do not like the result in *Rosenberger* have plenty of fine distinctions to cite in an effort to confine the holding to its specific facts.

In summary, concerning the constitutionality of general programs of direct aid, we learn from *Pinette* and *Rosenberger* that presently four justices are prepared to allow for a model of equal treatment for religion, four justices remain quite adamant about following separationism as their model, and Justice O'Connor is the swing vote. She was unwilling to commit to any general rule of law. Justice O'Connor appears to start from a presumption of no-aid, but then advises weighing all of the circumstances. If the program is equal on the face of it and if there are sufficient safeguards against the program becoming a subterfuge for the

48. 515 U.S. at 856-57.
49. 515 U.S. at 864-92.

channeling of tax monies to the support of religion, then she will uphold a rule of equal treatment.

In *Rosenberger,* as in *Widmar, Lamb's Chapel,* and *Pinette,* it was the free speech clause that required the equal treatment of religion. In the absence of the free speech claim, there was no indication that the Court would have required — as a matter of constitutional right — that religion be treated equally. I think it unlikely that it will do so in the near future. However, should a legislature choose to follow the equal treatment theory when designing a program-of-aid, then a slim majority of the Court will probably allow it. Accordingly, there now appears to be no right to the equal treatment of religion, but it is permitted.

It might also be asked whether the Court majority would still have found the establishment clause defense unsuccessful in *Widmar, Lamb's Chapel, Pinette,* and *Rosenberger* in the absence of the claimants' successful free-speech claims. Logically, the free-speech and no-establishment questions are independent of each other; thus the Court presumably would have rejected the establishment clause defense even if there had been no free-speech claim. For example, if the university in *Rosenberger* had elected as a matter of administrative judgment to design its limited forum in a manner that offered funding on an equal basis to all student newspapers, any resulting aid to an overtly religious newspaper such as *Wide Awake* would not violate the establishment clause. It follows that if a lawsuit ever comes before the Supreme Court challenging a legislature's equal funding of religion, a claim under the free speech clause should not be essential to the Court's upholding equal funding.

Conclusion

The current state of the U.S. Supreme Court's interpretation of the establishment clause can be summarized by contrasting the various lines of case-law precedent that follow a strict separation model with those that follow an equal treatment model. Three different types of situations appear:

1. constitutionally mandated equality, as in the situation of equal access for private religious speech (e.g., *Widmar, Pinette,* and *Rosenberger);*
2. constitutionally mandated strict separation, as in the situations of

government religious speech (e.g., *Stone* and *Schempp*) and direct funding of pervasively sectarian organizations (e.g., *Nyquist* and *Lemon*); and

3. instances where the Court's rule is to leave the matter to the discretion of the appropriate legislative body, as in the situations of religious exemptions from regulatory burdens (e.g., *Amos* and *Walz*) and aid to individuals who elect to "spend" a benefit at the religious institution of their choice (e.g., *Mueller* and *Witters*).

Only the future will reveal whether the Supreme Court will expand application of the equal treatment theory. If it does, it is likely to take the form of permitting direct funding of what now would be considered pervasively sectarian social-service organizations, as well as permitting individuals to elect to "spend" government-issued vouchers at both religious and secular schools.

CHAPTER 2

Equal Treatment and Religious Discrimination

MICHAEL W. McCONNELL

*In this chapter, Michael McConnell argues that Supreme Court inter-
pretations based on strict church-state separation and no aid to religion
make religion an object of discrimination. He also argues that if equal
treatment became the Court's guiding principle, religion would be
neither discriminated against nor placed in a position of special advantage. McConnell is Presidential Professor at the University of Utah
College of Law. This chapter was originally given as written testimony
before the Senate Judiciary Committee on September 29, 1995. It has
been edited for inclusion in this book.*

By any realistic standard of comparison, religious liberty in the United
States is in excellent shape. There is no official state religion; Americans
are free to practice their faith — for the most part — without fear or
hindrance and with a diversity and freedom that does not exist anywhere
else in the world. But for many Americans, especially those in public
schools and other parts of the government-controlled sector, religious
liberty is not all it should be, or all that our Constitution promises. All
too often, religious Americans, young and old, are finding that their
viewpoints and speech are curtailed because of their religious character.
In the past few decades, there has been an extraordinary secularization

of American public life, especially in the schools. Religious and traditionalist parents are finding that their viewpoints and concerns are ruled out-of-order, while at the same time the schools can be used to promote ideas and values that are sometimes offensive and hostile to their own.

Tolerance and diversity, it often seems, are one-way streets. There is scrupulous concern lest any child (and increasingly, any adult) be exposed to unwanted religious influence, but little or no concern for the religious or traditionalist child (or adult) who objects to the far-more-prevalent proselytizing that is carried on under the banner of various progressive causes. To object to foul language, relativistic values education, or inappropriate sex education is to risk being branded as a censor. To object to a moment of silence at the beginning of the classroom day, or to the singing of the Hallelujah Chorus, makes one a champion of civil liberty. Students who circulate scurrilous underground newspapers or who interrupt the school day with political activities receive the full protection of the First Amendment; but students who circulate Bible verses or try to meet with their friends for prayer or Bible study are often silenced. In reported cases in state and federal courts (outlined below), valedictory speeches have been censored, student research topics have been selectively curtailed, distribution of leaflets has been limited on the basis of religious content, and public employees have been forced to hide their Bibles. All too often, the freedom of religion protected by the First Amendment has been twisted into a one-sided freedom *from* religion.

If the polls are correct, many Americans attribute the enforced secularization of public life to the Supreme Court's decisions on school prayer, and see adoption of a school prayer amendment as the solution. For reasons I will outline below, I think that diagnosis is incorrect and disagree with that proposed remedy. But there is no question in my mind that the discontent with the status quo reflected in support for school prayer has a real and legitimate cause, and that constitutional doctrine has played a part in it.

In the decades preceding World War II, the dominant Protestant majority in this country not infrequently ran roughshod over the rights of others: Catholics, Jews, and non-Christians generally. Public schools were the vehicle for transmission of majority values, which were heavily imbued with a Protestant orientation. Aid to non-public schools was opposed because such schools were generally Roman Catholic. Prayer,

Bible reading, and the celebration of holidays were often conducted without regard to the coercive impact on children of other faiths. Much of the religion clause jurisprudence of the past forty years has been a response to this. And properly so. Who can read accounts by those who grew up in the era of Protestant hegemony without sensing the injustice and casual cruelty of the system?

But — largely in response to the prodding of courts with little understanding of or appreciation for the place of religion in the lives of ordinary Americans — we adopted the wrong solution to this very real problem. We should have opened up the government sector to a wider range of voices, promoted diversity and choice in education, sought pluralistic approaches to public activities with a cultural and religious aspect, and reduced the ability of those with power over public institutions to monopolize channels of education and influence. Instead, we preserved the structures by which Protestant Christians had dominated the public culture, and only changed the content. Secular ideologies came into a position of cultural dominance. The tables were turned. The winners and losers changed places. But the basic injustice — the use of government authority, over education and elsewhere, to favor and promote the values and ideals of one segment of the community — continued unabated.

Some have responded with a call to cultural warfare: if one worldview or another is to be in the ascendancy, let it be ours. Hence the persistent calls for a return to a "Christian America." But I think there is a better way. The solution is to insist, in a rigorous and principled way, on the rights of all Americans, without regard to faith and ideology, to participate in public life on an equal basis. No more double standard. When speech reflecting a secular viewpoint is permitted, then speech reflecting a religious viewpoint should be permitted, on the same basis. And vice versa. When the government provides benefits to private programs and activities — whether charitable endeavor, health care, education, or art — there should be no discrimination or exclusion on the basis of religious expression, character, or motivation. Religious citizens should not be required to engage in self-censorship as a precondition to participation in public programs. Public programs should be open to all who satisfy the objective purposes of the program. This is already the rule for controversial secular ideas and viewpoints; it should be the rule for religious ideas and viewpoints as well.

The beginning of wisdom in this contentious area of law is to recognize that neutrality and secularism are not the same thing. In the marketplace of ideas, secular viewpoints and ideologies are in competition with religious viewpoints and ideologies. It is no more neutral to favor the secular over the religious than it is to favor the religious over the secular. It is time for a reorientation of constitutional law: *away* from the false neutrality of the secular state, *toward* a genuine equality of rights.

This will require a great deal of forbearance, for toleration of the expression of others does not come easily. But toleration must be evenhanded. I am hard-pressed to understand why traditionalist citizens should be expected to tolerate the use of their tax dollars for lewd and sacrilegious art, while others go to court to ban even privately sponsored nativity scenes and menorahs from public property in December. The proper task of the establishment clause of the First Amendment is to ensure that no religion is given a privileged status in American public life — indeed, that religion in general is not given a privileged status. There is no basis in the history or purpose of the establishment clause for the secularization of society, or for discrimination against religious voices in the public sphere. As Justice William J. Brennan, Jr., wrote in *McDaniel v. Paty,* "Religionists no less than members of any other group enjoy the full measure of protection afforded speech, association, and political activity generally. The establishment clause . . . may not be used as a sword to justify repression of religion or its adherents from any aspect of public life."[1]

As I will show below, Justice Brennan's words are, unfortunately, not so much a description of current law as they are a prescription for reform.

Why Not School Prayer?

One reaction to the discontent just described is to amend the Constitution to permit organized prayer in public school classrooms. When I speak with religious leaders, lawyers, and laypersons concerned about the state of religious liberty in America — and especially about the effects of the

1. 435 U.S. 618, 641 (1978).

33

Supreme Court's school prayer decisions — I have given them this advice: it would be a mistake to attempt to overturn the school prayer decisions, but equally a mistake to believe that constitutional doctrine today adequately protects our rights of religious expression and participation, especially in public schools and other parts of the public sphere.

I believe that a narrow focus on a "school prayer amendment" would be a mistake for two reasons. First, whatever its merits in an earlier and more homogeneous era, the practice of officially sponsored and led prayer in public school classrooms would be impossible to maintain today in a way that would be either spiritually valuable or noncoercive. In order to be broadly acceptable, a prayer would have to be so general and abstract that it would be largely meaningless. Religious Americans are justified in attempting to integrate their faith into their ordinary lives, including the spheres of work and education, but a watered-down civil religion serves no one's interest. If anything, civil religion denigrates and trivializes religion by subordinating the forms of worship to the needs of the state. Moreover, no matter how abstract and how general the prayer may be — and for some, precisely because it has become so abstract and so general — it will remain unacceptable to some children in this world of diverse beliefs. I do not believe that officially sponsored, vocal classroom prayer can be offered without effectively coercing those in the minority. And that should not be permitted.

Indeed, I think there has come to be a widespread recognition among religious Americans that to allow school-sponsored prayer would cede partial control over the religious upbringing of their children to agents of the state. Speaking personally, I do not want my children to be taught prayers composed or selected by the government, and I do not think public school teachers are the proper parties to lead my children in acts of public worship. And I think these sentiments on this subject are coming to be shared by many Americans whose initial reaction to the *School Prayer* decisions was largely negative.

The second reason that a narrow focus on school prayer would be a mistake is that it would distract from far more serious questions of religious expression and participation in American public life, both in the public schools and elsewhere. The great problem is not that public officials are failing to sponsor prayers, but that — in a well-meaning but mistaken commitment to what they think is a constitutional ideal of a secular public sphere — teachers, principals, school board members, and other public officials often engage in discrimination against religious expression. In short, the point should not be to get the government into the business of prayer but to open up the public sphere to the free and equal participation of all citizens, religious and nonreligious alike.

Some of this anti-religious discrimination is blatantly unconstitutional; some of it has been upheld under current constitutional doctrine; all of it thrives on the uncertainty and confusion of Supreme Court decisions over the past forty years. And however problematic Supreme Court decisions have been, the effect "in the trenches" has been much, much worse. Among lower courts and governmental administrators, the nuance and confusion of Supreme Court rulings tend to be resolved by a wooden application of the three-part test of *Lemon v. Kurtzman:*[2] secular purpose, no "primary effect" of "advancing religion," and no "excessive entanglement" between church and state. This leads to a reflexive invalidation of anything that might be thought to "advance" religion or "entangle" religion and government — no matter how neutral, voluntary, or fair that religious participation might be.

Separation versus Equality of Rights

Interpretation of the establishment clause of the First Amendment during the past forty years has wavered between two fundamentally inconsistent visions of the relation between religion and government. Under one vision, which has gone under the rubric of the "no aid" view or the "strict separation" view, there is a high and impregnable wall of separation between government and religion. Religion is permitted — indeed, it is constitutionally protected — as long as it is confined to the private sphere of home, family, church, and synagogue. But the public sphere must be strictly secular. Laws must be based on strictly secular premises, public education must be strictly secular, public programs must be administered in a strictly secular manner, and public funds must be channeled only to strictly secular activities. This vision is reflected in the "*Lemon* test," which states that all law must have a "secular purpose"; that governmental action may not "advance" religion; and that religion and government must not become excessively "entangled."

2. 403 U.S. 602, 612-13 (1971).

This "secularist" or "separationist" model may be contrasted with what I think is the authentic vision of church-state relations in America: one of equality of rights. Under this vision, no individuals, groups, or ideas are given special status on the basis of their religion or philosophy. All are treated equally. The result is not a secular public sphere but a pluralistic public sphere in which every viewpoint and worldview is free to participate and "to flourish according to the zeal of its adherents and the appeal of its dogma," to borrow the words of Justice William O. Douglas in *Zorach v. Clauson*.[3]

Under this view, the two parts of the religion clause play a consistent and mutually supportive role in protecting religious liberty. The purpose of the First Amendment is to protect the religious lives of the people from unnecessary intrusions of government, whether promoting religion (establishment) or hindering it (free exercise). This approach will foster religious pluralism — as opposed to either majoritarian religion on the one hand or secularism on the other. It seeks to preserve what Madison called the "full and equal rights" of religious believers and communities to define their own way of life, so long as they do not interfere with the rights of others, and to participate fully and equally with their fellow citizens in public life without being forced to shed or disguise their religious convictions and character.

Under the separationist view, the various parts of the First Amendment are at war with one another. The free-exercise clause forbids the government from inflicting penalties for the practice of religion. As the Court stated in *Sherbert v. Verner*, "the liberties of religion and expression may be infringed by the denial of or placing of conditions upon a benefit or privilege,"[4] just as they may by the imposition of a "fine" for the exercise of religion. But the establishment clause (under the separationist interpretation) requires the government to withhold otherwise available benefits if the beneficiaries would use it for a religious activity. For example, under the Child Care and Development Block Grant (42 U.S.C. §9858k), a qualifying child-care facility can receive government assistance if and only if it refrains from "any sectarian purpose or activity." This means that a church-based child-care center would have to cease such innocuous (and to many parents, desirable) practices as

3. 343 U.S. 306, 313 (1952).
4. 374 U.S. 398, 404 (1963).

offering a prayer before snacks or a program of reading Bible stories. Under the principle of *Sherbert v. Verner,* this looks very much like a denial of the free exercise of religion: denial of funding is the equivalent of a "fine" for engaging in acts of religious speech. It diminishes the freedom of the indigent parent to obtain child care under religious auspices if that is the family's preference, and it creates an incentive for child-care centers to secularize themselves if they wish to serve the low-income population. Yet it is said to be required by the establishment clause.

Thus, the establishment clause is said to require precisely what the free-exercise clause prohibits: withholding of benefits on account of the exercise of a constitutional right. In a world in which the government aids or advances many different causes and institutions, this interpretation means, in effect, that the government *must* discriminate against religion. The separationist reading of the establishment clause poses an increasingly serious threat to religious liberty as the government sector increases in its scope and activity. When the government was little more than the "watchman state," it could be strictly secular, and no one's rights were invaded. But as the government becomes involved with more and more areas of life that previously were private, such as health, charity, education, and culture, a secular state becomes tantamount to a secular culture.

When different parts of the same constitutional amendment are in conflict, the results inevitably will be confusing, inconsistent, and unpredictable. Constitutional historian Leonard Levy has commented that "the Court has managed to unite those who stand at polar opposites on the results that the Court reaches; a strict separationist and a zealous accommodationist are likely to agree that the Supreme Court would not recognize an establishment of religion if it took life and bit the Justices."[5] Worse yet, in the hands of school administrators, local officials, and lower courts, the effect is all too often to deny religious citizens opportunities to which they would otherwise be entitled. In the public schools in particular, this means that religious references in the curriculum have been comprehensively eliminated and religious students forced to shed their constitutional rights at the schoolhouse gate — meanwhile, advo-

5. Levy, *The Establishment Clause: Religion and the First Amendment* (New York: Macmillan, 1986), p. 163.

cates of various "progressive" ideologies are free to use the schools to advance their ideas of public morality, even when it means running roughshod over the desires and convictions of religious and traditionalist parents. It is no wonder that many parents have come to believe that the First Amendment works against them.

Denial of Equal Rights of Expression

Lest this account seem too abstract or alarmist, let me give some examples from litigated cases. I choose these examples because the facts can be verified from the case reports. But only a small fraction of cases can be litigated; these are only the tip of the iceberg. My examples fall into two categories. The first involves denial of equal access to students and other persons who wish to engage in religious speech or expression at times when and places where nonreligious expression is allowed. The second involves denial of government benefits to individuals or groups on the basis of their religious viewpoint, character, or motivation. These are two faces of the same problem.

Guidry v. Calcasieu Parish School Board.[6] In this case, the class valedictorian informed the school principal of her intention to devote a portion of her graduation speech to the importance of Jesus Christ in her life. The principal ordered her to remove the offending portion; she refused and was eliminated from the graduation program. The district court upheld the principal's action and the court of appeals affirmed on jurisdictional grounds. There have been similar incidents elsewhere, including a case now proceeding in Ohio.

Bishop v. Aronov.[7] In this case, a tenure-track professor of exercise physiology at a public university made occasional references in class to his religious beliefs and offered an optional, after-class lecture entitled "Evidences of God in Human Physiology." The dean ordered him to cease these activities, despite the fact that the professor had an undoubted academic-freedom right to make personal remarks during class so long as they were not excessive, disruptive, or coercive, and despite the fact that the lecture

6. Religious Freedom Report, 118 (E.D. La. 1989), *aff'd on jurisdictional grounds sub nom. Guidry v. Broussard,* 897 F.2d 181 (5th Cir. 1990).
7. 926 F.2d 1066 (11th Cir. 1991), cert. denied, 112 S. Ct. 3026 (1992).

was within his professional expertise. The court of appeals affirmed the dean's order, hinting that allowing a professor to express his or her views in this way might violate the establishment clause.[8]

Settle v. Dickson County School Board.[9] In this case, students were permitted to choose their own topic for a research paper, so long as the topic was "interesting, researchable, and decent." Among the subjects approved by the teacher were spiritualism, reincarnation, and magic throughout history. One student, however, asked to write on the life of Jesus Christ, was refused permission, and ultimately received a grade of "zero" on the paper. The teacher gave a smorgasbord of reasons for her refusal, all of them uninformed, bigoted, or selectively applied. In particular, the teacher said that "we don't deal with personal religion — personal religious beliefs. It's just not an appropriate thing to do in a public school." Indeed, she said that "the law says we are not to deal with religious issues in the classroom." This is — or at least should be — an erroneous statement of the law. When a research topic is otherwise appropriate, as this one was, the fact that it involves religion is not a legitimate basis for exclusion. Nonetheless, the Sixth Circuit Court of Appeals held that "all six of Ms. Ramsey's stated reasons for refusing to allow Brittney to write the paper fall within the broad leeway of teachers to determine the nature of the curriculum and the grades to be awarded to students, even the reasons that may be mistaken."[10] If even the teacher's "mistaken" reasons fall within the school's "broad leeway," that means that students have no constitutional rights in the matter. While I have much sympathy for keeping the courts out of the business of supervising teachers' curricular decisions, I have little doubt that the case would have come out the other way if a racist teacher had forbidden a paper on Martin Luther King, Jr., or an anti-communist teacher had forbidden a paper on the evils of capitalism.

Perumal v. Saddleback Valley School District.[11] In this case, students at a southern California public high school were forbidden to distribute leaflets inviting other students to their Bible study group, despite a

8. I represented Professor Bishop in his unsuccessful petition for certiorari in the Supreme Court.

9. 53 F.3d 152 (6th Cir. 1995).

10. 53 F.3d at 156.

11. 198 Cal. App. 3d 14, 243 Cal. Rpt. 245 (Ct. App., 4th Dist.), cert. denied, 488 U.S. 933 (1988).

California statute permitting students to distribute petitions and other printed materials. The state appellate court upheld the school's action, holding that permitting the students to distribute the leaflets would violate the establishment clause. "The inevitable consequence of the establishment clause when applied to religious ritual on school property," the court reasoned, "is to restrict that activity to preserve the wall between church and state."[12]

Roberts v. Madigan.[13] In this case, a fifth-grade public school teacher was ordered by the assistant principal to remove a Bible from the surface of his desk, to refrain from reading the Bible during the class's silent reading period, and to remove two illustrated books of Bible stories from a classroom library of over 350 volumes. The Court of Appeals upheld the principal's action, holding that the teacher's conduct violated the establishment clause.

Brown v. Polk County.[14] Although some restrictions on religious speech are justified, governments have imposed and courts have upheld restrictions that go far beyond what should be constitutionally legitimate. In *Brown v. Polk County,* for example, a supervisor regularly held Bible studies with co-religionists in his office, engaged in religious counseling, and used office resources to promote his religious ministry, all to a degree that might well be considered excessive and disruptive to morale. The First Amendment would seem to require that a carefully tailored remedy be applied; instead, the supervisor was ordered to remove all religious objects from his office, including removing a Bible from a desk drawer, to cease any activity that "could be considered" to be religious proselytizing, witnessing, or counseling in the workplace, and even to refrain from meeting with like-minded co-workers before work in his own office for prayer. On appeal, a panel of the Eighth Circuit Court upheld these remarkable restrictions over a dissent that started with the statement that the action of the County "seems to me so egregious and obviously illegal as almost to furnish direct evidence of an anti-Christian animus on their part."[15] It took rehearing en banc

---

12. 243 Cal. Rpt. at 549. I represented the students in their unsuccessful petition for a writ of certiorari in the Supreme Court.
13. 921 F.2d 1047 (10th Cir. 1990), cert. denied, 112 S. Ct. 3026 (1992).
14. 61 F.3d 650 (8th Cir. 1995).
15. 37 F.3d 404, 412.

in the Court of Appeals to reverse many of these restrictions. Even then, the employees were forbidden to meet for prayer in their offices, and four of the judges would have upheld the entire ban on religious expression in the workplace.

Hedges v. Wauconda Community School District.[16] While lower courts are less protective of religious expression than the Supreme Court, local governments and school boards are often even less protective than the lower courts. It is remarkable how many local school boards, libraries, and other local institutions have content-based restrictions prohibiting religious expression on their premises. In *Hedges v. Wauconda Community School District*, for example, an eighth grader attempted to hand out to her fellow students a religious leaflet entitled *Issues and Answers* before the start of the school day. The principal retrieved the leaflets and ordered her not to distribute such literature again. The written school policy prohibited distribution of material that is obscene, pornographic, pervasively indecent, invasive of the privacy of others, disruptive, or religious, while permitting distribution of nonlibelous and nondisruptive secular materials. It says something about the state of mind of the modern school board that "religious" materials are lumped together with obscenity, pornography, and libel. This rather transparent form of viewpoint discrimination was struck down by the district court. But even after the district court decision, the school board issued a new policy, equally discriminatory, spelling out in greater detail what kinds of religious publications are prohibited (including materials that constitute "an effort to proselytize other students"). Once again, the student was forbidden to distribute *Issues and Answers*. The National School Boards Association submitted an *amicus curiae* brief in support of the board's anti-religious policy, which demonstrates that policies of this sort — far from being aberrant — are common among school administrators. In a similar case in Florida, a principal confiscated and destroyed invitations that an elementary school student had given to her friends, inviting them to a church-based alternative to a Halloween party.[17]

Fortunately, in these two cases the courts intervened on behalf of the students. In a particularly strong opinion by Judge Frank Easter-

16. 9 F.3d 1295 (7th Cir. 1993).
17. See *Johnston-Loehner v. O'Brien*, 859 F. Supp. 757 (M.D. Fla. 1994).

brook in *Hedges,* the Seventh Circuit Court held that "no arm of government may discriminate against religious speech when speech on other subjects is permitted in the same place at the same time."[18] This, it seems to me, is a worthy statement of constitutional principle, which ought to be substituted for the restrictive doctrine imposed by most school boards and lower courts under the "*Lemon* test."

Hedges is an illustration of the extraordinary persistence of some school officials in attempting to prevent religious expression on school property. It should not be necessary for eighth graders to make two separate trips to the federal courthouse to have their basic First Amendment rights recognized by their school principals. Most students do not have the resources or the courage to confront the system in this way. All around the country, there are reports that students in public schools have been prohibited from meeting with others for prayer at the flagpole, from expressing religious views or addressing religious themes in school reports, from praying at meals, and from distributing religious literature. In many such instances, the school officials yield upon being confronted by legal counsel. In other instances, they spend great sums of money on legal fees to defend their right to discriminate against religious speech, with a surprising degree of success in the courts. We can only assume that most students confronted with this sort of restriction, not having ready access to lawyers and not being accustomed to bringing lawsuits against their principals, simply acquiesce and are silenced.

Garnett v. Renton School District.[19] This is another example, from my own experience, of the persistence of school boards in resisting religious expression. I represented a group of high school students in Renton, Washington, who wanted to form a prayer and Bible study club after school. Immediately after passage of the Equal Access Act in 1984, they sought permission to meet, and were denied. Thus began a Kafkaesque trial by ordeal in the federal courts, in which the students, backed by volunteer lawyers from the Christian Legal Society, were opposed by paid counsel of the school board supported by energetic efforts by the local chapters of the ACLU and the American Jewish Committee. It was to take nine years — including three trips to the district court, four trips to the court of appeals, and two trips to the

18. 9 F.3d 1297 (7th Cir. 1993).
19. 987 F.2d 641 (9th Cir.), cert. denied, 114 S. Ct. 72 (1993).

Supreme Court — before the students ultimately won vindication of their rights. At the bitter end, the ACLU and the American Jewish Committee made the extraordinary argument that the school district should shut down its entire extracurricular program rather than allow the students to meet. This is just one illustration of the hostility and opposition that religious students sometimes encounter when they seek to express their faith on public school property.

I have heard it said that cases of discrimination against religious speech are rare. It is sometimes suggested that the cases are concocted by activist groups for newspaper consumption. This is not true. In each of the cases in which I have been involved, the students or (in one case) the professor had been stymied by the system long before they ever turned to lawyers. In each case, the precedent has been against them. Outside the narrow compass of the Equal Access Act, the rights of religious speakers are rarely understood and frequently denied. If cases of this sort are so rare, why is it that the federal courts of appeals for the Second, Fourth, Sixth, Eighth, Ninth, Tenth, and Eleventh Circuits — not to mention state courts and district courts — have all decided cases in the past few years holding that religious speakers are *not* entitled to equal treatment, and in many cases that religious speakers *must* be excluded from participating in forums for expression that are open to similar speech of a secular orientation? And how many more denials of free speech rights have occurred in situations where no one had the inclination, sophistication, or determination to take the case to court?

Denial of Benefits on Account of Religion

Discrimination against religious expression does not always take the form of denial of access to a forum for speech. Often it consists of denials of government benefits of various sorts to those whose expressive activity is deemed to be religious. This form of discrimination is powerfully supported by a line of precedent in the Supreme Court based on *Lemon v. Kurtzman*,[20] which prohibits the use of public funds for what are called "specifically religious activities" or by "pervasively religious" organizations. In those instances in which nonreligious and even

20. 403 U.S. 602 (1971). Also see *Hunt v. McNair*, 413 U.S. 734, 743 (1973).

43

anti-religious activity receive government support, however, it is rank discrimination to exclude activity that expresses religious character, ideas, or motivation. I fully concur with the view that the government may not fund organizations or activities *because they are religious,* or single out religious groups or activities for special favor; but the Constitution should not be read to require discrimination against religion. Neutrality, not secularism, is the key to a proper interpretation of the establishment clause as it applies to government benefits. The government should not be permitted to use its power of the purse to favor secular over religious voices, any more than it may favor religious over secular voices.

As Justice O'Connor stated in a 1994 concurring opinion, "The Religion Clauses prohibit the government from favoring religion, but they provide no warrant for discriminating *against* religion."[21] Unfortunately, this position, which I believe would strike most Americans as being obvious and commonsensical, was in a portion of a concurring opinion in which Justice O'Connor was calling for a *reconsideration* of current doctrine. The Court should "be prepared" in a "proper case," she said, to reconsider its doctrine, "in order to bring our Establishment Clause jurisprudence back to what I think is the proper track — government impartiality, not animosity, toward religion."[22] This has not yet happened.

The following litigated cases exemplify the problem.

Fordham University v. Brown.[23] In this case, the Department of Commerce rejected the application of the public radio station operated by Fordham University for federal funding, under the Public Telecommunications Facilities Program, for construction of a new radio tower. Although the review process gave the Fordham station the highest possible recommendation, the Department rejected the application because, for the past forty-seven years, the station has broadcast Catholic mass from the Fordham University chapel for one hour each Sunday morning. This broadcast, according to the Department, offends the regulation against the use of funded facilities "for essentially sectarian purposes." The district court upheld the decision. Amazingly, the court

21. *Bd. of Education of Kiryas Joel v. Grumet,* 114 S. Ct. 2481, 2498 (1994).
22. *Bd. of Education of Kiryas Joel v. Grumet,* 114 S. Ct. 2481, 2498.
23. 856 F. Supp. 684 (D. D.C. 1994).

44

found that the restrictions against carrying religious programming "do not inhibit religion."[24] Rather, it held, "the challenged regulations are a product of the Secretary's efforts to comply with Supreme Court jurisprudence in this area."[25] This is precisely the problem: government officials are under the impression, too often confirmed by the courts, that discrimination against religious speech is not only constitutionally permissible but constitutionally required. (This case was later settled on appeal on terms favorable to Fordham.)

Scores of federal and state programs contain restrictions similar to the regulation in the Fordham case, which in practice amount to discrimination explicitly on the basis of religion. Congress needs to investigate the extent to which the federal government itself is the originator and instigator of anti-religious discrimination in the administration of public funds.

Witters v. Department of Services for the Blind.[26] In this case, the state of Washington had a program to pay for vocational education for the blind. Larry Witters, an eligible individual, wished to use these benefits to study for a career in the clergy. Because of the religious nature of his proposed field of study, the Washington Supreme Court held that funding would violate the establishment clause. In an extremely important decision, the United States Supreme Court unanimously rejected that position, holding that state assistance for religious training does not violate the First Amendment so long as the aid is "made available generally without regard to the sectarian-nonsectarian, or public-nonpublic nature of the institution benefited, and is in no way skewed toward religion."[27] On remand to the state court, however, the state Supreme Court again ruled that Witters could not be included in the program, this time on the basis of the state constitution. Again, Witters petitioned the United States Supreme Court, but this time the petition was denied. While the Court was prepared to reject the view that the First Amendment does not *compel* anti-religious discrimination in this context, it was not prepared to hold that the First Amendment *prohibits* anti-

24. 856 F. Supp. at 698.
25. 856 F. Supp. at 699.
26. 112 Wash. 2d 363, 771 P.2d 1119, cert. denied, 110 S. Ct. 147 (1989). 474 U.S. 481 (1986).
27. 474 U.S. at 487-88.

religious discrimination. Witters never received the vocational assistance to which he was entitled.

The Witters case illustrates an important point: that the erroneous separationist understanding of the First Amendment has extended to many state constitutions as well as the federal constitution. It is not sufficient to obtain reversal of federal establishment-clause doctrines like the "*Lemon* test"; protection should be extended to those whose rights are violated under state interpretations of church-state separation as well.

Aguilar v. Felton.[28] No discussion of problems in this area would be complete without reference to the Supreme Court's disgraceful record with regard to educational choice. Much of the problematic precedent in this area arose in the context of state efforts to provide some assistance to parents who choose to educate their children under religious auspices. The Supreme Court, in a series of decisions beginning with *Lemon v. Kurtzman,* has made these efforts virtually impossible. The most egregious decision, in my opinion, was *Aguilar v. Felton,* in which the Court struck down those portions of the Elementary and Secondary Education Act that provided remedial English and math training by public school teachers to educationally and economically disadvantaged students on the premises of their schools, both public and private. The effect has been to deny less affluent parents the practical ability to exercise choice in education, as is their constitutional right, and to deny to urban school districts the more practicable way to provide remedial services to some of their neediest children. This makes no sense, either pedagogically or constitutionally. In a pluralistic nation, the parents — not the voting majority — should determine the content of their children's education, and they should not be penalized for it. Diversity and choice are far more consistent with the purposes of the First Amendment than the present system.[29] (In the summer of 1997, after this essay was written, the Supreme Court overruled *Aguilar v. Felton.*)

28. 473 U.S. 402 (1985). As Assistant to the Solicitor General, I was the principal author of the brief in support of the program, and I argued the companion case, *Grand Rapids School Dist. v. Ball,* 473 U.S. 373 (1985).

29. I have set forth my views on educational choice at greater length in several articles, including "The Selective Funding Problem: Abortion and Religious Schools," *Harvard Law Review* 104 (1991): 989; and "Multiculturalism, Majoritarianism, and Educational Choice: What Does Our Constitutional Tradition Have To Say?" *University of Chicago Legal Forum,* 1991 (1991), 123.

Miller v. Benson.[30] Even today, when most expert observers believe the Supreme Court would uphold a well-drafted, genuinely neutral educational-choice plan, the lower courts continue to rule to the contrary. A recent example is *Miller v. Benson,* in which the federal district court ruled that the state of Wisconsin may not extend its private school choice plan to so-called sectarian schools. In Milwaukee, students qualifying for the program can attend the private school of their choice, including progressive schools, Afrocentric schools, or other schools reflecting the philosophical orientation of the parents, teachers, and administration. But they cannot attend schools where the philosophical orientation is religious. This obviously excludes a large number of the schools parents would like to choose in Milwaukee, schools that deliver an excellent education, something that public schools have all too often failed to do.

Two explanations are usually offered in defense of the idea that tax-supported benefit programs must not be extended to religiously affiliated activities, even on a neutral basis. Neither, in my opinion, is persuasive.

First, it is argued that such participation would violate the religious freedom of taxpayers because it would compel them to support schools or activities propagating ideas in which they do not believe. But this is a valid objection only when funding is provided to a religious activity on a preferential basis, because it is a religious activity. That is what the battle over disestablishment among our founders was about. The principle has no application when the government funds a wide variety of private groups that have a secular purpose, and religious groups are included on a neutral basis. No one suggests that churches or synagogues should not enjoy — on an equal basis with other property and other nonprofit institutions — the valuable benefits of police and fire protection, roads, sewers, and tax benefits. There is no principled reason to deny a similar equality to citizens who choose religious schools or the services of other religious institutions. Justice Brennan stated the principle well in his plurality opinion in *Texas Monthly, Inc. v. Bullock:* "Insofar as [a] subsidy is conferred upon a wide array of nonsectarian groups as well as religious organizations in pursuit of some legitimate secular end, the fact that religious groups benefit incidentally does not

30. 878 F. Supp. 1209 (E.D. Wis.).

47

deprive the subsidy of the secular purpose and primary effect mandated by the Establishment Clause."[31] The underlying requirement should be one of neutrality — that is, equality of treatment. The government must not favor religion, but neither is it required to discriminate against religion.

Second, it is suggested that religious recipients would be made worse off by inclusion in neutral aid programs because the aid would come with "strings." These "strings," it is argued, would create incentives for the recipients to comply with governmental policy even at the expense of their own autonomous principles. There are two answers to this argument. First, this ought to be a choice left to the recipient. Any aid program has costs as well as benefits, and ordinarily we allow the affected individuals and groups to weigh the costs and benefits for themselves. There is no reason to assume that religious individuals and groups have any less competence to make the choice than others. Second, and more important, is the fact that the present system creates even more severe incentives for potential recipients to betray their principles. Under current doctrine, they can obtain aid if and only if they renounce their religious character. The Fordham radio station will receive hundreds of thousands of dollars — so long as it agrees to cease broadcasts of the mass. A child-care center serving low-income clients can receive federal assistance — if it eliminates Bible stories and prayers before the snack. These conditional "strings" are far worse than the strings that ordinarily come with the aid, because they interfere with the fundamental religious character of the recipient. The current system makes government grant programs relentless engines of secularization. I believe that government programs should have as neutral an effect as possible, which means that the programs should be administered without discrimination on the basis of religion.

Recent Developments

Since proposals for a Religious Equality Amendment or other congressional action to protect religious freedom surfaced in 1995, there have been several encouraging developments — in court, in Congress,

31. 489 U.S. 1, 14-15 (1989).

and in the executive branch. Unfortunately, these developments fall far short of full vindication of constitutional rights.

In 1995, the Supreme Court decided two cases with a direct bearing on the question of religious equality, *Rosenberger v. Rector* and *Capitol Square Review Board v. Pinette*.[32] I represented the petitioners in the Rosenberger case, a group of students at the University of Virginia who started a magazine with a religious editorial viewpoint and were for that reason denied access to the Student Activities Fund, which subsidizes the printing costs of other student publications and activities that express a wide variety of viewpoints. The university's position was that it must fund publications expressing controversial viewpoints of a secular nature (including gay, racist, pro-choice, Marxist, or whatever), without discrimination on the basis of viewpoint, but that publications addressing similar issues from a religious perspective are not allowed. (Notwithstanding its prohibition of "religious" activities, the university funded the Muslim Students Association and the Jewish Law Students Association; it said the activities of these groups were "cultural" rather than "religious.") The Court of Appeals upheld the university's action on the ground that otherwise impermissible viewpoint discrimination against religious speech is justified by the "compelling" governmental interest of avoiding a violation of the establishment clause. In other words: the free speech clause and the establishment clause mean opposite things, and the establishment clause trumps the free speech clause.

The Supreme Court reversed the decision of the Court of Appeals, holding that "the Establishment Clause [does not] justif[y], much less require[,] a refusal to extend free speech rights to religious speakers who participate in broad-reaching programs neutral in design."[33] This is an excellent statement of what should be the operative constitutional principle. Unfortunately, the precedential weight of this decision is considerably diminished by three factors.

First, the majority opinion limited its holding to the narrow factual context of the case, suggesting that the principle of neutrality quoted above may not apply when tax funds are involved or when payments are made directly to the religious speakers and not (as in *Rosenberger*) to an independent third party, such as the printer.

32. 115 S. Ct. 2510 (1995) and 115 S. Ct. 2440 (1995).
33. 115 S. Ct. at 2522.

Second, a crucial fifth vote for the decision was provided by Justice O'Connor, who wrote a concurring opinion specifically disavowing any "categorical" answer to the constitutional question, instead suggesting that courts in the future must "draw lines, sometimes quite fine, based on the particular facts of the case."[34] For lower courts, government officials, and would-be speakers who need to conform their conduct and their decisions to the Constitution, this refusal even to attempt to state operative principles is extremely problematic, for they cannot know (without litigation) what their rights and responsibilities are. As Justice O'Connor herself stated in another context, "Liberty finds no refuge in a jurisprudence of doubt."[35]

Third, there were four justices in dissent who took a hard, uncompromising separationist position. This opinion warrants attention, because it confirms the central point I have made here: that this mode of interpretation of the establishment clause is inherently inconsistent with the ideal of neutrality toward religion. With commendable candor, the dissent by Justice Souter openly attacks the idea that "evenhandedness" — Justice Souter's synonym for neutrality — is required, *or even permitted,* by the First Amendment. Even if "aid is distributed generally and on a neutral basis," otherwise eligible recipients *must be excluded if they are religious.*[36] (The dissent recognizes only that in "doubtful" cases, mostly involving "indirect" aid, neutrality may be the operative principle.) Ordinarily, one might not be too concerned about a dissent, which is, after all, only a dissent. But a dissent joined by four of the justices (including three of the four most recent appointees), in the face of a wavering five-justice majority, could easily influence lower courts and future cases, and even become the majority position within a few years. This should be a cause for alarm for all lovers of religious liberty, because the message is clear: religious citizens are *not* entitled to equal treatment, but *must* be excluded from the benefit of public programs otherwise open to all.

Similarly, in *Pinette,* the Court ruled that private speakers who wished to display a religious symbol on public property on exactly the same terms and conditions as secular symbols have a constitutional right

34. 115 S. Ct. at 2526.
35. *Planned Parenthood v. Casey,* 505 U.S. at 844 (1992).
36. 115 S. Ct. at 2541.

to do so. But again, the precedential value of the opinion was undermined by a concurrence by Justice O'Connor, who, as in *Rosenberger*, resisted a clear statement of principle in favor of case-by-case judgment under an "endorsement" test.

Thus, *Rosenberger* and *Pinette* repudiate separationist interpretations of the establishment clause and advance the protection of an equality of rights for all persons, religious as well as nonreligious. But the lack of clear-cut statements of principle in majority opinions means that ordinary citizens still do not know where they stand. All that can be predicted is that much more litigation will be necessary before First Amendment rights are secured.

As part of the 1996 welfare reform legislation, Congress adopted a provision protecting the rights of private groups, religious as well as nonreligious, to assist in dealing with the grave problems of poverty without being forced to sacrifice their religious (or other) commitments and character. This, too, is a major step toward securing an equality of rights, and a major break with past programs in which religiously affiliated service providers were either excluded or forced to secularize themselves — even when they would be among the most effective participants in the program. Unfortunately, this provision applies to only a few federal programs, and it has yet to be tested in the courts.

Finally, the President made a major statement in 1995 on the issue of the rights of religious students in public schools, and the Secretary of Education distributed guidelines (drafted by a wide spectrum of outside groups) advising school administrators on the current state of the law.[37] This was a positive development, because much of the discrimination against religious speech is a product of misinformation and ignorance. The guidelines themselves, of course, have no legal status.

Is Congressional Action Appropriate?

I do not want to minimize the importance of the developments I have just described. But they are far from a full solution to the problem. Many millions of Americans remain concerned — justifiably so — that

37. See Steven Homes, "Clinton Defines Religion's Role in U.S. Schools," *New York Times*, 26 August 1995, pp. A1, A8.

their rights of religious expression, participation, and practice remain at risk. The question is whether or not there is anything Congress can do to secure these rights.

Some may argue that interpretation of the Constitution is a matter belonging solely to the courts, and that it would be inappropriate for Congress to play a role in enforcing religious citizens' rights to equality of treatment. But this argument misconceives the historic role of Congress under our constitutional system as an enforcer of rights and as a corrective to judicial misconstruction. Both by constitutional amendment and by statute, Congress has frequently intervened when the courts have failed to provide adequate protection for constitutional rights or have otherwise misinterpreted the Constitution.

Congress has been particularly attentive to religious liberty in recent years, enacting three major statutes on the subject in the past decade, each of them designed to change or overrule judicial interpretations: the Equal Access Act, the Religious Freedom Restoration Act,[38] and the Native American Free Exercise of Religion Act.

Most pertinent for present purposes is the Equal Access Act, which most observers consider to have been a tremendous success. Even most groups who opposed the idea of equal access at the time have now come to appreciate the wisdom and justice of the proposition that students should be able to form noncurricular clubs and meet on school grounds without discrimination on the basis of the political, philosophical, or religious content of their speech. The only problem with the Equal Access Act is its narrow scope. It applies only to one public benefit (access to meeting rooms), only to high school students, only to particular times. But if high school students should not be denied otherwise available privileges on the basis of the religious character of their speech, why should not *all* citizens be protected from the denial of *any otherwise available public benefit* on the basis of their religious character? In my view, the principle of the Equal Access Act should be understood not as a narrow solution to a particular problem, but as a general principle of equal access to public benefits.

At a minimum, I submit, Congress should survey existing federal

38. The Supreme Court subsequently held the Religious Freedom Restoration Act unconstitutional, at least as applied to state and local governments (*City of Boerne v. Flores*, 117 S. Ct. 2157 [1997]).

programs to identify those in which religious citizens are denied rights to equal treatment. The Fordham case, which I described earlier, is a shocking example of this. If Congress does nothing else, it should at least clean house to ensure that the federal government is not itself discriminating against religious citizens.

As a second step, expanded equal-access legislation could be passed to provide effective legal remedies against state and local — as well as federal — governments and agencies. Congress should consider whether statutory penalties, patterned after those in the Federal Access to Clinic Entrances Act, would be appropriate to ensure that government actors have the incentive to comply with the law, and thus reduce the need for litigation.[39]

Finally, Congress should give serious consideration to a constitutional amendment embodying the fundamental principle of religious equality. This obviously would require a greater effort to achieve proposal and ratification, but to the extent that the problems are caused by misinterpretations of the establishment clause, it would be a more secure approach than mere legislation (which could, after all, be held unconstitutional). It is to be expected that some separationist groups would fight such an effort with great vigor, but the principle of religious equality will no doubt strike a chord with the American public as reflecting a fair and workable approach to church-state problems. Obviously, an amendment to the Constitution should not be proposed lightly, and would require great care. After some forty years of confusing and often erroneous decisions by the Supreme Court in this area, however, it is understandable that many Americans perceive a need for dramatic action.

In 1996 the Judiciary Committee of the House of Representatives considered a proposed amendment to the Constitution that was introduced by Representative Richard Armey. It read: "In order to secure the right of the people to acknowledge and serve God according to the dictates of conscience, neither the United States nor any State shall deny

---

39. The Federal Access to Clinic Entrances Act, passed in 1994, was patterned after civil rights laws and prohibits the use of force, the threat of force, or obstruction to interfere with access to abortion clinics and houses of worship. It provides that civil and criminal action can be initiated by federal or state attorneys general and by persons whose rights under the law were violated. See "Abortion Clinic Access Accord Heads for Final Passage," *Congressional Quarterly Weekly Report,* 30 April 1994, p. 1070.

any person equal access to a benefit, or otherwise discriminate against any person, on account of religious belief, expression, or exercise. This amendment does not authorize government to coerce or inhibit religious belief, expression, or exercise."[40] An amendment such as this or one of a similar nature has great potential to overcome the confusions and mixed signals coming out of the courts, and thereby restore religious equality and freedom.

Even if such a proposal were not ultimately adopted, public deliberation of it would bring these important questions to the forefront, and — like the proposed Child Labor Amendment and Equal Rights Amendments in the past — might well be a stimulus for reform that would make ultimate ratification unnecessary. Because of a lack of interest among the press and the often arcane language of legal decisions, the public has not been made aware of the extent to which our constitutional freedom *of* religion has been transformed into a freedom *from* religion. Public deliberation over these issues would in itself be salutary. Indeed, there is reason to believe that some of the recent positive developments, such as the President's statement and the Secretary of Education's guidelines, have been responses to the amendment proposal. That is all to the good. The problem has occurred in large part because religious discrimination has been cloaked in language of "the separation between church and state," the "*Lemon* test," and other legal formulas that disguise what is really going on. It is time to bring these issues out into the open. Congress needs to play a major role in doing so.

40. House Joint Resolution 184, 14th Congress, 2d Session. An earlier version of this amendment was introduced by Representative Henry Hyde of Illinois.

CHAPTER 3

The Theoretical Roots of Equal Treatment

JAMES W. SKILLEN

In this chapter, James Skillen argues that modern liberal thought provides an inadequate theoretical base for an approach to religious freedom that assures all religious and philosophical worldviews will have equal access to the public arena. He suggests pluralist thought offers a better theoretical base for achieving full religious freedom. Skillen is the executive director of the Center for Public Justice in Annapolis, Maryland, and the author of many books and articles, including Recharging the American Experiment: Principled Pluralism for Genuine Civic Community.

The chief political and constitutional questions in dispute today in regard to religion involve whether citizens are free to practice their religions (both inside and outside churches) with the assurance of fair and equal protection under the law. This dispute, I believe, will not be settled as long as the strict separationist perspective defines religion narrowly and confines most religious expressions to a private sphere while giving majoritarian control to an equally religious view of life that escapes the tag "parochial" by virtue of its self-designation as secular or nonsectarian.

The strict separationist position on issues of church and state is necessarily committed to the belief that keeping religion and religious organizations strictly separate from the political realm does no harm to — and even helps — the well-being of both religion and society as a whole. But underlying that belief lies a host of assumptions about the nature of religion, society, and government, most of which are rooted in Enlightenment liberalism. For liberalism emphasizes individual autonomy and choice, liberation from tradition, and the privatizing of religion. Just as the founders of the early federal Republic decided to disestablish the church in order to obtain an independent, more clearly defined, and more just civic community, so today I believe the United States needs to disestablish the dominant, liberal civil religion that shapes society by means of the bipolar dichotomy of sacred and secular, nonsectarian and sectarian, rational neutral and religiously biased.

The way to resolve deep religious disputes about public life is not to grant a privilege to secularism in public life while pushing other views of life out of the public arena, but rather to assure all religions equal access to the public square regardless of their majority or minority status. In a pluralistic society, organized under a constitutionally limited government, the argument for the equal treatment of religion can be understood as an extension of the argument for "justice for all" or for "equal treatment under the law." To recognize that government has limited responsibilities with respect to the life of citizens should lead to the conclusion that government ought to protect equal access of all citizens to the public square without discriminating among them for reasons (such as faith) that do not belong to government's own jurisdictional obligations.

The argument of this chapter will be that a just political order is characterized, among other things, by its adherence to two pluralist principles, which should govern two types of human diversity. The first type of diversity is the wide range of human responsibilities and social institutions, and the first pluralist principle is that the laws of the land should acknowledge and do justice to this societal diversity by upholding an open, nontotalitarian, and pluralist social order. The second type of diversity is the variety of faiths and philosophies by which people direct their public and private lives, and the second pluralist principle requires that the laws of the land do justice to these faiths and philosophies by means of their equitable and nondiscriminatory treatment in public as well as in private spheres of life.

56

In this chapter I will argue that modern liberal beliefs and the strict separationist approach to church-state issues to which they have given rise do not satisfy these two pluralist principles. Instead, I suggest alternative beliefs, rooted in pluralist thought, that give rise to an equity-based approach to church-state issues and more adequately meet the demands of pluralist norms.

What Kind of Pluralism?

Arguments for a twofold principled pluralism (or pluralism as a matter of public-legal principle) have developed during the past two centuries primarily in critical response to secularizing, liberal individualism on the one hand, and to collectivist totalitarianism on the other. The sources of what I am calling principled pluralism are largely Christian — particularly Reformed Protestantism and more recent Catholic social teaching, though each of these traditions in America has accommodated itself to liberalism by way of democratic pragmatism. However, there are now emerging movements in Protestant and Catholic circles — as in some others — to try more consistently to work out the implications of what we might call simply "structural" and "confessional" pluralisms.[1]

These two pluralist principles, which call for public-legal recognition of independent, nongovernmental institutions (structural pluralism) and of religious diversity expressed in both public and private life (confessional pluralism), typically do not receive consideration when pluralism is discussed in individualist or collectivist circles. Yet they are crucial for laying a theoretical base for religious freedom and the equal access of religion to the public realm. For example, when David Nicholls set out to distinguish different meanings of pluralism, he concluded

---

1. Illustrative of the movements mentioned are the following books: *Positive Neutrality: Letting Religious Freedom Ring* by Stephen V. Monsma (Westport, Conn.: Greenwood Press, 1993); *Catholicism, Liberalism, and Communitarianism,* ed. Kenneth L. Grasso, Gerard V. Bradley, and Robert P. Hunt (Lanham, Md.: Rowman & Littlefield, 1995); *Recharging the American Experiment: Principled Pluralism for Genuine Civic Community* by James W. Skillen (Grand Rapids: Baker Books, 1994); and *Political Order and the Plural Structure of Society,* ed. James W. Skillen and Rockne M. McCarthy (Atlanta: Scholars Press, 1991). The present essay draws upon the Introduction in the last-mentioned book.

57

that there are three varieties.[2] One variety, he explains, was developed by the so-called English pluralists at the start of the twentieth century. A second is connected with the interest-group politics of American liberalism. And a third he associates with less-differentiated, non-industrialized societies. None of these, however, describes what we are after with the phrase "principled pluralism" or "structural and confessional pluralisms."

Nicholls' second variety of pluralism, for example, is associated with the development of behavioral social science in the United States and particularly with the names of Arthur Fisher Bentley, David Truman, and Robert A. Dahl. These scholars thought of social groups as mere collections of individuals who share a common *political* interest or purpose. In his book *The Process of Government* (1908), Bentley describes politics as the process of intergroup conflict in which each group tries to gain or maintain some particular interest of its members.[3] From this point of view, our two pluralist principles do not even come into view.

In the decade following World War II, social philosopher Robert A. Nisbet began to question the individualist starting point of American idealism. Nisbet recognized a strong current of doubt and pessimism running through the West. After all, two world wars and at least two kinds of ideological fanaticism had produced unprecedented human destruction in a supposedly enlightened Europe. Western liberalism, Nisbet concluded, with its confident assumption "that history is a more or less continuous emancipation of men from despotism and evil,"[4] could offer no satisfactory account of evil on such a grand scale. Belief in the inevitable progress of history is a modern myth — a new faith — emerging from the Enlightenment of the late eighteenth and early nineteenth centuries. According to that myth, says Nisbet, individuals are supposed to become ever more independent, happy, and self-determining as they

2. Nicholls, *Three Varieties of Pluralism* (New York: St. Martin's Press, 1974). For a better and broader view of pluralism, see Kenneth McRae, "The Plural Society and the Western Political Tradition," *Canadian Journal of Political Science* 12 (December 1979): 676ff.

3. Bentley, *The Process of Government,* newly edited by Peter H. Odegaard (Cambridge: Harvard University Press, 1967 [1908]).

4. Nisbet, *The Quest for Community* (New York: Oxford University Press, 1953), p. 214.

are liberated from the past constraints of aristocratic and ecclesiastical bondage. This faith, however, leads its adherents to reject much of what is good about traditional associations and community life. A chief consequence is that "liberated" individuals may fall prey to bureaucratic and even totalitarian governments which make them less free than their predecessors had been. "The conception of society as an aggregate of morally autonomous, psychologically free, individuals, rather than as a collection of groups, is, in sum, closely related to a conception of society in which all legitimate authority has been abstracted from the primary communities and vested in the single sphere of the State."[5] Commitment to the full autonomy of individuals has *not*, in fact, liberated everyone but has led instead to a new enslavement — powerlessness, insecurity, and loss of social meaning on a mass scale.

Although Nisbet does not explore the question of how to do justice to competing public faiths that are active in the same society, his criticism of individualist and statist ideologies throws into relief the diversity of basic views of life that citizens hold. At this juncture we can see the close connection between faith and social order, between the fundamental convictions of diverse faith communities and their different ways of trying to shape the social and legal order. Any discussion of religious freedom and of equal access of diverse faiths to public life must pay attention to the way these faiths contend with one another in all spheres of life.

If, as Nisbet argues, one consequence of individualistic idealism has been the emergence of the custodial state, then one consequence of the growing custodial state — at least as it emerged in the United States — has been the triumph of interest-group politics. This is the argument of Theodore J. Lowi in his book *The End of Liberalism*.[6] American citizens, says Lowi, have increasingly turned to the state to secure the protection and benefits of their freedom. In the process, they have organized more and more as political interest groups, as Bentley and others anticipated. Yet they hide from or deny the expansion of government which this movement helps create. They try to maintain the conviction that government is simply an extension of their own freedom and self-governance. But that is an illusion.

5. Nisbet, *The Quest for Community,* p. 228.
6. Lowi, *The End of Liberalism: The Second Republic of the United States,* 2d ed. (New York: W. W. Norton, 1979).

What was set in motion following the Great Depression was a gradually expanding process of interest-group competition. Under the pressure of the scramble for power and public influence, government's ability to decide what is just and unjust — what is good policy and bad — has been seriously undermined. Interest-group liberalism, according to Lowi, seeks a form of government "in which there is no formal specification of means or of ends." In a government so divided, "there is, therefore, no substance. Neither is there procedure. There is only process."[7] The more ubiquitous and intrusive government has become, the more undefined and lacking in authority it has become. Interest-group politics, as Lowi sees it, corrupts democracy because it gives the impression that people are adequately represented in government simply because they have access to the interest-group process. This kind of liberalism leads to the impotence of government because government's power has been delegated to a process without standards or limits. Citizens as well as public officials become demoralized as they find themselves caught in a process that makes them mere interest-group brokers.[8] Among other things, this means that a principled legal basis for distinguishing the identities of different social organizations and for protecting the religious freedom of diverse faith communities in all spheres of society is either lost or exposed to the constantly shifting battle lines of interest-group politics.

By the 1970s, not only was it evident that interest-group politics had become regnant in America, but other problems with the American liberal tradition were also coming more clearly into view. Sociologist Peter Berger and commentator-activist Richard John Neuhaus, among others, took a "neoconservative" turn away from the liberal ideal of individual autonomy insofar as the latter ignores or refuses to acknowledge social boundaries and moral standards.[9] They faulted many government social programs for ignoring the "mediating structures" of society where genuine and original community exists. They called for the redirection of public policy toward the empowerment of families,

7. Lowi, *The End of Liberalism*, p. 63.
8. Lowi, *The End of Liberalism*, p. 296.
9. Berger and Neuhaus, *To Empower People: The Role of Mediating Structures in Public Policy* (Washington: American Enterprise Institute, 1977). A second edition of this book was published together with twelve additional essays in *To Empower People: From State to Civil Society*, ed. Michael Novak (Washington: AEI Press, 1996).

churches, neighborhoods, and voluntary associations and away from direct government programs created in response to interest-group demands that spawned new public bureaucracies. Neuhaus and Berger were in search of a view of society with different presuppositions from those of either liberal individualism or socialist collectivism. Neuhaus would soon gain a wide reputation for his book *The Naked Public Square*, in which he argues strongly for religion's rightful place in the public arena and against the idea that religion may be confined to private life.[10] His argument is not simply that religious faith should be revived but that its expression should be recognized as essential to public society.

In 1983, Michael Walzer joined the debate over the purpose and limits of government with his book *Spheres of Justice*. Equality, he argues, is a legitimate standard pointing toward "a society free from domination."[11] But liberty and equality do not have simple, singular meanings in a complex, differentiated society. Walzer develops an argument from history to the effect that modern government should not try to become the sole distributor of all social goods. If a central authority seeks to make all individuals free and equal in all respects, it will inevitably become tyrannical by invading other spheres of social life in which different kinds of goods ought to be distributed according to other legitimate principles and authorities.

Echoing some of the critical judgments of Nisbet, Lowi, Berger, and Neuhaus, Walzer contends that distributive justice must take into account the actual diversity of social spheres. To overcome the inadequacies of both individualist and collectivist logic, Walzer argues, we need to recognize "complex equality":

> The regime of complex equality is the opposite of tyranny. It establishes a set of relationships such that domination is impossible. In formal terms, complex equality means that no citizen's standing in one sphere or with regard to one social good can be undercut by his standing in some other sphere, with regard to some other good. Thus, citizen X may be chosen over citizen Y for political office, and then the two of them will be unequal in the sphere of politics. But

10. Neuhaus, *The Naked Public Square* (Grand Rapids: William B. Eerdmans, 1984).
11. Walzer, *Spheres of Justice: A Defense of Pluralism and Equality* (New York: Basic Books, 1983).

61

they will not be unequal generally so long as X's office gives him no advantages over Y in any other sphere — superior medical care, access to better schools for his children, entrepreneurial opportunities, and so on.[12]

Walzer, in effect, sees society's historical differentiation into multiple spheres as one of the essential safeguards against tyranny — whether that be the tyranny of a totalitarian dictator or of an indiscriminate majority that tries to level all social boundaries in an attempt to secure simple equality for every individual. What Walzer does not explore sufficiently, however, is the principled basis for such pluralism and the fact that people with different basic views of life interpret social diversity quite differently.

In 1985, Robert N. Bellah and his team (Richard Madsen, William M. Sullivan, Ann Swidler, and Steven M. Tipton) released their best-selling *Habits of the Heart,* which not only exposed and criticized individualism gone awry but also sought to show that important communitarian traditions, particularly religious traditions, had been and still are important for American life.[13] Reminding their readers of the important insights of Alexis de Tocqueville about religion and community in nineteenth-century America, the Bellah team urged Americans to recover rather than relinquish community and religious commitment. The Bellah team's 1991 book, *The Good Society,* went even further to argue for the critical importance of diverse institutions for a healthy society.[14]

In various ways, what all of these scholars have done over the past several decades is to call into question the simplistic and often counterproductive ideals of individual autonomy, liberation from traditional authorities, the privatizing of religion, and egalitarianism maintained through a democratic process of interest-group politics — all of which underlie the strict separationist position on church-state issues. They have pointed, in essence, to the emptiness of an ideal of freedom that promises to liberate people from all social obligations except the uni-

12. Walzer, *Spheres of Justice,* p. 19.
13. Bellah et al., *Habits of the Heart* (Berkeley and Los Angeles: University of California Press, 1985).
14. Bellah et al., *The Good Society* (New York: Knopf, 1991).

versal and ubiquitous political ones. They have affirmed the importance of a limited state constrained in part by its recognition of the boundaries of other social spheres and by clear standards of justice. Furthermore, their suspicions about, and criticisms of, the myth of perpetual liberal progress have helped heighten public consciousness of the multiplying and competing faiths now at work shaping America's multicultural public square. Many, for example, now interpret Enlightenment liberalism as simply one among many competing worldviews or fundamental approaches to life, rather than as the one, truly universal, public perspective that transcends all parochial, religious traditions. To the extent that this is the case, the strict separationist position is called into question.

Religious Diversity and the Common Good

Partly in response to the growing crisis of liberalism, another mode of moral argument has been gaining strength in the American context. It focuses particularly on the contradictions internal to liberalism's basic faith and assumptions. Alasdair MacIntyre contends that Enlightenment liberalism aimed to create a "social order in which individuals could emancipate themselves from the contingency and particularity of tradition by appealing to genuinely universal, tradition-independent norms."[15] In fact, however, those who have taken up this project have not been able to transcend tradition but have simply gotten caught in a new, more problematic tradition of their own making. What "began as an appeal to alleged principles of shared rationality against what was felt to be the tyranny of tradition, has itself been transformed into a tradition whose continuities are partly defined by the interminability of the debate over such principles."[16]

MacIntyre would say that Nisbet, Lowi, and Walzer illustrate perfectly the "interminability" of the debates within our liberal context. Each raises criticisms of the existing social order and urges the adoption of other values so that justice can be done to individuais and groups in

15. MacIntyre, *Whose Justice? Which Rationality?* (Notre Dame: University of Notre Dame Press, 1988), p. 335.
16. MacIntyre, *Whose Justice? Which Rationality?*

our society. But each one believes that his argument appeals to universal principles of practical reasoning. The truth, however, is that conceptions of both justice and practical rationality differ depending on fundamental presuppositions about reality. And those presuppositions are tied to particular social-political contexts and religiously deep commitments.

The structure of liberal societies is such that even as individuals appeal to universal principles, they undermine the hope of achieving universal agreement about justice and rationality. Liberalism's view of the "common good," according to MacIntyre, is that every individual should be free to express his or her preferences in a variety of ways. Under these conditions, practical rationality turns out to be a method of justifying individual preferences and setting constraints on the bargaining process among self-asserting, competitive individuals. The kind of reasoning and bargaining that Lowi criticizes as interest-group politics is precisely what one should expect to see in a liberal society. Thus, the centrifugal tendencies of this individualizing and relativizing mode of thought contradict its claim to a universal rationality. It represents only one approach to life, only one faith among others.

Liberalism cannot foster a mode of practical reasoning that proceeds from and moves toward a genuine *common good* in the area of justice because it does not accept the idea of a common *natural* social order that precedes individual claims to autonomy. Consequently, under liberalism, individual preferences multiply to create a diverse range of interest groups, each compartmentalized in its own sphere. MacIntyre points out that the heterogeneity of this type of society means that "no overall ordering of goods is possible. And to be educated into the culture of a liberal social order is, therefore, characteristically to become the kind of person to whom it appears normal that a variety of goods should be pursued, each appropriate to its own sphere, with no overall good supplying any overall unity to life."[17]

MacIntyre believes that in order to reach agreement about the demands of justice for a structurally complex society, we need more than an argument to defend the historical emergence of different social spheres, each of which expresses different individual preferences. The Walzers and Lowis of this world will find themselves in a never-ending argument about their diverse valuations of historically relative prefer-

17. MacIntyre, *Whose Justice? Which Rationality?* p. 337.

ences. What is needed is a mode of practical reasoning that emerges from a community that accepts justice and other standards as natural or transcendent to the historical process. Practical reasoning can succeed only in a community that agrees on the moral virtues appropriate to the different social roles performed by its members. The liberal tradition provides no such context in which to reason in this fashion.

MacIntyre believes that the Aristotelian-Thomist tradition can justifiably lay claim to an authority greater than that to which the liberal tradition lays claim because, among other things, it has recognized itself as a tradition of practical rationality within a particular context of order and meaning. Since diverse ethical and social traditions do in fact exist, the strongest kind of practical rationality will be one that recognizes its grounding in a tradition of virtues within an overall, integrated view of a just society.[18] In turning to Aristotle and Thomas Aquinas, MacIntyre thus indicates his commitment to an ordered, natural (or natural/supernatural) hierarchy within which reasoning can find its moorings and proceed coherently. He aims to go beyond the limits of liberal individualism not by reaching for a rationality that supposedly transcends all past communities and traditions. Rather, he takes his stand in a tradition of thought that is both conscious of itself as a tradition and able to direct practical reasoning toward truth and justice.

Not all Catholics and Protestants would agree with MacIntyre's interpretation of the Aristotelian/Thomist tradition. Nevertheless, his turn in this direction is coincident with a revival of Catholic social thinking in the United States, grounded in the events of the Second Vatican Council and the work of both European and American thinkers, including Jacques Maritain and John Courtney Murray.[19] At Vatican II, the Catholic Church committed itself to religious freedom in society by reinterpreting its own commitment to the dignity of the human person and freedom of conscience, not by adopting a liberal individualist view of humanity and society. In fact, according to Kenneth L. Grasso, "the

18. MacIntyre, *Whose Justice? Which Rationality?* pp. 402-3.
19. See Jacques Maritain, *The Person and the Common Good* (New York: Scribner's, 1947) and *Man and the State* (Chicago: University of Chicago Press, 1951); John Courtney Murray, *We Hold These Truths: Catholic Reflections on the American Proposition* (New York: Sheed & Ward, 1960); and Keith J. Pavlischek, *John Courtney Murray and the Dilemma of Religious Toleration* (Kirksville, Mo.: Thomas Jefferson University Press, 1994).

Catholic human rights revolution makes it clear that a gulf separates Catholic social thought from both the classical and the liberal traditions."[20] Grasso believes that Catholic social thought offers a stronger foundation for human rights, constitutional democracy, social pluralism, and human solidarity than does liberalism.[21] Contemporary Catholicism seeks religious freedom, not a publicly imposed position of privilege, but it also seeks equal access for its views in all spheres of life and the recognition that there is more to the structure of society than individuals and the state. Catholic social thought, in other words, represents a distinct, religiously framed understanding of society, not simply a revival of private religiosity.

Another ethicist much engaged in the debates over the plural structure of society is Jeffrey Stout, who appreciates MacIntyre's criticism of philosophical individualism and Catholicism's commitment to religious freedom and social solidarity.[22] But Stout fears that MacIntyre may be throwing the baby out with the bathwater. The fact is, says Stout, that contemporary American society is not the expression of a purely individualist philosophy. Despite the impact of liberalism, American society has not yet dissolved into anarchy; it displays degrees of social agreement about the nature of the common good and about the virtues needed in diverse spheres of social life. Those elements of agreement are themselves the fruit of our long Western tradition in which earlier disagreements, especially those expressed through religious warfare, were overcome by decisions to limit the political order in ways that allow all citizens to share certain public rights along with the freedom to disagree peacefully and to pursue a diverse range of goods.

Modern liberal societies, therefore, are not as individualistic and relativistic as MacIntyre imagines. They reveal a certain kind of practical rationality at work that produces meaningful if not completely homogeneous public communities. By tracking the inner logic of actual social differentiation and institutional formation, says Stout, we can work to achieve levels of rational agreement higher than MacIntyre thinks

---

20. Grasso, "Beyond Liberalism: Human Dignity, the Free Society, and the Second Vatican Council," in *Catholicism, Liberalism, and Communitarianism*, p. 52.

21. Grasso, "Beyond Liberalism," p. 54.

22. Jeffrey Stout, *Ethics after Babel: The Languages of Morals and Their Discontents* (Boston: Beacon Press, 1988), p. 220.

possible. Such agreement will not be exhaustive with respect to a comprehensive understanding of the political common good. But it can be sufficient for building both a "thin" conception of the political community and a commitment to the protected freedom we all require in order to carry on diverse activities in other spheres of social life.

Much like Walzer, Stout sees a "thin" agreement about the nature of the common good as a manifestation of our practical Western agreement not to try to achieve a complete or morally undifferentiated community through politics. Room has been made for "complex equality" — a rich complexity of life lived out in many social spheres where people can continue to nurture virtues proper to each sphere — schooling, church, health care, family, and more. Stout calls for a "stereoscopic" view of society in which the *political* common good is interpreted as an agreement to protect both individual freedoms and the integrity of diverse spheres of social life.

Stout conceives of society as a diversified, complex order, not as a simple, collective unity. His foundation is not Aristotelian or Thomist, though he wants to use some of MacIntyre's and Walzer's language of multiple virtues appropriate to distinct social spheres. His vision is not individualistic, though it includes a liberal conception of individual rights and limited government; he wants an open public order that will not demand "deep" civic agreement about a comprehensive common good. His vision is not socialist, but it is critical of the power of marketplace values when they overwhelm nonmarket spheres of life. Stout claims to engage in a form of pragmatic social criticism with both eyes open, and he believes that certain principles and practices transcend his personal preferences. "The languages of morals in our discourse are many, and they have remarkably diverse historical origins," he writes, "but they do not float in free air, and their name is not chaos. They are embedded in specific social practices and institutions — religious, political, artistic, scientific, athletic, economic, and so on."[23]

Does Stout's argument answer the questions and criticisms posed by MacIntyre? Has he offered a solid basis, apart from his own self-assertive preferences, for the best social practices in each of many differentiated institutions and organizations? Living face-to-face with a

---

23. Stout, *Ethics after Babel*, p. 291.

wide range of religious, political, artistic, scientific, medical, and economic institutions, do we not need to articulate the norms or standards by which to distinguish good from evil, healthy from unhealthy, just from unjust, in each sphere of society? If this complex array does not "float in free air" or go by the name of "chaos," then what order of nature or divine creation allows human beings to develop society's complex shape while holding them accountable within it? And if people living in the same society hold different basic views of this reality, how can public justice be done to all of them? The answers to these questions have enormous importance for religious freedom and how one understands the meaning of the equitable treatment of religion. Defining and protecting religion's legitimate role in society necessitates norms or standards by which to differentiate the various spheres of human endeavor and to judge what is just and equitable.

In his book *Political Liberalism*,[24] John Rawls seeks to answer this question on liberal terms by clearly delimiting the political arena. In this book, in contrast to the more comprehensive and undifferentiated argument for liberalism he offered in *A Theory of Justice*,[25] Rawls proposes a differentiated, restricted *political* liberalism. Rawls still believes that liberalism provides the best political philosophy for our day, but if it is to work, it must be able to sustain a reasonable political order for a society in which there is a diversity of incompatible, comprehensive views of life, both religious and philosophical. At first glance it appears that Rawls is working toward a framework for religious pluralism in society that meets the demands of our second pluralist principle of equal treatment of all faiths and philosophies in both public and private life.

That is not exactly what Rawls has in mind, however. Instead of recognizing that diverse, comprehensive faiths also typically include some elements of incompatibility even with regard to the political order itself, Rawls assumes that since all citizens share in the same political community, it should be possible to develop a method of shared public reasoning that will, in essence, allow for the marginalization of deeper differences. The aim of his political philosophy, which he summarizes with the phrase "justice as fairness," is practical:

24. Rawls, *Political Liberalism* (New York: Columbia University Press, 1993).
25. Rawls, *A Theory of Justice* (Cambridge, Mass.: Harvard University Press, 1971).

68

It presents itself as a conception of justice that may be shared by citizens as a basis of a reasoned, informed, and willing political agreement. It expresses their shared and public political reason. But to attain such a shared reason, the conception of justice should be, as far as possible, independent of the opposing and conflicting philosophical and religious doctrines that citizens affirm.[26]

But how can Rawls expect that a strictly delimited political agreement can be upheld independent of the deeper, comprehensive views of life to which people are committed and from which their conceptions of justice arise? Like Thomas Jefferson, he can believe this only on the basis of his own deep, comprehensive view of life, according to which faith and religion can be subordinated to public-moral reasoning. As I see it, Rawls is correct when he says that the political order can be distinguished from ecclesiastical, familial, and other spheres of social life, but it is a mistake to confuse the religious/political distinction with the private/public distinction. If we are to take religion and other comprehensive philosophies of life seriously and accord them equal access to the public square, then they cannot be marginalized by public moral reasoning.

In fact, Rawls thinks he can have it both ways. On the one hand, he believes he is doing justice to the comprehensive character of differing fundamental views of life by seeking to build political agreement only on the "overlapping" consensus that exists among all of them. On the other hand, as he moves toward the construction of that overlapping consensus, he argues that differing comprehensive views should "give way in public life" in order to allow the common, political conception to become "freestanding."[27] What finally becomes freestanding in Rawls's construction, however, looks very much like something quite compatible with Rawls's own comprehensive liberal view of life and not so much like something that overlaps comfortably with Christian social theory or with a number of other comprehensive religions and philosophies. Moreover, if diverse religious and philosophical views of a comprehensive character can truly overlap politically, why should they have to give way at all in the political commons?

26. Rawls, *Political Liberalism*, p. 9.
27. Rawls, *Political Liberalism*, p. 10.

Rawls seems to confuse "political conception" with "political order." Given his own liberal starting point, the political order has its grounding in the reasoning of the autonomous individuals who construct it. Political order is the construct of a rationally developed consensus. For this reason, Rawls looks for a way to make *political* reasonableness independent of the differing comprehensive views of life that people hold; otherwise, the political commons may not exist.

From a principled pluralist viewpoint, however, political order should not be confused with, or made so entirely dependent on, the political reasoning of citizens. Citizens may continue to disagree over the very nature of a political order even while they live together in it. Their comprehensive views of life cannot always be marginalized or privatized. Instead of seeking to specify the norms of a just political order in distinction from nonpolitical communities and institutions, Rawls takes the tack of trying to delimit the qualities of public reasonableness that will be sufficient to produce the political order. In the end, what he means by the political commons is whatever can be constructed by those who are politically reasonable, and this may require excluding from the public dialogue some people who refuse to participate on Rawls's terms of political reasonableness. This does not sound like equal access of diverse religions to the public square.

By seeking to distinguish the political from the nonpolitical and by realizing that incompatible, comprehensive views of life run very deep, Rawls has certainly moved closer to a recognition of our two pluralist principles articulated at the outset of this chapter. And yet he cannot fully affirm those two principles because he does not admit that religions and comprehensive philosophies will express themselves in all spheres of life and that the political order ought to recognize those comprehensive commitments in public as well as in private spheres of society. Thus his view cannot support an approach to issues of church and state that advances a fulsome role for religious and other philosophical systems in the public arena.

Ronald F. Thiemann works to expose some of these shortcomings of Rawls and other contemporary liberals in his book *Religion and Public Life: A Dilemma for Democracy*.[28] The truth about contemporary

28. Thiemann, *Religion and Public Life: A Dilemma for Democracy* (Washington: Georgetown University Press, 1996).

democracies, says Thiemann, who sounds much like MacIntyre at this point, is that the very principles of democracy and social order are being contested. Thus Rawls's hope of fashioning a "freestanding" public reasonableness will not hold up. Recognition of the distinct and limited sphere of politics is important, but the distinctiveness of the political order does not imply the independence of political concepts from the comprehensive views of life held by citizens. "If it is the case that a 'political conception [of justice] must draw upon various ideas of the good,'" says Thiemann, "then the claim concerning the conceptual independence of the political seems unjustified."[29]

The challenge of our day, according to Thiemann, is to find common ground among citizens who are culturally diverse to the point of being unlikely to agree on universal principles for such a common ground. We need to agree on some kind of "public space in which acceptable arguments are justified by criteria claiming less than universality but more than mere subjectivity."[30] Thiemann makes the constructive argument that most religions cannot be privatized and marginalized. Faith is a communal affair, not a narrowly individual one, and thus it will always have a public character. The question for politics in a pluralistic society, therefore, is not first of all who is reasonable enough to be granted entrance into civic debate, but rather what the demands of citizenship are regardless of the faith one holds. Religious traditions have a distinct contribution to make to the nurturing of these civic virtues.

Thiemann, however, is not as far from Rawls as his criticism might imply. He, too, stresses the qualities of mind, of discourse, of personal habit and civility required for good citizenship. He does not go very far in distinguishing the characteristics peculiar to the political sphere in contrast to those of various nonpolitical spheres of life. Thus, Thiemann is less helpful in clarifying the conditions for a just structural pluralism than he is in showing that religion will play itself out in all spheres, including the political. The old idea of "separation of church and state" is simply inadequate to deal with the public character of religious life, he argues. The question is how to overcome the privatization of religion and to develop the habits of genuine dialogue among citizens who may continue to differ at a fundamental level. "Religious voices," Thiemann

29. Thiemann, *Religion and Public Life*, p. 89.
30. Thiemann, *Religion and Public Life*, p. 126.

concludes, "should be welcomed into the pluralistic conversation of democracy as long as they agree to abide by the fundamental values of this republic: a commitment to freedom, equality, and mutual respect."[31]

At this concluding point, one can see how little Thiemann differs from Rawls. He is intent on affirming the *values* to which citizens should be committed in order to be allowed to enter the public conversation. He is less intent on trying to articulate the responsibilities of government in terms of which it may hold citizens accountable to fulfill their obligations regardless of the values they hold. Obviously the nurturing of civic responsibility is crucial to an open society, but the grounds on which citizens might be committed to freedom, equality, and mutual respect are likely to be quite different, as Thiemann's argument implies. What we need in the United States today, then, is a clarification, and in some cases a redefinition, of government's responsibility in relation to the nongovernmental spheres of civil society in which people of differing faiths live out their lives.

Conclusion

If a just society is one in which multiple institutions and diverse spheres of responsibility can function together in freedom, under protection of the law, then part of the legal obligation of a just government is to recognize and protect that complex diversity of society. This is the first principle of structural pluralism articulated above. Closely related to this principle, and mutually interdependent with it, is the principle of religious freedom. If, as presupposed here, government should be limited in authority and should not have the responsibility to legislate or adjudicate theology, true faith, and correct ecclesiology, then government should act in accord with the principles of justice by treating all faiths and faith communities with equal public protection. Government cannot do this, however, without respecting the freedom and diversity of those faiths.

Some religions (or comprehensive philosophies, or ways of life) are, by self-definition, public in character. That is to say, they function not simply through the practice of religious ceremonies but also by the way

31. Thiemann, *Religion and Public Life*, p. 173.

72

in which their adherents educate their children, or farm their land, or organize their families, or develop political arguments. In this respect, Catholics, secularists, Muslims, New Age religionists, Jews, and different camps of Protestants may differ in their views of society and even of government itself. The U.S. Constitution gives government no authority to predefine religion, or to require that all religions function in the way that Christians or Muslims or Enlightenment secularists believe religion should function. True religious freedom, then, requires freedom for different communities of shared faith or philosophy to live out their convictions in all spheres of life. This is to restate the second pluralist principle articulated at the outset: confessional pluralism.

A strict separationist position on religion cannot do justice to these principles of pluralism, because it insists that religion can be predefined as a private affair and that the public order is neutrally secular. While this position aims to shut out other views of religion from public life, it remains unselfconscious about the deep religious character of its own comprehensive point of view, which it wants to impose. The fact is that what underlies the religious/secular division of life is a comprehensive view of reality, with roots in the Enlightenment, that designates traditional religion as private and modern politics as secular. It is this comprehensive view of life, therefore, that ought to be compared with comprehensive Christianity or comprehensive Judaism. Strict separationists would no more want their view of public life to be confined entirely to private spheres than would Christians, Muslims, and Jews want their views of life to be so confined. The only way to treat all positions fairly, then, is by protecting the full freedom of all to express themselves, to exercise their convictions, in public as well as in private life — in other words, in all spheres of life.

If one religion or comprehensive view of life is closer than others to the truth, then this truth needs to work its way out in freedom — in the freedom of argument and the freedom of conscientious practices in public and private life. Consequently, the kind of political order needed to permit an ongoing, free-flowing, public debate about the truth concerning life in this world is one that neither cuts short the debate by force nor interferes with human responsibility in the wise diversity of social spheres. Such a political order would be a constitutionally limited government obligated to protect religious freedom for all. The principle of confessional pluralism is enshrined in the U.S. Constitution's First

Amendment, but that principle has been challenged and sometimes violated by the interpretation that religion is a purely private or ecclesiastical affair. In this chapter, I have tried to show that such an interpretation not only misunderstands the First Amendment, but also does an injustice to many nongovernmental institutions and organizations by overlooking their independent character or forcing on them a secularized identity. Genuine religious freedom can be achieved only by means of equal legal treatment of all religions and religiously equivalent views of life, a treatment which recognizes that they have the right to express themselves in diverse ways in every sphere of life.

CHAPTER 4

What Would Equal Treatment Mean for Public Education?

CHARLES L. GLENN

In this chapter, Charles Glenn argues that equal treatment would allow more room in public schools for an honest discussion of the important role of religion in American history and culture. What is even more significant, he contends, is that the principle of equal treatment encourages a discussion of much-needed reform of the public educational system. Glenn concludes that religiously based schooling within public education is needed to allow parents to exercise genuine choice in the education of their children. Charles L. Glenn is Professor of Educational Policy and chairman of the Department of Administration, Training, and Policy Studies at the School of Education at Boston University.

The trend in recent Supreme Court decisions — to treat "religious expression" as entitled to the same protection as other forms of expression, and thus to the same degree of acceptance and even support by government — seems likely to have an effect on k-12 education as it has on other institutions. However, public schools (those operated by local government) will be affected not so much by the new legal precedent as by a gradually changing attitude on the part of their staff to be more open to religion in a public school setting. The law already recognizes the right of religious expression by students, and practice is slowly responding. For religious schools, equal treatment as a theory for interpreting the establishment clause has its greatest potential impact in the area of public finance. This new understanding of what the Constitution requires could lead to a consideration of religiously based schooling within the public sector.

Religion in Government-operated Schools

The courts and the law established the right of students to express their religious faith to their classmates when not under the instructional supervision of teachers well before the *Rosenberger* decision. One of the legal cases arose when two students were prevented from distributing religious tracts in the hallways and cafeteria of their high school in Pennsylvania.

Scott Slotterback, who was in the tenth grade, and his friend Keith Ferry, who was in the ninth grade, attended Interboro Senior High School (ISHS) in Prospect Park, Pennsylvania. They began to distribute religious tracts in school; "designed like comic strips, the tracts depicted a twentieth-century man's death and resurrection. Under each frame was a quotation from the Bible."[1] They handed out these materials on nearly fifty occasions in the halls or cafeteria. One of the teachers confiscated the materials on several occasions and finally took one of the boys to the principal, who "ordered him to cease his hallway distributions or risk suspension."[2] After consulting with the school system's lawyer, the principal met again with Scott Slotterback and gave him "a handwritten note setting forth the permissible time, place, and manner of future distributions. Such distributions would be permitted only twice during the remainder of the school year; would be restricted to the area around the exit doors of ISHS; and would have to occur after school hours,"[3] with advance notice given to the principal.

In response to the threat of legal action, the school system then adopted a formal policy governing distribution of materials on school property; this provided for advance review and written approval by the

1. *Slotterback v. Interboro School District,* 766 F. Supp. 280 (1991) at 284.
2. 766 F. Supp. at 285.
3. 766 F. Supp. at 285.

principal, unless the materials fell into one of seven prohibited categories. "Such distribution [was] to be made at the time of normal dismissal of the students from the buildings where the distribution is to occur, . . . inside or outside the exit doors of the buildings," on as many days as requested, but in a "peaceful . . . non-argumentative manner, without littering." Among the seven categories of "unacceptable non-school written material(s)" were "materials that proselytizes [sic] a particular religious or political belief."[4]

The Federal District Court found that this prohibition was "unconstitutionally overbroad and invalid on its face. Although the school district has a compelling interest in preventing material, substantial interference with the work of the schools and with the rights of other students, that interest is protected under other portions of the new policy, and the blanket ban on religious and political literature is unnecessary."[5] The court also found that the provision for advance review was too stringent, and declared its intention of reviewing the merits of the restrictions on when and where distribution of materials could occur to determine whether school officials had good "reason to anticipate substantial interference with work at the high school should distributions of religious tracts continue at exit doors before and after school and in the cafeteria area at lunchtime."[6]

High school pupils who attend a school that allows for student-run activities also have a right to gather on school grounds to express their religious interests or beliefs. Concern that many high schools were not allowing pupils to meet for religious purposes during time set aside for extracurricular activities led to passage of national legislation, the Equal Access Act of 1984, which begins,

> It shall be unlawful for any public secondary school which receives Federal financial assistance and which has a limited open forum to deny equal access or a fair opportunity to, or discriminate against, any students who wish to conduct a meeting within that limited open forum on the basis of the religious, political, philosophical, or other content of the speech at such meetings.

4. 766 F. Supp. at 285.
5. 766 F. Supp. at 297.
6. 766 F. Supp. at 300.

77

The constitutionality of this law was upheld in 1990 by the Supreme Court in *Board of Education v. Mergens,* which stated that such meetings could occur

> if the school uniformly provides that the meetings are voluntary and student-initiated; are not sponsored by the school, the government, or its agents or employees [such as teachers]; do not materially and substantially interfere with the orderly conduct of educational activities within the school; and are not directed, controlled, conducted, or regularly attended by nonschool persons [such as adult religious leaders].[7]

Mergens was cited repeatedly in the Supreme Court's ruling in the Rosenberger case.

While the "Rosenberger doctrine" could ensure that religious viewpoints have equal rights with other viewpoints in some settings in the public school, it is not likely to lead the court to reconsider recent cases that have upheld limits on student religious expression based upon a concern not to overrule the authority of teachers in managing the instruction in their classrooms.

The most celebrated of these cases involved Brittney Kaye Settle, a ninth grader in Tennessee.[8] Her teacher, Ms. Ramsey, assigned a research paper on a topic to be selected by the student, subject to the teacher's approval; she required only that each topic be "interesting, researchable and decent"[9] and draw upon at least four sources. Brittney submitted an outline for a paper entitled "The Life of Jesus Christ." The teacher refused to accept it and told Brittney she would have to select another topic. Her father intervened to complain. Ms. Ramsey told him that she would accept a paper on religion as long as it did not deal solely with Christianity or the life of Christ. (However, other students reportedly were allowed to write on witchcraft, black magic and the occult, and spiritualism.) Brittney submitted another outline with the title "A Scientific and Historical Approach to Jesus Christ." Ms. Ramsey rejected this outline as well, explaining later to the school board that she "just knew

7. 496 U.S. 226 (1990).
8. *Settle v. Dickson County School Board,* 53 F.3d 152 (1995).
9. 53 F.3d at 153.

78

that we don't deal with personal religion — personal religious beliefs. It's just not an appropriate thing to do in a public school. . . . People don't send their children to school for a teacher to get in a dialogue with personal religious beliefs. They send them to learn to read and write and think. And you can do that without getting into personal religion." The teacher also said that because Brittney knew a lot about Jesus Christ, she could produce an outline without doing any significant research, and thus defeat the purpose of the exercise. "It was a lot easier to write a quick little preliminary outline on Jesus Christ, which she knew a lot about, which most of my students knew a lot about." In addition, Ms. Ramsey told the school board that "the law says we are not to deal with religious issues in the classroom."[10]

As a result of her refusal to comply with Ms. Ramsey's requirements, Brittney received a zero for the assignment. This, her lawyer later argued, violated her free speech rights under the First Amendment; like the lawyer in the Rosenberger case, her lawyer invoked free speech rather than free exercise rights. Brittney lost both in court and on appeal.

What was the basis of this decision? It was not that there was anything wrong with the topic Brittney selected: Ms. Ramsey was wrong in her belief that religion had to be kept out of the classroom or that a religious figure was not an appropriate subject for an assignment in public school. But the court ruled against Brittney on different grounds. "Had Ms. Ramsey rejected the paper on the ground of its religious content alone," Judge Batchelder wrote in concurring with the opinion of the appeals court, or if this had been an opinion essay rather than a research paper, "Brittney's freedom of speech truly would have been violated."[11] But "this case is not about Brittney Settle's First Amendment right to express her views, opinions or beliefs, religious or otherwise, in the classroom. This case is about whether Brittney's ninth-grade English teacher may determine what topic is appropriate to satisfy a research paper assignment in that class."[12]

According to the Sixth Circuit Court majority

10. 53 F.3d at 154.
11. 53 F.3d at 159.
12. 53 F.3d at 157.

Free speech rights of students in the classroom must be limited, because effective education depends not only on controlling boisterous conduct, but also on maintaining the focus of the class on the assignment in question. . . . Teachers may frequently make mistakes in grading and otherwise, just as we do sometimes in deciding cases, but it is the essence of the teacher's responsibility in the classroom to draw lines and make distinctions — in a word to encourage speech germane to the topic at hand and discourage speech unlikely to shed light on the subject. Teachers therefore must be given broad discretion to give grades and conduct class discussion.

Later the majority noted, citing *Epperson* (another Tennessee case), "Students do not lose entirely their right to express themselves as individuals in the classroom, but federal courts should exercise particular restraint in classroom conflicts between student and teacher over matters falling within the ordinary authority of the teacher over curriculum and course content."[13]

The unifying theme in judicial reasoning in this and other related cases is to ask whether a classroom is an "open forum" for the expression of opinions, and the consistent answer is that it is not. It seems unlikely that the courts will interpret *Rosenberger* to undermine the authority of teachers to make prudential judgments — wise or unwise — about assignments and grading, but it is possible that gradually America's two million teachers will come to understand that religious themes are not inappropriate in their classrooms and will grow more comfortable with dealing with them in an evenhanded way. Whether public schools become more open to religious themes in the classroom depends largely, it would seem, on the extent to which the idea of equal treatment reaches teachers, administrators, and school board members. There are some hopeful signs that opinion-makers in the educational establishment are concerned enough about the alienation of millions of Americans from the public schools to begin to throw their influence behind something like fair treatment of religion in the curriculum.

A decision handed down by the Fifth Circuit Court in December 1995, *Doe v. Duncanville Independent School District*, illustrates the subtlety of distinguishing between free exercise of religion in a school

13. 53 F.3d at 155.

context and (unconstitutional) promotion of religion by the school.[14] "Jane Doe," a high school student, and her father brought a complaint that (1) the basketball team on which she played engaged in prayer before and after games, (2) the school chorus, of which she was a member, sang "The Lord bless you and keep you, the Lord lift his countenance upon you, and give you peace; the Lord make his face to shine upon you, and be gracious unto you" (based on Numbers 6:24-26) as its theme song, and (3) an outside organization was allowed to distribute free Bibles to students who wanted them. The third claim was dismissed for lack of standing; the court's ruling on the other two is interesting in different ways.

The Fifth Circuit Court found that the team prayers were unconstitutional if the coaches "initiated or participated" in the prayers, but within the rights of the players if they wished to pray together. This illustrates the careful judgments that must be made as public school authorities seek to accommodate the desire of many students to pray in the context of significant events in their young lives, and the awkward position of teachers who serve as the instruments of public policy and representatives of government, yet have their own convictions and rights and are mentors who share sympathetically in those events. Judge Edith Jones wrote a partial dissent to the Fifth Circuit's formulation of the role of coaches or other teachers in relation to student religious observances, like prayers before a game:

> There is practically no doubt that the trend in Supreme Court establishment clause cases . . . prevents teachers from actively joining in the student-led prayers, e.g., by joining hands in the prayer circle. Such actions would . . . too easily connote official endorsement and would imply coercion of non-participants. . . . However, teachers are not prohibited from exercising deference and respect toward student-initiated prayers . . . the line between deference and sympathetic reverence is a fine one that cannot and should not be policed, if teachers' individual freedom of conscience is to retain any meaning.[15]

14. *Doe v. Duncanville Independent School District*, 70 F.3d 402.
15. 70 F.3d at 409-10.

The district court had allowed songs with religious texts to be used "for their artistic and historic qualities if presented objectively as part of a secular program of education," but not as the "theme song" of the school's chorus. The appeals court concluded, however, that "legitimate secular reasons exist for maintaining The Lord Bless You and Keep You as the theme song"; this decision was based upon testimony by the chorus director that it was "a good piece of music . . . by a reputable composer" and useful for teaching sight reading. The majority opinion made this point:

> [The chorus director] estimated that 60-75 percent of serious choral music is based on sacred themes or text. Given the dominance of religious music in this field, DISD [Duncanville Independent School District] can hardly be presumed to be advancing or endorsing religion by allowing its choirs to sing a religious theme song. . . . Indeed, to forbid DISD from having a theme song that is religious would force DISD to disqualify the majority of appropriate choral music simply because it is religious. Within the world of choral music, such a restriction would require hostility, not neutrality, toward religion. . . . Where, as here, singing the theme song is not a religious exercise, we will not find an endorsement of religion exists merely because a religious song with widely recognized musical value is sung more often than other songs. Such animosity towards religion is not required or condoned by the Constitution.[16]

In this case, equal treatment of religious material was not held to be simply passive and reliant upon student initiative (as in *Mergens*), but was held to fall within the appropriate decision-making of school authorities. On the other hand, in this decision there was no suggestion that equal treatment obligated the school system to include religious music in the interest of neutrality between religious and secular content. Instead, the court deferred to the administrative authority of public school officials and found a secular educational justification for the use of the school's religious song.

This stress on an appropriate educational justification has been noted as crucial in cases involving decisions by school authorities to display

16. 53 F.3d at 407-8.

material with religious associations. Perhaps the high point of court hostility to religion in schools (at least so far) was the Supreme Court's ruling in *Stone v. Graham*, which struck down a Kentucky law requiring the posting of the Ten Commandments (a privately contributed poster bearing a notice that it served a secular purpose of illustrating the basis of the fundamental legal code of Western civilization) in every classroom.[17] "The recitation of a supposed secular purpose," the Court found, "cannot blind us to the undeniably religious nature of such material," which could create an unconstitutional appearance of endorsement of religion by a public school. The schools had not integrated the Ten Commandments into the curriculum, and the Court found that the effect of displaying them could be "to induce the schoolchildren to read, meditate upon, perhaps to venerate and [horrors!] obey" them.[18] The Court concluded that it did not believe the assertion of the state legislature that it considered familiarity with the Ten Commandments to serve a useful educational purpose unrelated to promotion of religion. Dissenting from this judgment, Justice Rehnquist wrote that "the Establishment Clause does not require that the public sector be insulated from all things which may have a religious significance or origin."[19]

In a more recent case, *Washegesic v. Bloomingdale Public Schools*, the court found that hanging a "portrait" of Jesus in the hallway of a high school violated the First Amendment, since

> any action of the state which, either directly or indirectly, conveys that religion, or a particular type of religion, is more accepted, respected, or tolerated than another value system has the potential to subtly coerce students to acquiesce to the promoted religion. The Court finds that the school's display of the portrait of Jesus may well have such a coercive influence and that it is therefore unconstitutional.[20]

The district court judge suggested that the painting would have been acceptable if it had been "part of a larger display" or "incorporated into

17. 449 U.S. 39 (1980).
18. 449 U.S. at 41-42.
19. 449 U.S. at 45-46.
20. *Washegesic v. Bloomingdale Public Schools*, 813 F. Supp. 559 at 564 (Mich. 1993).

a class, lecture, or other context"; apart from such a context, it "advances Christianity because it exposes students to the fundamental figure of the Christian religion without providing them access to portrayals of leaders, prophets, or divinities of other religions or to depictions of advocates of nonreligion." As was the case with the Ten Commandments in *Stone,* the picture of Jesus had not been placed in a historical, ethical, or artistic context. It stood alone on the school wall, where its effect could be to make children "look at, meditate upon, and perhaps revere Jesus Christ."[21] The ruling in this case was similar to that in *Stone*: "However desirable this might be as a matter of private devotion, it is not a permissible state objective under the Establishment Clause."[22]

While *Washegesic,* like *Stone,* required removal of a religious display from a public school, they both left the door open to inclusion of religious materials and themes in educational programs with a legitimate secular purpose. Simply asserting such a purpose in legislation was not enough — after all, legislators do not ordinarily design the curriculum and educational goals for schools — but it seems likely that school authorities prepared to advance a non-pretextual instructional argument for including material of religious significance would prevail if challenged on establishment-clause grounds. Indeed, the courts have frequently echoed Justice Clark's insistence, in *Abington v. Schempp,* that

> one's education is not complete without a study of comparative religion or the history of religion and its relationship to the advancement of civilization. It certainly may be said that the Bible is worthy of study for its literary and historic qualities. Nothing we have said here indicates that such study of the Bible or of religion, when presented objectively as part of a secular program of education, may not be effected consistently with the First Amendment.[23]

Whether such a comparative and "objective" presentation of matters of religious faith can be satisfactory to many parents with strongly held religious convictions remains to be seen, but there can be no question that it would be a positive change — in the interest of intellectual

21. 813 F. Supp. at 566, 562, n. 8, and 563.
22. 813 F. Supp. at 563 (quoting Stone, 449 U.S. at 42n.9).
23. 374 U.S. 203 (1963).

honesty, if nothing else — from the prevailing embarrassed silence about such matters. What is less clear is whether the Court will interpret the equal treatment doctrine to imply a positive obligation on the part of public schools to include, or at least allow, religious instruction in the absence of a clear secular justification. This does not seem likely, but what could prove to be as significant is that the idea of equal treatment might permeate the educational establishment, and public schools would become less hostile and more open to teaching about religion.

This raises the difficult question of the rights of teachers to religious expression in schools. John Peloza, a biology teacher in a public high school in California, contended that the school district's requirement that he teach evolution violated his constitutional rights because evolution is a religious theory; he was made "an unwilling agent of the school district in the establishment of the religion of secular humanism, in violation of the First Amendment."[24] However, the Federal District Court held that "there is a compelling state interest for secondary school teachers to adhere to the curriculum set forth by the appropriate school district."[25]

Peloza also asserted that "even if he is not permitted to teach his theory of creationism in the classroom, he should be permitted to privately discuss religion and his theory of creationism in conversations with students during private, non-instructional time on the campus, during lunch, class breaks, and before and after school hours." The court found that "the plaintiff's right to free speech must be balanced 'against his student's right to be free of religious influence or indoctrination in the classroom.'"[26]

Public school teachers are unlikely to gain greater freedom of religious expression in school under the *Rosenberger* decision because they are considered representatives of their schools and thus of local government and, ultimately, of the state, performing an official function in relation to a "captive audience" of children. Writing for the majority in the *Rosenberger* decision, Justice Kennedy noted that "we have permitted the government to regulate the content of what is or is not expressed

24. *Peloza v. Capistrano Unified School District,* 782 F. Supp. 1412 at 1414 (1992).
25. 782 F. Supp. 1412 at 1416.
26. 782 F. Supp. 1412 at 1419.

when it is the speaker or when it enlists private entities to convey its own message."27

Finding Room for Religion in Public Schools

At several points in this chapter, I have noted that the *Rosenberger* decision is not likely to create a new legal precedent that will significantly alter the place of religion in the public schools. On the other hand, there could be a profound change in public education if the idea of genuine equal treatment for religious ideas becomes more commonly discussed and accepted among public school administrators and public policymakers. I want to turn now to a discussion of how equal treatment, as a form of public policy, might affect religious instruction in the public schools, and what problems and opportunities this new role for religion might entail.

Over recent decades there has been an attempt to render public schools inoffensive to all parents by progressively removing from curriculum and school life any elements to which there could be objections from any quarter. This includes, pre-eminently, discussion of religion as something other than a historical curiosity. Although often traced to the post–World War II rulings of the Supreme Court on religious observances in school, this process in fact began in the mid-nineteenth century. In an attempt to meet the objections of Roman Catholics to public schooling (in order more effectively to socialize their children and thus to reduce the "papist threat"), many communities voluntarily reduced the religious content of that schooling to vestigial observances empty of doctrinal content. The "neutralization" of the common school has been considered, by those who articulate the position of the educational establishment, the only solution to the oppressiveness of single-value education. If a particular conviction causes tension for those who don't share it, then the complete absence of conviction — the lowest common denominator — should resolve the tension.

No responsible educator would explicitly endorse "value-free" education, of course, nor would a good teacher seek to keep her own values out of the classroom. Public schools commonly endorse persistence,

27. *Rosenberger v. University of Virginia*, 115 S. Ct. 2510.

honesty, consideration, and above all tolerance as traits that they should seek to develop in their pupils, and to which no right-thinking person should object. To many in society who hold religious convictions, however, an education that declines to take positions on fundamental aspects of human life as they wish their children to understand and live it is by no means neutral; they perceive it as directly hostile to the convictions by which they live and a violation of "perhaps the most fundamental human right — the right to make a world for one's children."[28]

The fact that "neutrality" has not led to universal support for the common public school genuinely bewilders members of a secularized elite for whom religiously based truth claims are a relic of an earlier stage of human development. Thus the organization called People for the American Way has warned of the collapse of public education if religiously based concerns are accommodated in any way. But is it fair to characterize as "the American Way" the exclusion, from the schools that children attend, of the values that are most important to their parents?

Over the past decade there has been an emerging chorus of support for curriculum revision that would do justice to the values by which most Americans live. In 1987, for example, a broad spectrum of distinguished Americans endorsed a Statement of Principles stressing that

> students need an honest, rigorous education that allows them to penetrate Orwellian rhetoric. . . . Such a goal is compromised when the drawing of normative distinctions and values is frowned upon as a failure of objectivity. . . . It is absurd to argue that the state, or its schools, cannot be concerned with citizens' ability to tell right from wrong, and to prefer one over the other in all matters that bear upon the common public life. That would be utterly to misunderstand the democratic vision, and the moral seriousness of the choices it demands of us.[29]

But a lowest-common-denominator moral education is unlikely to satisfy parents for whom religion and moral decision-making based

28. Peter L. Berger and Richard John Neuhaus, "To Empower People," in *To Empower People: From State to Civil Society,* ed. Michael Novak (Washington: American Enterprise Institute, 1996), p. 180.

29. *Education for Democracy: Guidelines for Strengthening the Teaching of Democratic Values* (Washington: American Federation of Teachers, 1987).

upon religion are of fundamental significance. As Richard Baer, Jr., has noted, "When it comes to the *Big Questions* — questions regarding the meaning and purpose of life, who we are, and how we ought to live in light of our deepest religious and metaphysical commitments — Americans today hold very different views about reality and what is appropriate belief and behavior."[30]

One aspect of doing justice to religion is to ensure that its role in history and in contemporary American life is presented fully and fairly. Historian Paul Gagnon and others have demonstrated that a desire to avoid controversy has led to an expurgation of religion from textbooks as an element of fundamental significance for many individuals and societies. "Students are left with the impression that toleration is the only 'religious' idea worth remembering. . . . Modern readers, always ready to mistake their own indifference to religion for the virtue of toleration, could profit from better perspective. . . . The teaching of toleration, as with any other democratic virtue, must be done in relation to matters we feel strongly about." Gagnon concludes that "without preaching or indoctrination, texts need to demonstrate, for example, that ideals and values are important."[31] To do less is simply a distortion of reality, a form of censorship no less objectionable than the earlier failure to mention the role of women and of members of minority groups. A number of groups have urged that history and social-studies texts be changed to reflect our history more accurately.

It is worth noting that this position, first held by conservatives, has in a very few years become a mainstream position, and is even supported by the fiercely "separationist" People for the American Way (PAW). Most notably, an all-star cast of religious, civic, and political leaders endorsed the "Williamsburg Charter" and called for schools to do justice to the role of religion in American life. This support is not without nuances. PAW has chosen to stress teaching about "religious freedom," which may translate into presenting history as a series of protests against orthodoxy. Thus Roger Williams would be portrayed as a dissenter from the Calvinism of Massachusetts Bay but not as a devout Baptist. Although

30. Baer, Jr., "The Supreme Court's Discriminatory Use of the Term 'Sectarian,'" *The Journal of Law and Politics* 4 (Spring 1990): 465.

31. Gagnon, *Democracy's Half-Told Story: What American History Textbooks Should Add* (Washington: American Federation of Teachers, 1989), p.198.

teaching about religion raises issues of interpretation and emphasis, schools could implement such teaching in a relatively noncontroversial way. It is, however, subject to several objections, which may be illustrated from the British experience.

The Education Reform Act of 1988 continues the requirement of religious education in all publicly supported schools in England and Wales; in schools run by local education authorities, this teaching is based upon a locally established syllabus which "must reflect the fact that religious traditions in the country are in the main Christian whilst taking account of the teaching and practices of other principal religions." The religious education syllabus for the London borough of Ealing states, "Whilst our children need to understand that Christianity is a living faith which has shaped the history, institutions, art and culture of Britain, they also need to explore the other living faiths in our borough so that the richness of our religious experience can be shared and appreciated." Some Christian parents have attacked the suggestion that the effect of Christianity is more appropriate for study than is its content. Others urge that religious education should focus not just on "vague 'traditions,' but on the peculiar substance of Christianity." If religious teaching is to be in the school at all, let it be explicit, "withered fig trees and all."[32]

A school may teach about religion on such a superficial basis that nothing of its real power comes across. Reviewing American history texts, Harriet Tyson noted that "words such as *faith, love, heart, soul, sorrow, pain, pride, greed,* or *evil* are hardly ever used. One gets the impression that religion is nothing more than a fun spoiler, like parents and teachers."[33] On the other hand, a comparative religions approach (like that of the required course in "spiritual currents" in Dutch schools) threatens to trivialize each of the religious traditions discussed. Should children be taught that all beliefs and values are a matter of opinion? Richard Baer, Jr., comments that "the position that the [elementary school] child should be exposed to a multiplicity of values . . . presup-

32. Charles L. Glenn and Joshua L. Glenn, "Making Room for Religious Conviction in Democracy's Schools," in *Schooling Christians,* ed. Stanley Hauerwas and John H. Westerhoff (Grand Rapids: Eerdmans, 1992), p. 105.

33. Tyson, "The Values Vacuum: A Provocative Explanation for Parental Discontent," *Religion and Public Education* 16 (Fall 1989): 386-87.

poses that, for the sake of what is viewed as a good cause, the state has the right to violate the parents' wishes for the child's moral and religious development. This position also prejudges the very difficult psychological question of how much exposure to diversity of values is good for the moral development of the child."[34] An approach that relativizes all religions and value systems will satisfy no one but the historian — and those who wish to convey a radical individualism that rests upon the rejection of shared convictions.

What many parents seem to be looking for is the presence of religion itself in the school. In England, where this is not only permitted but actually required by law, the results have been generally unsatisfactory to all. The results have dissatisfied both nonbelievers and believers: the former fear that their children will be indoctrinated, while the latter dislike what they see as a distortion and trivialization of their faith by a focus upon easily accessible and uncontroversial customs and symbols: "Jews have dreidels, Christians have manger scenes. . . ."

The Williamsburg Charter signatories agreed that any attempt to find a religious "lowest common denominator" for the public schools can lead only to "the folly of endless litigation and further flight from public education" by those parents (and children) who can't accept that version of religion as representing fairly the stubborn particularity of their own faith. To respond adequately to this "new stage and new stress in America's public philosophy" requires an entirely new structure of public education.[35]

Some of us believe that this can be achieved only by true structural pluralism, which would allow parents to select schools corresponding to their own convictions, and allow those responsible for each school to develop and maintain a clear and coherent identity, as is to some extent possible in the Netherlands . . . but that would be another essay.

We could also imagine a government-operated school which, in the name of equal treatment or a dynamic and positive neutrality toward religious convictions, sought to provide an open educational forum in which the deeply held beliefs of teachers and parents as well as of students

34. Baer, Jr., "Censorship and the Public Schools," unpublished paper, Cornell University, 1984.

35. "Chartered Pluralism: Reforging a Public Philosophy for Public Education" (Washington: The Williamsburg Charter Foundation, 1988).

were given free expression within a framework of mutual respect and openness. Some years ago in the Netherlands, opponents of the denominational divisions of that nation's system of public education called for the development of what they called "encounter schools" *(ontmoetings-scholen)*, in which the whole range of religious expression present in Dutch society would find a place. On first consideration, the idea seems attractive, since surely we want to allow Christian, Islamic, and secular humanistic convictions to be fully expressed in a climate of mutual respect, especially considering present practice. But the effective implementation of this idea poses difficulties. Maintaining a balance among teachers who are expressing different convictions (and, inevitably, differ in their ability to convey and to convince) would be an enormously sensitive and challenging task. Creating a unified vision among the staff, a vision essential to an effective school, would be extremely hard. Nevertheless, a balanced encounter among religious and moral perspectives seems essential to higher education (though in practice neither traditional faith nor traditional virtues seem to be treated with much respect), and it would be worthwhile to find ways of exposing secondary students to the conflict of convictions in a way that did not trivialize them.

In elementary education, an emphasis upon how groups and individuals in society differ in their convictions and loyalties does not seem appropriate. Developmentally, what is more important to learn at this stage is that convictions and loyalties are important, and that people the children respect are morally responsible actors. "The most liberated adult," John Coons suggests, "could turn out to be one who, throughout his school life, has experienced the steady and uncompromising faith of his fathers — religious or secular. . . . A strong value position defended by intelligent and committed adults could prove an exhilarating and toughening experience for a young person weaned on Fred Flintstone; it might do more for the possibility and practice of liberty than even a prolonged immersion in socratic dialogue."[36]

Children need not share the convictions by which their teachers live in order to learn that such convictions are important. Parents often select religiously based schools for their children even though they are not adherents of that religion. Many inner-city Protestant parents in the

36. Coons, "Intellectual Liberty and the Schools," *Journal of Law, Ethics and Public Policy* 1 (1985): 521.

United States send their children to Catholic schools, and many Muslim parents in the Netherlands and Britain select Christian schools in preference to secular schools for their children.

What does seem critically important to the quality of a school, and especially to its capacity to *educate* in the fullest sense, is whether it is a community of purpose informed by an ethos that is shared by staff and at least accepted by the parents who entrust their children to them. The *ethos* of a school is that coherent set of beliefs about education, relationships, and the meaning of human life which underlies the character of good schools. In other — perhaps most — schools, both ethos and the distinctive character in which ethos finds consistent expression are simply missing, never having been thought through or considered necessary; the definition of their work is "based on decades of interest group negotiation and mandated responses to particular problems." For teachers and administrators in such schools, "accountability means doing as well as possible on the statistics kept by the central office. It does not mean reaching and implementing a contract with individual students, teachers, or families,"[37] much less developing a coherent *ethos* to guide their practice.

Describing several Catholic schools that serve poor and minority children, Gerald Grant writes of

[an] orientation . . . emphasized not only in catalog rhetoric but at every important juncture in the life of the school. Much effort is spent in communicating the ideals for which the school stands, and in encouraging a dialogue with a public about those ideals. There is a deeply embedded belief that education is inseparable from the concept of what constitutes a good life and a good community.[38]

In good schools, "intellectual and moral virtue are seen as inseparable. . . . Teachers must have equal concern for mind and for character, schools should be neither morally neutral factories for increasing cognitive output nor witless producers of obedient 'well-adjusted' young-

37. Paul T. Hill, Gail E. Foster, and Tamar Gendler, *High Schools with Character* (Santa Monica, Calif.: The Rand Corporation, 1990), pp. ix, 53.
38. Grant, *The World We Created at Hamilton High* (Cambridge, Mass.: Harvard University Press, 1986), p. 173.

sters." Teachers in such schools "expressed a belief in the saving power of the community and expressed great reluctance to expel or give up on a difficult student." Anthony Bryk insists upon the centrality of such orientations for effective schools:

> Most of the recent research on school organization has focused on consequences either for student academic achievement or for teacher commitment and sense of self-efficacy. Both of these streams of research point toward the communal character of good schools and how life within these institutions is shaped by underlying value commitments. When the social form and daily life of a school derive from and extend basic beliefs, normative environments are created that have powerful educative effects. This organizational coherence is captured in the phrase "good schools have a distinctive ethos."[39]

Every aspect of a school — not just the formal lessons — educates, but it is to be feared that the education provided by a school without a shared ethos will be incoherent, even though the curriculum may be highly prescribed. *Only a school of character can aspire to develop the character of its pupils.*

The question raised by Grant and others is whether schools that are constrained to function as subordinate units in a bureaucracy can develop and articulate such an ethos:

> Is it possible to create schools with such an ethos where there is less agreement about ends, where a substantial proportion of students and even many teachers did not select the school, and where some may be attending against their will? In such instances, must we settle for weakly normed schools tied together by a system of rules and procedures that at best can only ensure that none of the disparate elements within the school gains an edge or a preference over the other? Or is it possible to create diversified public schools with a strong ethos in both intellectual and moral terms?[40]

39. Bryk, "Musings on the Moral Life of Schools," *American Journal of Education* 96 (February 1988): 273.

40. Grant, *The World We Created at Hamilton High*, p. 179.

The answer seems obvious: No, it is not possible to create such schools unless there are changes in the environment within which they function. Yes, it may be possible to do so, if such changes occur. School autonomy, what Grant calls "authentic local control — local in the sense of the school itself, not the district or the city — "[41] is essential. So is free choice by both parents and teachers that leads to a convergence of educational intentions:

> Students and staff members must be able to sort themselves among focus schools and between focus and other schools. Choice will not create focus schools, but it is an indispensable part of a focus-based educational reform. . . . From the fact that students choose to enroll, the school creates a presumption that they are willing to accept the school's goals and rules. . . . The school sees itself as responsible for the development not only of a student's mind but also of his or her character.[42]

But autonomy and choice do no more than create the possibility of authentic education by making room for a school to display in its character (that is, how it goes about its work and its daily life as a purposeful community) the ethos that animates it. Autonomy and choice cannot take the place of such an ethos, nor do they ensure, when an ethos exists, that it is consistent with the needs of children and the requirements of justice and freedom.

Is it conceivable that a government-operated school could rest upon an ethos shaped by religious belief? We can expect to see some enrichment of the curriculum for the sake of doing justice to the role of religion in American history and in current society. This is a long-overdue reform, essential not only to make the curriculum more even-handed but also to ensure that it is accurate and adequate to the reality of our society. This is very different, however, from providing schools that view religious convictions as important in shaping their underlying ethos.

All of this suggests that even if the idea of equal treatment became the governing norm for American public schools, thereby providing

---

41. Grant, *The World We Created at Hamilton High*, p. 202.
42. Hill, Foster, and Gendler, *High Schools with Character*, pp. xi, 28.

teachers and administrators with greater free-exercise-of-religion rights and opening the doors of public schools to more religious instruction, it would not easily solve the many perplexing issues about how best to incorporate religion into the public schools as they currently are configured. What is essential is a fundamental restructuring of publicly supported education that will provide schools with the autonomy necessary to develop in ways that are sensitive to the myriad moral and religious viewpoints of the parents who send their children to them. It is this understanding of the concept of equal treatment that I will now consider.

Opening Up the Educational System

The only way to have a publicly supported educational system that can truly *educate* through dealing seriously with the profound stuff of life, while avoiding paralyzing conflict over the basis and content of this education, is to encourage a real diversity among schools, based upon parent and teacher choice among meaningful alternatives. Teachers must be allowed to do their intricate work in schools that provide collegial support based upon shared values and goals. Parents must be allowed to select schools whose teachers share their own values. Parents, teachers, and children should be encouraged to form communities in support of real education. This is, not coincidentally, also the best formula for the fundamental reform that American education so urgently requires.

The solution is not simply a "disestablishment" of American public education to release energy for reform and to restore the alliance of families and teachers in the interest of particular children, though that has much to recommend it.[43] Those who assume that market forces are all that is needed have an insufficient understanding of the common good that is served by schools. What is needed is a carefully crafted

43. See Rockne M. McCarthy, James W. Skillen, and William A. Harper, *Disestablishment a Second Time: Genuine Pluralism for American Schools* (Grand Rapids: William B. Eerdmans, 1982); and John E. Coons and Stephen D. Sugarman, *Education by Choice: The Case for Family Control* (Berkeley and Los Angeles: University of California Press, 1978).

system of educational provision, with the state exercising its appropriate role as the guarantor of justice rather than the primary provider of schooling. As David Osborne and Ted Gaebler wrote in their influential book *Reinventing Government,*

> The public sector tends to be better, for instance, at policy management, regulation, ensuring equity, preventing discrimination or exploitation, ensuring continuity and stability of services, and ensuring social cohesion. . . . The third sector tends to be best at performing tasks that generate little or no profit, demand compassion and commitment to individuals, require extensive trust on the part of customers or clients, need hands-on, personal attention . . . and involve the enforcement of moral codes and individual responsibility for behavior.[44]

By the "the third sector" they mean "organizations that are privately owned and controlled, but that exist to meet public or social needs, not to accumulate private wealth." These are the nonprofit organizations, associations, churches, and other institutions that provide the rich texture of the civil society, and that can — as Osborne and Gaebler point out — do better than government those things that make up the human care of human beings. Schools are, or should be, prototypically third-sector organizations. It was more than twenty years ago that Robert Nisbet pointed out the urgent need of "the creation, or re-creation, of *intermediate* associations" in place of "the systematic flouting by government of the richly varied groups and institutions in the social order which could so easily become themselves the channels or instruments of governmental funding,"[45] and Peter Berger and Richard John Neuhaus made a similar plea for a greater reliance upon "mediating structures," the "value-generating and value-maintaining agencies in society."[46]

It may be that the fundamental problem of American public schools is the misguided effort to subject them to the bureaucratic rationality

---

44. Osborne and Gaebler, *Reinventing Government* (Reading, Mass.: Addison-Wesley, 1992), pp. 45-46.

45. Nisbet, *Twilight of Authority* (New York: Oxford University Press, 1975), p. 278.

46. Berger and Neuhaus, "To Empower People," p. 163.

of large school systems and extensive — and intrusive — state and federal regulation rather than to empower them as institutions of the civil society. The belief that magnet schools provide this kind of empowerment may explain why they have been so successful, and why charter schools, the logical next step in school-level autonomy, have aroused such enthusiasm. But those who develop or seek to enroll their children in charter schools are already coming up against the limits created by the prevailing doctrine of religious neutrality. It is no accident that the great majority of nonpublic schools in the United States have a religious basis: those motivated to make the efforts that these schools demand of their sponsors, staff, and clients alike are typically concerned that the meaning of life not be "off limits."

It is not enough to talk about the importance of families, if the educational system is so organized as to deny parents the opportunity to make significant decisions. The present system of assignment of pupils to schools in the United States is almost unique among nations with universal schooling in its refusal to acknowledge the right of parents to choose schools for their children. This right is spelled out explicitly in the major international covenants protecting human rights. For example, the *Universal Declaration of Human Rights* (1948) states that "parents have a prior right to choose the kind of education that shall be given to their children." The nations signing the *International Covenant on Economic, Social and Cultural Rights* (1966) agreed "to have respect for the liberty of parents . . . to choose for their children schools, other than those established by public authorities, which conform to such minimum educational standards as may be laid down or approved by the State and to ensure the religious and moral education of their children in conformity with their own convictions." Similarly, the First Protocol to the *European Convention for the Protection of Human Rights and Fundamental Freedoms* provides that "in the exercise of any functions which it assumes in relation to education and teaching, the State shall respect the right of parents to ensure such education and teaching in conformity with their own religious and philosophical convictions" (article 2).

John Coons has argued eloquently that American education frustrates parents in their attempts to exercise this right and duty:

From top to bottom its structure effectively frustrates the choices of parent and child which the law protects in every other realm of

97

life. Parents choose shoes, food, games, hours and every other important feature of a child's life. In education this liberty is not only opposed but squelched. Ordinary families with all their rich variety in culture and values are forced to accept the form, content and ideology of a politically dictated education.[47]

Some assert that government should make the decisions about the education of children because some parents — and poor parents in general — are incapable of doing so and indeed simply don't care. Of course there are some inadequate and irresponsible parents of every social class, and society must have ways of intervening to protect individual children from situations of clearly established abuse and neglect, including neglect of their need for an education. Policy for the great majority should not, however, be guided by exceptional cases.

Federally funded research that I have directed found that inner-city parents of all racial/ethnic groups are keenly interested in making school choices for their children, and use a variety of means of obtaining information and reaching conclusions about which schools would best meet their needs.[48] The major impediment to allowing them to exercise such choices is the disrespect for the family that is unfortunately widespread among professional educators. Children from middle-class families are easy to teach, it is often said, though their parents may be too pushy and interfere with what educators alone are capable of deciding. On the other hand, there is a perception that children from working-class or poor families are difficult, and that their parents don't care about education — fortunately, since schools can't be expected to do much with their children.

Policies that treat parents as incapable of responsible decision-making do not serve children well. A system that expects parents to be passive conveys a message that responsible choice, the expression of character or virtue, is exercised *for*, not *by*, the individual — a lesson that encourages personal irresponsibility. An opportunity is thereby lost to engage parents and their children together in making decisions whose consequences are immediately apparent to both.

47. Coons, "Intellectual Liberty and the Schools," p. 515.
48. C. L. Glenn, K. McLaughlin, and L. Salganik, *Parent Information for School Choice: The Case of Massachusetts* (Boston: Center on Families, Communities, Schools and Children's Learning, 1993).

Normative judgments are the essential stuff of successful family life, and of successful education. They cannot be avoided. Neither can they be imposed by the state. That is why only a system of schooling based upon family choice of schools would permit the uninhibited expression of particular perspectives on the truth in schools.

There is a new openness to what a few years ago would have been inconceivable in elite policy circles: to consider religiously based schooling *within public education* as a viable alternative to the supposedly neutral schooling provided by local government. This is surely the question that needs to be answered first, before the question of the constitutionality of this or that funding arrangement. We can be sure that when the legal question is posed, it will be in the form of whether it is legitimate for public funds to be made available for the religious schools that some parents choose, not whether government has an obligation to make funds available to support what Carl Esbeck calls "religious choice" if it funds other choices.

We could imagine, in a strictly logical world, that the second form of the question would be posed on the basis of the free exercise clause of the First Amendment. After all, once the precedent has been established — and it is now very well-established indeed — that government provides extensive choice of publicly funded schools, without (in Quentin Quade's phrase) financial penalty to the parents, a case could be made that drawing the line on the basis of religious content alone violates the principle of equal treatment suggested by the Rosenberger case. That is, government could legitimately decide to support some choices and not others on the basis of educational quality considerations, for example, or health and safety concerns, but should leave it up to parents to inquire and form judgments about the religious or philosophical perspective of the schools among which they are free to choose.

Realistically, however, the courts are unlikely to reach the point of articulating a right to publicly funded religious schooling until a lot more water has flowed under the bridge. Even in Europe, the human-rights high court has declined to rule that the right to choose a religiously based school implies a right to public funding for that school, though in fact most European governments do provide such funding as a policy matter. It seems likely that a similar sequence of political and legal decisions will be followed in the United States. First, governments will decide to support religiously based choices as a matter of fairness and good policy. Then the courts will rule that this does not violate the establishment clause if the decision about which schools should receive public funds rests entirely in the hands of parents. When state governments decide not to include religiously based choices among the options that they will support, it is unlikely in the short term that the courts will order them to do so on the basis of equal treatment and content neutrality. Down the road, if publicly funded school choice continues to grow as rapidly as it has in recent decades, and if some states support religious options and others do not, an articulated right could emerge.

Accordingly, we should look to the political process — and above all to changing public opinion — rather than to the courts for a breakthrough. First the "myth of the common school" must be dispelled by a recognition that a government "monopoly on the generation and maintenance of values" — to use Berger and Neuhaus's phrase — is inconsistent with a free society. Only then can we create the framework for educational freedom and the equal treatment of all religious and secular worldviews.

CHAPTER 5

Equal Treatment: Implications for Nonprofit Organizations

ROBERT A. DESTRO

The equal treatment approach to establishment clause interpretations has implications for religiously based nonprofit service organizations as well as for education. In this chapter, Robert Destro considers the nature of nonprofit associations in the United States and weighs how equal treatment, if it were fully developed and applied to them, would affect their activities and relations with government. He argues that the First Amendment guarantees of religious freedom must be read in conjunction with guarantees of other civil liberties of the Constitution if an appropriate, freedom-protecting concept of equal treatment is to be reached. Robert Destro is a professor of law at the Columbus School of Law, The Catholic University of America.

In no country in the world has the principle of association been more successfully used, or applied to a greater multitude of objects, than in America. . . . In the United States, associations are established to promote the public safety, commerce, industry, morality, and religion. There is no end which the human will despairs of attaining through the combined power of individuals united into a society.[1]

1. Tocqueville, *Democracy in America*, ed. Richard D. Heffner (New York: Mentor Books, 1956), pp. 95-96.

By the time Alexis de Tocqueville wrote these words in 1832, Americans had been living on the frontiers for over two hundred years. Life was hard. The environment was hostile, and cooperation with neighbors was the key to survival. Associations were organized to attend to the tasks at hand, and communities — both social and political — grew up around them. Though we rarely think of it as such, the Constitution of the United States is the organic document of one such association, the United States of America, and its Preamble speaks to its purposes:

> We the People of the United States, in Order to form a more perfect Union, establish Justice, insure domestic Tranquility, provide for the common defence, promote the general Welfare, and secure the Blessings of Liberty to ourselves and our Posterity, do ordain and establish this Constitution for the United States of America.

America has changed considerably since Tocqueville's tour of America, but its reliance on private, quasi-private, and quasi-public associations to get the community's business done has, if anything, kept pace with those changes. Government, at all levels, simply could not operate without the assistance of private-sector contractors. Both for-profit and nonprofit organizations[2] supply everything from business cards, cleaning services, and computer software to aircraft carriers and reusable re-entry vehicles for space exploration.

The private, nonprofit sector of the U.S. economy is enormous, and is a significant contract and grant partner with the government. The

---

2. The Uniform Nonprofit Association Act defines a "nonprofit association" as "an unincorporated organization consisting of [two] or more members joined by mutual consent for a common, nonprofit purpose" (Uniform Unincorporated Nonprofit Association Act §1(2)), but does not define the term "nonprofit organization" because the drafters concluded that the common definition would limit the range of associations eligible to take advantage of the benefits such a structure embodies (*Accord*, Cal. Corp. Code §21000 [West, 1996]). The common definition of the term "nonprofit organization" is "an association whose net gains do not inure to the benefit of its members and which makes no distribution to its members, except on dissolution." See Uniform Act Comment to §1. A "nonprofit organization" can therefore be organized for any purpose, as long as the members do not seek to "profit" in the pecuniary sense. Its activities can include religious, scientific, social, literary, educational, recreational, benevolent, or political activities; the organization may also serve any other purpose not that of pecuniary profit" (*Accord*, Cal. Corp. Code §21000 [West, 1996]).

nonprofit sector includes churches, charities, labor unions, much of the nation's health care system, virtually all of its private schools, colleges, and universities, and a myriad of other organizations and activities. In 1992, it accounted for 6.7 percent of the GNP. In 1993, tax-exempt public charities alone were generating "$500 billion in revenues, ha[d] assets of about $1 trillion, employ[ed] seven million people, and [had become] the fastest-growing sector of the U.S. economy."[3] In 1994, private, nonprofit associations employed 11 percent of all American workers.

Figure 1: Major Types of Tax Exempt Organizations

Type	Number
Religious, charitable	599,745
Social welfare	140,143
Fraternal beneficiary societies	92,284
Business leagues	74,273
Labor, agriculture	68,144
Social and recreation clubs	65,273
War veterans	30,292

Source: Internal Revenue Service[4]

Although government agencies are not generally considered to be a part of the nonprofit sector, it is sometimes difficult to know where "the government" ends and the "private" (or "nongovernmental") sector begins. There is considerable overlap in the modern administrative state. Congress has created some very high-profile agencies but organized them as private nonprofits, even though it continues to provide a considerable proportion of their funding. Two of the most widely known of these are the Legal Services Corporation (LSC), which provides legal services for the poor at public expense, and the Corporation for Public Broadcasting (CPB), which collects and distributes public and private

3. John Connor, "IRS Asks Congress for Flexible Clout on Tax Exemption," *The Wall Street Journal*, 16 June 1993; reported in WESTLAW at 1993 WL-WSJ 696265.

4. John R. Emshwiller, "More Small Firms Complain about Tax-Exempt Rivals," *The Wall Street Journal*, 8 August 1995, Enterprise Section; reported in WESTLAW at 1995 WL-WSJ 8737198.

funds to support public broadcasting stations. The Public Broadcasting Service (PBS) and National Public Radio (NPR) are private, nonprofit organizations as well, even though they were created by CPB. CPB provides major funding, derived from public resources, for both.

Developments such as these bear witness to the vitality of America's penchant for delegating the community's tasks to associations of every type. And why not? Government does not have unlimited resources, and both state and federal governments operate under constitutions that limit the types of activities for which they may undertake direct responsibility. Thus, even were there a constituency for operating an organization like PBS as an agency in the executive branch of the federal government, there are many reasons why Congress might want to defer to the private sector. Purchasing services is often a less complicated way to acquire a superior product than trying to develop it in-house.

My task in this chapter is to explore the implications of a legal regime in which nonprofit associations that are, in some significant way, religious in character may be *considered* contractors or grantees on an equal basis when the political community allocates responsibility and funds to the private sector for the acquisition of goods or services. This would include, among other things, the "product" produced by a sheltered workshop, education of both children and adults, health care, social services, and job training. In short, virtually any good, commodity, or service that government is empowered to purchase with public funds is included. Specifically excluded, however, is any implication that the government may purchase items of religious ritual (Bibles, sacramental items), ministerial services for the purposes of religious teaching or worship in nonmilitary settings, or property to be devoted exclusively to religious use.

In this chapter I also assume that the United States Supreme Court has accepted the proposition that neither the states nor the federal government may discriminate against religious individuals or organizations on the basis of either the content or the viewpoint of speech that takes place in a state-created, quasi-public forum;[5] and that the establishment clause has been construed to permit direct payments to any association — including those that might have a religious identity, character, or mission — for

5. *Rosenberger v. The Rector & Visitors of the University of Virginia,* 115 S. Ct. 2510 (1995).

goods, services, or programs that meet generally acceptable standards for quality, cost, design, or professionalism.[6]

In Part One I will briefly identify the "institutional identity and integrity" problems that can arise for religiously oriented nonprofits under this (very) speculative hypothesis. In Part Two I will discuss several of the key nondiscrimination principles that govern, or should govern, the decisions of political communities when they entrust private associations with the responsibility to act in the public interest and support that decision by allocating funds from the public treasury. In Part Three I will relate those provisions to current discussions of "equal treatment" and access for religious organizations or speakers. I will conclude the chapter with the observation that the promise of "equal treatment" will remain just that — a promise — unless the Supreme Court is willing to reconsider the way in which it views its own role as the ultimate arbiter of both the "value" of speech and the "proper" relationship of the state and citizens who take their religious commitments very seriously.

I. Grasping the Nature of the Problem: Government Power and the Maintenance of Institutional Integrity

Constitutions, both state and federal, rather clearly delineate the tasks reserved for government alone. Among the most obvious of these are the coinage of money, regulation of commerce and foreign affairs, the levy and collection of taxes, and law enforcement. Constitutions may speak as well to other services deemed essential to the public welfare, such as the provision of public infrastructure services (roads, highways, electricity, gas, and water), education, social services, and medical care, but legislatures are generally given broad authority to decide the degree of public-private cooperation that will best suit the public interest, convenience, and necessity.

It was precisely this allocation of responsibility that led to the initial debates over the need for a federal Bill of Rights, and, in particular, to a demand for a guarantee that the federal government would not use

---

6. The courts have approved such arrangements, but the Supreme Court never indicated that the Constitution *requires* such an approach.

its enumerated powers to inhibit freedom of religion. There were two points of view. The Federalists took the position that a federal religious-freedom guarantee was unnecessary because they "drew a nonestablishment sum from the lack of federal jurisdiction over religion plus the [religious] test ban" of Article VI. In their view, the provision of Article VI that there shall be no religious test for holding public office was "enough [of a religious liberty guarantee] for a federal government of specific enumerated powers."[7]

The anti-Federalists and the states were not so trusting. Many anti-Federalists viewed the no religious test clause and the supremacy clause as threats to religious liberty.[8] The states were unwilling to entrust enormous power and discretion to a sovereign that had power to pre-empt local law and custom concerning freedom of religion, speech, press, assembly, and petition whenever Congress deemed it "necessary and proper" to the attainment of its delegated responsibilities. Viewed from the perspective of the communities that would dissent from any federal attempt to impose a "politically correct" view of religion or its place in the community, any constitution that did not state *explicitly* that the federal government had no power to vex religious liberty, or to set national policy on the subject, would be fatally defective.

Even though the First Amendment was the guarantee sought by those who were not sanguine about the ability of the federal government to control its appetite for power over religion, speech, press, and politics, the current case law demonstrates that they were right to be skeptical. And nowhere are the dangers implicit in "an establishment of religion" more clear than in the complex First Amendment questions that will arise if and when the Court can be convinced to reconsider its long history of discrimination in the treatment of religious organizations.

The nonprofit organizations that would benefit from a rethinking of the Supreme Court's perspective are principally concerned about two things: (1) their ability to maintain an organizational identity and character that comports with their religious mission or outlook; and

7. Gerard V. Bradley, "The No Religious Test Clause and the Constitution of Religious Liberty: A Machine That Has Gone of Itself," *Case Western Reserve Law Review* 37 (1987): 709.

8. Bradley, "The No Religious Test Clause," pp. 694-711.

(2) their ability, in practice, to freely integrate their faith-based perspectives into their day-to-day operations and activities without fear that government will view that integration as professionally improper. I will consider each of these in turn.

Will Religious Associations Be Able to Maintain Their Identity, Character, and Mission?

The answer to this question depends on two factors: (1) the commitment of the organization to maintain its character through recruitment, hiring, and training of its key employees and volunteers; and (2) the propensity of the government to foster institutional homogeneity in the name of "cultural diversity." Both concerns are significant. The first, however, is beyond the scope of this chapter.

The second concern arises from the unthinking manner in which the government understands the concepts of religion, secularity, neutrality, and nondiscrimination.[9] To the extent that a government agency concludes that religion or religious identity is not related to the purpose of an association, or that a particular program or policy is not essential to the maintenance of its identity as an association with a religious character, it is likely that both labor and employment-discrimination law will be invoked to prevent or severely curtail attempts by the organization to maintain that character through its hiring, training, and program development activities.

The assumption that a government agency, usually a court, is either qualified or empowered by the First Amendment to make such determinations seems not to be questioned. Occasionally, however, the ironic nature of that assumption becomes the centerpiece in an actual case or controversy. Take *EEOC v. Townley Engineering & Mfg. Co.*[10] as an example. This was an employment discrimination case in which a for-profit manufacturer of mining equipment argued, without contradic-

---

9. See Michael S. Ariens and Robert A. Destro, *Religious Liberty in a Pluralistic Society* (Durham, N.C.: Carolina Academic Press, 1996), pp. 947-94; and Robert A. Destro, "Equality, Social Welfare and Equal Protection," *Harvard Journal of Law and Public Policy* 9 (1986): 53.

10. 859 F.2d 610 (9th Cir. 1988); cert. denied 489 U.S. 1077 (1989).

tion from the government, that its owners had dedicated their entire operation to the service of God. They included scriptural verses and tracts with their mailings, took great pains to accommodate the religious needs of their employees, and required mandatory attendance at prayer meetings during working hours.

The court, however, rejected the proposition that a for-profit manufacturing business can have a religious character. In the court's view, the organization must have an essentially religious purpose, not a financial one, in order to claim the protection of the religious accommodation provisions of the nation's civil rights laws. Calling that conclusion "a theological judgment," U.S. Circuit Court Judge John T. Noonan, Jr., made this observation in dissent:

> Secular men and women take secular values seriously. Men and women of the world believe that the world's business is important. When Congress elevates this business to a national priority it has been all too easy for officers of the government and even judges to ignore the countervailing command of the Constitution. In the Supreme Court, the Constitution has been no shield for the spirit when Congress has ordained that the spirit must yield to secular needs. . . .
>
> The [Equal Employment Opportunity Commission] and the court appear to assume that there must be a sharp division between secular activity and religious activity. The theological position is that human beings should worship God on Sundays or some other chosen day and go about their business without reference to God the rest of the time. Such a split is attractive to some religious persons. It is repudiated by many, especially those who seek to integrate their lives and to integrate their activities. Among those who repudiate this theology is the Townley Manufacturing Company. The integration of work and religious purpose that the Townleys and their company seek was captured centuries ago in exquisite devotional verse:

> *Who sweeps a room as for Thy cause*
> *Makes that, and the action, fine.*

> George Herbert, "The Elixir,"
> *The Writings of George Herbert*, 185.

What is notable for present purposes is that the tendency condemned by Judge Noonan is well established in case law.[11] To the extent that indirect pressures might be brought to bear on an association through manipulation of contract or grant eligibility requirements, that pressure would be imposed *in addition to* pre-existing pressures to eliminate religion from the "secular" workplace. Equal treatment might therefore have a dark side: a relentless effort on the part of the government to restrict any overt evidence of religious belief or practice in any aspect of an organization that it views as "essentially secular." At least insofar as government *regulation* is concerned, the much-vaunted wall of separation between church and state becomes illusory. The government can decide which activities are "secular" and which are "religious," and the criteria favor government authority rather than religious freedom.

In *EEOC v. Kamehameha Schools*,[12] for example, the issue was whether or not the Kamehameha Schools would be permitted to comply with a requirement of the will of their founder and benefactor, the late Bernice Pauahi Bishop, a member of the Hawaiian royal family and, at the time of her death in 1884, the largest landowner in Hawaii. It provided that the bulk of her estate should be placed in a charitable trust "to erect and maintain in the Hawaiian Islands two schools, each for boarding and day scholars, one for boys and one for girls, to be known as, and called the Kamehameha Schools." It also directed that "the teachers of said schools shall forever be persons of the Protestant religion," but made it clear that Mrs. Bishop did "not intend that the choice be restricted to persons of any particular sect of Protestants."[13]

When Carole Edgerton, who is not a Protestant, sought a position as a substitute French teacher, she was informed of the Protestant-only requirement. She filed a charge of religious discrimination with the Equal Employment Opportunity Commission (EEOC). The schools' defense was that the nation's key employment discrimination law, Title VII of the Civil Rights Act of 1964,[14] permitted its "Protestants-

---

11. See Ariens and Destro, *Religious Liberty in a Pluralistic Society*, especially pp. 581-674.

12. 990 F.2d 458 (9th Cir.) (as amended, May 10, 1993); cert. denied, 114 S. Ct. 439 (1993).

13. 990 F.2d at 459.

14. 42 U.S.C. §2000e-2(a).

only" hiring policy. Its case was based on three assertions: first, that the schools were religious educational institutions; second, that they were entitled to claim the religious curriculum exemption;[15] and third, that, given the terms of Mrs. Bishop's will, religion was a bona fide occupational requirement for teachers at the schools she established.[16]

The United States Court of Appeals for the Ninth Circuit rejected each defense, holding that religious exemptions are to be narrowly construed, and that the burden of proving that they apply rests upon the institution claiming them.[17] Basing its analysis on *EEOC v. Townley Engineering & Mfg. Co.*, the court undertook an analysis of the facts to determine whether the secular characteristics of the schools outweighed their religious ones. The goal was, in the court's words, to determine "whether the 'general picture' of the institution is primarily religious or secular."[18] "Mere affiliation" with a religious organization, or the maintenance of a religious environment, are not enough. In the view of the Ninth Circuit Court, Title VII's religious exemption applies only to schools that are actively involved in the *propagation of a particular religion.* The court stated,

> The religious characteristics of the Schools consist of minimal, largely comparative religious studies, scheduled prayers and services, quotation of Bible verses in a school publication, and the employment of nominally Protestant teachers for secular subjects. References to Bible verses, comparative religious education, and even prayers and services are common at private schools and cannot suffice to exempt such schools; the addition of nominally Protestant teachers does not alter this conclusion. We conclude the Schools are an essentially secular institution operating within an historical tradition that includes Protestantism, and that the Schools' purpose and character is primarily secular, not primarily religious.[19]

15. The curriculum exemption in 42 U.S.C. §2000e-2(e)(2) provides: "It shall not be an unlawful employment practice for a school . . . to hire and employ employees of a particular religion . . . if the curriculum of such school . . . is directed toward the propagation of a particular religion."
16. 990 F.2d at 459.
17. 990 F.2d at 460.
18. 990 F.2d at 460.
19. 990 F.2d at 463-64.

What this means, in practice, is that an organization must concede that its primary purpose is the propagation of a particular religion before it will be permitted to take "affirmative action" to maintain its character. If it does, however, it is likely that it will make itself *ineligible* under current law to participate in the kinds of public-private partnership programs that the equal treatment concept appears to permit.

Freedom to Integrate the Faith-Based Perspectives of an Association into Its Day-to-Day Operations and Activities

This issue is by far the more difficult of the two mentioned in the introduction to this section. At bottom, this issue is one of professional legitimacy. Bluntly put, can a religiously committed institution provide really "professional" services, or will they be tainted by the religious commitments of the organization or its staff?

Institutional "Neutrality" and the Concept of "Professionalism." There is no better example of this problem than the world of academia, and none more explicit than the definition of "academic freedom" embodied in the Bylaws of the Association of American Law Schools (AALS) in Section 6-8(d):

> A faculty member shall have academic freedom and tenure in accordance with the principles of the American Association of University Professors. Those principles are defined by the American Association of University Professors' [AAUP] 1940 Statement on Academic Freedom and Tenure and the Interpretive Comments adopted in 1970. Specifically, the Association of American Law Schools adopts the position of the 1970 Interpretive Comments that 'most church-related institutions no longer need or desire the departure from the principles of academic freedom implied in the 1940 Statement, and we do not now endorse such a departure.'

In order to maintain its accreditation, a religiously affiliated law school must bear the burden of proving that it complies.

The assumption implicit in this requirement is that the AAUP's vision is both normative *and* neutral with respect to religion, and that whatever need or desire a religious institution might have to depart

111

from the principles *implied* in the AAUP statement has long since vanished. What the rule actually requires of a religiously affiliated institution, however, is not clear on the face of the regulation, nor can it be fully grasped without some consideration of the provisions of the AAUP's 1940 Statement on Academic Freedom and Tenure. The three "Principles on Academic Freedom and Tenure" at the core of that statement determine whether or not an educational institution is professionally legitimate:

1. The teacher is entitled to full freedom in research and in the publication of the results, subject to the adequate performance of his other academic duties; but research for pecuniary return should be based upon an understanding with the authorities of the institution.
2. The teacher is entitled to freedom in the classroom in the discussing his subject, but he should be careful not to introduce into his teaching controversial matter which has no relation to his subject. Limitation of academic freedom because of religious or other aims of the institution should be clearly stated in writing at the time of the appointment.
3. The college or university teacher is a citizen, a member of a learned profession, and an officer of an educational institution. When he speaks or writes as a citizen, he should be free from institutional censorship or discipline, but his special position in the community imposes special obligations. As a man of learning and educational officer, he should remember that the public may judge his profession and his institution by his utterances. Hence he should at all times be accurate, should exercise appropriate restraint, should show respect for the opinions of others, and should make every effort to indicate that he is not an institutional spokesman.[20]

The 1940 Statement has a long and interesting history. Thankfully, however, it is recounted elsewhere and need not be repeated here.[21] The

---

20. *Policy Documents and Reports* 3 (AAUP, 1984); see Appendix B, *Law & Contemporary Problems* 53 (Summer 1990): 407. The 1940 Statement was amended in 1989 and 1990 to remove gender-specific references in the text.

21. See Walter P. Metzger, "The 1940 Statement of Principles on Academic Freedom and Tenure," *Law & Contemporary Problems* 53 (1990): 3.

1940 Statement is relevant to the present discussion in two ways. First, it is the standard by which the academic legitimacy of law schools is to be judged, both by the schools themselves and by the agencies that accredit them. Second, religiously affiliated educational institutions are singled out for special scrutiny because the 1940 Statement leaves little doubt that institutional religious commitment is a factor that should be taken as calling into question the academic legitimacy of the institution.

In case there were any doubt that the religious character of these institutions is viewed as presenting unique "legitimacy" problems, consider Standard 211 of the American Bar Association's *Standards for the Approval of Law Schools*. It provides that a "law school shall maintain equality of opportunity in legal education, including employment of faculty and staff, without discrimination or segregation on ground of race, color, religion, national origin, or sex."[22] It adds the following proviso:

> This Standard does not prevent a law school from having a religious affiliation and purpose and adopting and applying policies of admission of students and employment of faculty and staff that directly relate to this affiliation and purpose so long as (1) notice of these policies has been given to applicants, students, faculty and staff before their affiliation with the law school, and (2) the religious affiliation, purpose and policies do not contravene any other Standard, including Standard 405(d) concerning academic freedom. The policies may provide a preference for persons adhering to the religious affiliation and purpose of the law school, but shall not be applied to preclude a diverse student body in terms of race, color, religion, national origin, or sex. This Standard permits religious policies as to admission and employment only to the extent that they are protected by the United States Constitution. It shall be administered as if the First Amendment of the United States Constitution governs its application.

The Association of American Law Schools has a virtually identical requirement. Executive Committee Regulation 6.17, which implements Bylaw 6-4(a), makes this proviso:

22. Cf. Calif. State Admissions Rule XVIII §2, Standards L and M (1994) ("Standards and Procedures for Preliminary Approval and Accreditation of Law Schools").

Law Schools with a Religious Affiliation or Purpose. It is not inconsistent with Bylaw Section 6-4(a) for a law school with a religious affiliation or purpose to adopt preferential admissions and employment practices that directly relate to the school's religious affiliation or purpose so long as (1) notice of the practices is provided to members of the law school community (students, faculty and staff) before their affiliation with the school; (2) the practices do not interfere with the school's provision of satisfactory legal education as provided for in these bylaws and regulations, whether because of lack of a sufficient intellectual diversity or for any other reason; (3) the practices are in compliance with Executive Committee Regulation Chapter 6.16, as well as all other Bylaws and Executive Committee Regulations; (4) the practices do not discriminate on the ground of race, color, national origin, sex, age, handicap or disability, or sexual orientation; and (5) the practices contain neither a blanket exclusion nor a limitation on the number of persons admitted or employed on religious grounds.

Since these "exemptions" apply *only* to religiously affiliated law schools, it follows that there must be something about their commitment to utilize hiring or admission practices as devices to maintain their religious character or identity that calls into question their legitimacy as professional schools. What is this factor that imposes upon these schools a duty of full disclosure?

Standard 211 and ECR 6.17 borrow their disclosure requirements from the "Limitations Clause" of Paragraph (b) of the AAUP Statement. It provides that "limitation of academic freedom because of religious *or other aims of the institution* should be clearly stated in writing at the time of the appointment" (emphasis added). The law accreditors, however, did not make an exact appropriation of the AAUP's language.

Because the phrase "or other aims of the institution" presupposes that there can be, at both religious and nonreligious institutions, *non*religious aims which could be inconsistent with academic freedom (e.g., "political correctness"), one might expect that *all* law schools should be compelled to make full disclosure. By its terms, the 1940 Statement applies to *any* "aims of [*any*] institution" which can be inconsistent with academic freedom, but the ABA and AALS single out

114

only institutions with a religious commitment or mission for special treatment. Why? The official attitude of the AAUP and much of the academy concerning religion itself is neither flattering nor religiously neutral.[23]

The 1940 Statement and its subsequent interpretations are based on a philosophical view of both the nature of freedom and the nature of the search for truth in an academic setting. Professor Walter Metzger of Columbia University notes that those who laid the groundwork for the 1940 Statement were

> utilitarian in temper and conviction, [and] did not view the expressional freedoms of academics as a bundle of abstract rights. They regarded them as corollaries of the contemporary public need for universities that would increase the sum of human knowledge and furnish experts for public service — new functions that had been added to the time-honored one of qualifying students for degrees.[24]

That utilitarianism was clearly reflected in the AAUP's 1915 Declaration of Principles,[25] but it is not apparent on the face of the 1940 Statement. The only vestige of a clear statement by the AAUP concerning "the compatibility of individual academic freedom with institutional religious or other doctrinal tests" is the "Limitations Clause" itself. As Metzger observes, "The words of this provision come from an every-day vocabulary . . . but they vibrate with mystery and ambiguity when read without the 1915 master key."[26] We must therefore take a brief look at that 1915 "master key" to the meaning of the Limitations Clause to see what view of religion or, more accurately, institutional commitment to religiously based truth claims the accreditation agencies have adopted. Professor Metzger provides the answer:

23. See generally Stephen L. Carter, *The Culture of Disbelief* (New York: Basic Books, 1993).

24. Metzger, "The 1940 Statement of Principles on Academic Freedom and Tenure," p. 13.

25. *General Report of the Committee on Academic Freedom and Academic Tenure, AAUP Bulletin* 1 (December 1915): 17; see Appendix A, *Law & Contemporary Problems* 53 (Summer 1990): 393.

26. Metzger, "The 1940 Statement of Principles on Academic Freedom and Tenure," p. 31.

The idea of institutional neutrality — the view that a university cannot put the stamp of its approval or disapproval on a disputed truth-claim and still be faithful to its social trust — was of such critical importance to these authors that they highlighted it in almost every paragraph, though they did not refer to it by that name. . . . Any university, they wrote, "which lays restrictions upon the intellectual freedom of its professors proclaims itself a proprietary institution, and should be so described whenever it makes a general appeal for funds; *and the public should be advised that the institution has no claim whatever to general support or regard.*"[27]

This is an important statement. In essence, it means that a faith-based commitment to the maintenance of an institutional culture hospitable to religion disqualifies the institution from participation in public finance programs, not because it is inappropriate to fund religious education on an equal basis, but because religiously committed institutions are not *educational* unless they are "neutral" with respect to precisely the truth claims they affirm. In this view, they can be either essentially educational or essentially religious, but not both at the same time.

Personal Faith Commitments and the Maintenance of "Professional Standards." The same problem exists, though less overtly, for professionals who work in associations that have strong faith commitments. Although the potential scope of this topic is enormous, only two basic points will be raised here. The first is the relationship of professional standards (however defined) to the discretion of a professional of any sort to bring the teachings or insights drawn from one's faith into one's professional activities. The second is the problem of self-censorship.

A good example can be found in the American Bar Association's *Model Rules of Professional Responsibility.* These rules clearly require that an attorney-advisor shall counsel the client concerning all relevant implications of a proposed course of behavior. They also make it clear that "in rendering such advice, a lawyer may refer not only to law but to other considerations such as moral, economic, social and political factors, that may be relevant to the client's situation."[28] Does this include

27. Metzger, "The 1940 Statement of Principles on Academic Freedom and Tenure," p. 14, emphasis added.

28. American Bar Association, *Model Rules of Professional Responsibility,* Rule 2.1,

an attorney's raising religious perspectives with the client without first having been given an opening (or permission) to do so? Some might answer this question in the affirmative. Others might suggest that there is a conflict of interest unless the client first consents to the raising of "extraneous" issues of this type.

The same problem exists for social workers, nurses, physicians, psychologists, and members of other "counseling" professions. If the survey data are correct, Americans are an "incorrigibly religious" people.[29] If they are, a professional might find it either appropriate or necessary to raise questions touching on religion or religious morality because the client or patient might find the discussion useful. To the extent that professional organizations consider such discussions to be "unprofessional" for any reason, there will be pressure to self-censor.[30]

As applied to nonprofit, religiously affiliated organizations providing such services, the question is this: Can, or should, a government agency condition the exercise of its grant or contract-making authority on a pledge by such agencies that they will *not* inject their religious perspectives into professional discussions without first seeking the client's permission to do so? If so, the implicit state-sponsored message to the organizations subject to those conditions is that religion is extraneous to professional discussions.

II. Overcoming the Conceptual Limits of Current First-Amendment Doctrine

It should be apparent by this point that the equal treatment model the Court appears to have adopted in *Rosenberger* and *Capitol Square Review and Advisory Board v. Pinette*[31] is not conceptually robust enough to

---

in Stephen Gillers and Roy D. Simon, Jr., *Regulation of Lawyers: Statutes and Standards* (Boston: Little, Brown, 1996), p. 182.

29. Richard John Neuhaus, *The Naked Public Square: Religion and Democracy in America* (Grand Rapids: William B. Eerdmans, 1984), p. 113.

30. Compare the discussion of the Supreme Court's treatment of the difference between running a soup kitchen and counseling pregnant teeenagers in Barry Lynn, Marc D. Stern, and Oliver S. Thomas, *The Right to Religious Liberty: The Basic ACLU Guide to Religious Rights,* 2d ed. (Carbondale: Southern Illinois University Press, 1995), p. 33.

31. 115 S. Ct. 2440 (1995).

deal with many of the issues raised by its opponents. The objections to it fall into three basic categories:

- objections centered on a legitimate concern for the institutional integrity of the affected religious organizations
- objections centered on a legitimate concern that organs of government cannot draw clear and predictable lines between the kinds of activities which can be funded because they are "not religious enough" to be disqualified, and those which should clearly be disqualified because they are "essentially religious"
- objections centered on a concern for the non-association rights of dissenters.[32]

Each of these concerns resonates in the current case law because each concern is valid. More to the point here, advocates of each position can take comfort in the knowledge that the jurisprudence of the religion clause is flexible enough for virtually any judge truly opposed to public-private partnerships involving religious institutions to find a "violation" of the establishment clause. Much of the opposition to the equal treatment principle, in this book and elsewhere, centers on precisely these issues.

Opponents of the equal treatment principle rarely examine either the biases or the power claims that undergird the Supreme Court's post-1937 jurisprudence of individual rights. In essence, opponents of equal treatment argue that the framers of the First Amendment intended to write a prophylactic exclusionary rule, the purpose and primary effect of which is to discriminate against any group of believers sufficiently orthodox to qualify, in the Court's view, as either pervasively sectarian or essentially religious. While the Court's sloppy and incomplete reading of history gives some support to that proposition, the language and structure of the Constitution do not.[33]

The First Amendment is not the only source of protection for reli-

---

32. See *Keller v. State Bar of California*, 496 U.S. 1, 15-16 (1990); and *Abood v. Detroit Board of Education*, 431 U.S. 209, 235-36 (1977).

33. A fair reading of the so-called Virginia experience does not support the Court's interpretation of either history or law. See Ariens and Destro, *Religious Liberty in a Pluralistic Society,* and supra note 9 at 469-73.

gious freedom. The federal government, including the Supreme Court,[34] is bound not only by the First Amendment but also by the test clause of Article VI, the due process clause of the Fifth Amendment, and the citizenship clause of the Fourteenth Amendment. State governments are bound by the religious freedom and nondiscrimination provisions of their own constitutions, and the provisions of the Fourteenth Amendment, including those incorporating the requirements of the First.

When a political community decides that certain goods, services, or commodities should be provided by private associations at public expense, it is the *Constitution* — not the First Amendment standing in isolation — that provides the rule of decision. And since "we must never forget that it is a constitution we are expounding,"[35] I will begin with the assumption that *all* guarantees relevant to the equal treatment of associations, including those with a religious character, should be considered. Thus, I will consider, in turn, the test clause of Article VI, the equal protection and citizenship guarantees of the Fourteenth Amendment, and the First Amendment's guarantee of freedom of peaceable assembly. I will then consider in context the First Amendment guarantees most commonly thought to control this question — the norms of the religion and speech and press clauses. The purpose of this exercise will be to set the stage for a brief examination of the validity of First Amendment arguments *against* equal treatment.

The Test Clause of Article VI

The test clause of Article VI is the nation's oldest anti-discrimination law. It provides that "no religious test shall ever be required as a Qualification to any Office or public Trust under the United States." Although federal case law discussing the test clause is sparse, state constitutions have similar provisions.

Given the large numbers of persons employed at the federal, state,

---

34. See Robert A. Destro, "The Structure of the Religious Liberty Guarantee," in *Symposium in Honor of Judge John Noonan, Journal of Law & Religion* 11 (1995): 355.
35. *McCulloch v. Maryland*, 17 U.S. (17 Wheat.) 316, 407 (1819).

and local levels of government, and the large number of projects funded in whole or in part by government money, the test clause is an under-appreciated tool in the arsenal of those who feel they have been victims of discrimination on the basis of religion. The question I will discuss in this subsection may be stated as follows: "To what extent does the no religious test clause of Article VI forbid the imposition of a neutrality paradigm as a precondition for becoming a federal contractor or grantee?" The answer depends on a three-part inquiry: (1) Is the condition a religious test?; (2) Is it utilized as a qualification?; and (3) Is the sought-after contract or grant a public trust under the United States?

What Is a Religious Test or Qualification? The most obvious and historic form of religious test was the test oath required under the English Act of Supremacy. In our day, a religious test is any device that operates to screen out persons whose religious beliefs or practices, including the taking of oaths, are thought, for reasons of policy or prejudice, to make them unfit to hold a public office or become the custodian of a public trust. If a government grant or contract recipient is the holder of a public trust either under the United States or the law of any state with a similar provision, the test clause not only is relevant but may be controlling.

What Is a Public Trust? Because the focus of this chapter is on associations rather than individuals, little attention need be given to the imposition of religious tests as a qualification for holding public office. Simply put, associations do not hold office. The concept of public trust, however, is broad enough to include associations.

Federal case law does not define the term "public trust," but the case law that does exist seems to support a broad reading of the term. The Claims Court has stated that "transactions relating to the expenditure of public funds require the highest degree of public trust and an impeccable standard of conduct."[36] Environmental Protection Agency grants for the construction of certain public works projects also constitute a public trust.[37] And finally, the corporate grantee of broadcasting

36. *Refine Construction Co. v. United States,* 12 Cl. Ct. 56, 63 (1987) (government contracts).

37. See 40 C.F.R. §§30.120, 33.300; and *Town of Fallsburg v. United States,* 22 Cl. Ct. 633, 641 (1991).

license is considered to be a public trustee who must serve the broad goals of the public interest, convenience, and necessity.[38]

In the modern administrative state, the dividing lines between public and private endeavor have been blurred. Not only has Congress created and financed a number of private, nonprofit organizations like the Corporation for Public Broadcasting, but the law requires that federal contractors and grantees submit to pervasive regulation and compliance review. Thus, it would be more than simply anomalous were the federal government to refuse to contract for cleaning or repair services with business associations run by Mormons or evangelical Christians, to buy wine for military-post exchanges or the White House from the Christian Brothers' winery, or to contract for printing services with a job-training program run by Jewish Vocational Services; it would be a direct violation of the explicit nondiscrimination norm embodied in the test clause of Article VI.

For present purposes, however, the important point is not the *quantum* of protection provided by the test clause. It is the fact that the structural implications of the test clause do not depend for their strength on the norms of either the First or the Fourteenth Amendment. Its language and history leave no doubt that the First Amendment was designed to *supplement* the protection offered by the test clause, not to supplant it. The test clause serves as an important source of protection for would-be judicial appointees, and it forbids discrimination on religious grounds by judges who appoint law clerks, secretaries, and other court personnel. The structural conclusion thus seems inescapable: any construction of the First Amendment that permits a judicially created *blanket* exclusion from eligibility for government contract or grant programs because of the religious activities, practices, or beliefs of the potential contractor or grantee is illegitimate.[39] Organizations staffed by individuals who are proudly atheist or agnostic should get no preference. Broad claims that a blanket exclusion would be more convenient,

---

38. *Red Lion Broadcasting v. FCC*, 395 U.S. 367, 383 (1969); *Office of Communication of the United Church of Christ v. FCC*, 707 F.2d 1413, 1427-28 (D.C. Cir., 1983).

39. Cf. *Bowen v. Kendrick*, 487 U.S. 589, 641 (1988). In the dissenting opinion it was argued that "there is a real and important difference between running a soup kitchen or a hospital, and counseling pregnant teenagers on how to make the difficult decisions facing them."

or that discrimination can be justified because it will enable government to avoid either an apparent endorsement of religion or an excessive entanglement with it, should not be enough.

Were such a rule applied by the Court, at least two key cases would need to be reconsidered:

- *Lemon v. Kurtzman*,[40] in which the Court held "that a dedicated religious person, teaching in a school affiliated with his or her faith and operated to inculcate its tenets, will inevitably experience great difficulty in remaining religiously neutral[, and] would find it hard to make a total separation between secular teaching and religious doctrine"; and
- *Ball v. School District of Grand Rapids*,[41] where the Court held that even though the record contained "no evidence of specific incidents of religious indoctrination in this case[,] the absence of proof of specific incidents is not dispositive [because] a teacher may knowingly or unwillingly" inject "improper ideological content" into the educational program.[42]

In *F.C.C. v. League of Women Voters*,[43] the Court ruled that Congress may not control the "ideological content" of programs run by government contractors and grantees. The holding in *Rosenberger* seems to support the application of that holding to grantees with a religious orientation as well, but the conclusion seems inescapable that the Court has serious doubts about whether or not professionals operating in an environment in which religion is a pervasive influence can be trusted to be ideologically "neutral."

Indeed, in *Lemon v. Kurtzman*, the Court stated that a state cannot "provide state aid on the basis of a mere assumption that secular teachers under religious discipline can avoid conflicts [with their public trust]. The State must be *certain*, given the Religion Clauses, that subsidized teachers do not inculcate religion."[44] But certainty with respect to ideo-

---

40. 403 U.S. 602, 618-19 (1971).

41. 473 U.S. 373 (1985).

42. 473 U.S. at 388.

43. 468 U.S. 364 (1984). This ruling struck down a ban on "editorializing" by public broadcasters.

44. *Lemon v. Kurtzman*, 403 U.S. 602, 619 (1971); emphasis added.

122

logical content is not possible, either in a religiously oriented organiza-tion or in a public school classroom. In either case, a public official or trustee might be tempted to abuse that trust by acting in an unpro-fessional manner. The court's approach is a classic example of a religious test imposed as a precondition for exercising a public trust. On its face, the rule requires certainty. All teachers subsidized with public funds are obligated to exercise their trust in a "secular" manner. The court, how-ever, has enforced the rule selectively, applying it only to subsidized teachers who associate themselves with persons or organizations having discernible religious commitments.[45]

The court remains badly divided on this issue. In *Agostini v. Felton*[46] it held, by a five-to-four margin, that a "no-aid" rule cannot be justified as a preventive measure. Following its decision in *Bowen v. Kendrick*,[47] the court held that taxpayers who object to the participation of organizations having a discernible religious perspective must prove that the funds have been misused. A mere "chance" that certain organizations might abuse their public trust is not enough. The dissenting justices in *Agostini*, by contrast, continue to want *certainty*. In their view, "The State is forbidden to subsidize religion directly and is just as surely forbidden to act in any way that could reasonably be viewed as religious endorsement."[48] In practice, this means that no person or association professing identifiably religious views will ever be eligible to administer public funds or public welfare programs. Why? Because government may not, in their view, pay money directly to a religious association or give public responsibility to any individual or association that could reasonably be seen as having a religious perspective. The majority's approach in *Agostini* is egalitarian, while that of the dissenters is discriminatory. The issue is clearly presented: Does the First Amendment's religion clause require precisely the kinds of discriminatory treatment that the "equality" provisions of the Constitu-tion appear to forbid?

---

45. *Aguilar v. Felton*, 473 U.S. 402 (1985), decided together with School District of Grand Rapids v. Ball, 473 U.S. 373 (1985).

46. 117 S. Ct. 1997 (1997).

47. 487 U.S. 589 (1988).

48. *Agostini v. Felton*, 117 S. Ct. at 2020 (Justices Souter, Breyer, Stevens, and Gins-burg dissenting).

Equal Protection of the Laws

Distinguishing Equal Protection from Equal Treatment. The rights most directly involved in nonprofit associational activity are those explicitly mentioned in the First Amendment itself: religious liberty, freedom of speech and press, the right to petition for redress of grievances, and the right to assemble peaceably. According to the Supreme Court's incorporation doctrine, protection of these rights against action by the states is guaranteed by the Fourteenth Amendment, which says, "No State shall make or enforce any law which shall abridge the privileges or immunities of citizens of the United States; nor shall any State deprive any person of life, liberty, or property, without due process of law; nor deny to any person within its jurisdiction the equal protection of the laws."

The amendment's introductory and most important provision, the citizenship clause,[49] is a model of unequal treatment. Even while establishing a uniform rule of citizenship, it differentiates between "persons born or naturalized in the United States" and all other persons. The former "are citizens of the United States and of the State wherein they reside"; others are aliens. Read together with the privileges and immunities, due process, and equal protection clauses which follow it, the citizenship clause recognizes that political communities can and do draw distinctions among those who live in the community, that rights and duties may differ according to legal status, and that such distinctions can and do serve legitimate purposes.

The history and structure of the amendment prove, however, that the purpose of drawing these distinctions was to eliminate state-sponsored discrimination that cannot be justified on the basis of either justice or the common good. The citizenship clause is substantive. Equal status in the nation's political community is acquired by birth or naturalization under "a uniform Rule of Naturalization" enacted by Congress pursuant to Article I §8. Congress is bound by a rule of equal treatment — it may enact only a uniform rule. Read structurally, the Constitution forbids the adoption of any policy that has as its purpose or effect the creation of second-class citizenship status.

But that is precisely the situation created by case law. A religiously

49. "All persons born or naturalized in the United States, and subject to the jurisdiction thereof, are citizens of the United States and of the State wherein they reside."

motivated dissenter who can convince a judge that an objective observer would view a program or policy as an endorsement of religion will get a decree that the establishment clause requires that the program or policy be discontinued. A religiously motivated dissenter who challenges policies that relegate religion to a subordinate status in the hierarchy of protected values,[50] the tendency of public institutions to disparage orthodox forms of traditional religion, or the penchant of government officials to deny the obvious generally has no recourse.

The privileges-and-immunities clause also utilizes a structural mechanism to create a baseline of protection for all citizens of the United States. By assuming that rights arise from membership in the national political community, the clause underscores the division of authority between the federal and the state governments. The states are free to add protections unavailable at the federal level as incidents of state citizenship, but they may not abridge any privileges and immunities protected by federal law. Equal treatment with respect to federally funded programs and opportunities is one of the most important of these immunities. The Supreme Court, however, appears to take a different view.[51]

---

50. See, for example, Kathleen Sullivan, "Religion and Liberal Democracy," *University of Chicago Law Review* 59 (1992): 195, 199-201. Professor Sullivan argues that "the affirmative implications of the Establishment Clause . . . entail[] the establishment of a civil order — the culture of liberal democracy." In her view, "the correct baseline [of the Religion Clause] is not unfettered religious liberty, but rather religious liberty insofar as it is consistent with the establishment of the secular public moral order" (p. 198). Acceptance of "secular liberalism" is, in this view, the "religious truce" which inheres in the establishment clause.

That such a truce "may well function as a belief system with a substantive content, rather than a neutral and transcendent arbiter among other belief systems" is freely admitted. See Naomi Maya Stolzenberg, "He Drew a Circle That Shut Me Out: Assimilation, Indoctrination, and the Paradox of a Liberal Education," *Harvard Law Review* 106 (1993): 581; and Larry Alexander, "Liberalism, Religion, and the Unity of Epistemology," in *Symposium: The Role of Religion in Public Debate in a Liberal Society, San Diego Law Review* 30 (1993): 763.

What is surprising (and refreshing) about Professor Sullivan's argument is both her candor and her apparent determination to ignore the history, language, and structure of the Constitution in an attempt to demonstrate that "the culture of liberal democracy" is ordained, albeit "implicitly," by the First Amendment itself as "the overarching belief system for politics, if not for knowledge" (pp. 198-201).

51. See *Aguilar v. Felton,* 473 U.S. 402 (1985); and *Wheeler v. Barrera,* 417 U.S. 402 (1974).

The requirement that a state provide equal protection of the laws to any person within its jurisdiction is both procedural and substantive. Noncitizens are entitled to the same *process* and *protection* as those who are members of the political community, but because certain rights and obligations are incidents of citizenship status, there is a wide range of cases in which unequal *treatment* can be justified.

An equal protection norm thus permits, and may require, that government work with people as it finds them, recognizing meaningful distinctions while ignoring others. This is why norms of government behavior that seek to foster equality, neutrality, or equal treatment can be problematic. Anatole France captured the essence of this difficulty in his oft-quoted statement that the "majestic equality" of the law "forbids the rich as well as the poor to sleep under bridges, to beg in the streets, and to steal bread."

Policies designed to foster equality can obliterate relevant differences. The application of civil rights laws in a manner that compels religious organizations to lose their religious identity is an example of this tendency. Blind adherence to a policy of equal treatment will ignore differences which should, in justice, be taken into account. Another example is the Supreme Court's holding in *Texas Monthly v. Bullock* that the establishment clause limits the permissible scope of free exercise clause claims to cases of empirically demonstrable, concrete, individual need.[52] Obviously, if the Constitution requires protection, then any version of a neutrality principle that results in unequal protection is illegitimate.

The interaction of the equality norms of the Fourteenth Amendment with the liberty norms of the First demonstrates that the First Amendment also contains implicit equality norms. Concepts such as neutrality and benevolent neutrality regarding religion are derived from them. One is an abstract equality norm, the other an abstract protective one. Because their focus is on an abstraction — namely religion — neither concept tells us what will happen to the rights of the *people* involved in any given controversy.

In this chapter I assume that *people* should be the focus of government policy, not abstractions such as speech or religion. The religious liberty of individuals and communities is the value enshrined in the

---

52. *Texas Monthly v. Bullock*, 489 U.S. 1, 18 (1989).

Constitution and the Bill of Rights. So, too, is the guarantee that they will be given equal protection of the laws. Proper respect for these constitutional principles requires an awareness that judges, administrators, and policy-makers are not empowered to strike "sensible balances" between these principles,[53] or rank them in terms of relative importance to our constitutional system. The government is obliged to protect every person within its jurisdiction. As a result, any policy that utilizes religious belief, affiliation, motivation, action, or lack thereof as justification for the disparate treatment of citizens and others persons should be viewed by the courts as presumptively invalid unless the government can prove that it has an unquestionably legitimate purpose for its policy.

Equal Protection: Individuals and Associations. The law draws distinctions among organizations and associations for the same reasons it differentiates among individuals: because the distinctions are thought to be useful in the formulation or implementation of public policy. Although the Constitution requires that government be evenhanded in its policies protecting the life, liberty, and property of persons, it is by no means self-evident that rules developed to protect individuals should also apply to associations.

Generally speaking, the law will draw distinctions based on the purpose of the association, the interests of its individual members, and its structural characteristics. The simplest are unincorporated associations; the most complex are large business corporations whose stock is held by the investing public. Churches, charities, and nonprofit associations fall somewhere in between.

Currently, each of the states provides a number of different methods that churches, religious organizations, and charities can utilize to constitute themselves for legal purposes. Most states provide special statutes to govern the corporate life of a religious or charitable organization; the others provide a more generalized opportunity to acquire legal status under state codes governing nonprofit corporations and unincorporated associations.

Equal protection doctrine requires that government have a principled basis for the regulatory lines it draws. In most cases, the existence of a rational basis for the distinction is simply assumed, but in cases

---

53. *Employment Division v. Smith,* 494 U.S. 872, 902 (1990) (O'Connor concurring).

involving race, national origin, religion, sex, and paternity status (il-legitimacy), a reviewing court will examine both the rationale for the classification and the degree to which it effectuates the policy goals it is designed to serve.

Unequal treatment designed to effectuate the fiscal, managerial, and democratic purposes of the associations themselves presents no prob-lems under the equal protection clause. The life of most associations consists of a complex web of interactions among individuals and fac-tions, and the dynamic nature of these interactions has a synergistic effect. Alexis de Tocqueville made this observation:

> An association consists simply in the public assent which a number
> of individuals give to certain doctrines; and in the engagement which
> they contract to promote in a certain manner the spread of those
> doctrines. The right of associating with such views is very analogous
> to the liberty of unlicensed printing; but societies thus formed
> possess more authority than the press. When an opinion is repre-
> sented by a society, it necessarily assumes a more exact and explicit
> form. It numbers its partisans, and compromises them in its cause;
> they, on the other hand, become acquainted with each other, and
> their zeal is increased by their number. An association unites into
> one channel the efforts of diverging minds, and urges them vigor-
> ously towards the one end which it clearly points out.[54]

The result of this convergence is an organizational identity and character distinct from that of the association's individual members, clients, and supporters.

The choice to adopt a civil-law corporate form is a logical outgrowth of that identity. The traditional view is that a corporation is an "artificial being, invisible, intangible, and existing only in contemplation of law."[55] In this view, corporations have only the rights given to them by the states. The opposing view recognizes that corporations are "merely as-sociations of individuals united for a special purpose, [who are] per-mitted to do business under a particular name, and have a succession

54. Tocqueville, *Democracy in America*, ed. Richard D. Heffner (New York: Mentor Books, 1956), pp. 95-96.
55. *Trustees of Dartmouth College v. Woodward*, 17 U.S. (4 Wheat.) 518, 636 (1810).

of members without dissolution."[56] Corporations thus have the same rights as their members.

All agree, however, that corporate status is a device that the members of an association utilize to effectuate their own goals. Religious associations organize for the same reasons that profit-oriented businesses do. Liability can be limited to association assets, members can own and control property in the name of the organization, and tax and regulatory provisions of state and federal law often provide special benefits to those doing business in the corporate form.[57]

The First Amendment and Freedom of Association

For First Amendment purposes, the initial question with respect to an organization is whether the form chosen by a group of individuals to effectuate their common purpose is enough to support unequal treatment. The assembly clause answers this question in the negative: "Congress shall make no law abridging the right of the people peaceably to assemble. . . ."

As construed by the United States Supreme Court, the right of peaceable assembly is one of a package of rights subsumed under the general rubric of freedom of expression. Its relevance for present purposes is that the right of peaceable assembly "includes the right to express one's attitudes or philosophies by membership in a group, or affiliation with it, or by other lawful means."[58] The members of an association should therefore have precisely the same rights when they act collectively as they do when they act individually.

Unfortunately, however, this is not always the case. The Court appears to be uncertain about the rights of individuals operating in the corporate form,[59] and the reason for that uncertainty lies in the Court's approach to the First Amendment itself.

---

56. *Pembina Consolidated Silver Mining & Milling Co. v. Pennsylvania,* 125 U.S. 181, 189 (1888). Corporations have also been called artificial entities. *Gulf, C. & S. F. Railway v. Ellis,* 165 U.S. 150, 154 (1897).

57. Ariens and Destro, *Religious Liberty in a Pluralistic Society,* chap. 8 (on labor law) and chap. 9 (on taxation).

58. *Griswold v. Connecticut,* 381 U.S. 479, 483 (1965).

59. See, for example, *Austin v. Michigan Chamber of Commerce,* 494 U.S. 652 (1990). A full discussion of this topic is beyond the scope of this chapter.

III. Religious Discrimination and the First Amendment in Context: Making the Case for Nondiscrimination

We are now in a position to examine how, and to what degree (if at all), the Court's jurisprudence of the First Amendment should be viewed as a limitation on a political community's discretion when it utilizes the powers granted in its charter or constitution to provide the public with goods, commodities, or services. Does the First Amendment require the government to discriminate between and among community-based associations that contribute to the common good by providing otherwise legitimate goods or services?

For purposes of analysis, it will be necessary to assume at the outset that the types of goods, commodities, or services to be provided are legitimately obtained and provided by the government, and that they would meet the most rigorous standards of quality control or professional oversight. We can thus eliminate at the outset any possibility that the programs in question are shams, the purpose of which is to further a purely private, political, financial, ideological, or religious agenda.

The goods and services that commonly come to mind in such an inquiry are those which might be deemed to have an ideological flavor: the operation of libraries and the purchase of books, the operation of educational services for children and adults, care of the sick, and unemployment services. Suppliers of tangible goods and services, such as the distributors of food or food coupons that do not have any sort of personal interaction with the recipients, would thus be judged by a more lenient standard. We will also assume at the outset that, were the community so inclined, the public, or "government," sector could provide these services and commodities only on its own property using only its own employees.

It is only when the community decides to broaden the distribution and operational base to include *non*-governmental associations that First Amendment problems are alleged to arise. But the scope of these alleged problems is a very limited one. A review of case law indicates that government may rely on virtually any association to provide services at public expense. It can contract with for-profit businesses (such as HMOs), nonprofit organizations, and charities to provide goods and services to the poor, the unemployed, and the elderly; it can provide funds directly to eligible individuals in the form of vouchers (such as food stamps), electronic debit cards, and scholarships; and it can embark upon joint ventures that draw on the strengths of both the public and the private sectors.

There is only one hotly debated exception. Many argue that the First Amendment itself requires the exclusion of associations that are "too religious" in character or mission.[60] Justice Brennan's concurring opinion in *Abington School District v. Schempp* is characteristic of the strict separationist view of the First Amendment:

> What the Framers meant to foreclose, and what our decisions under the Establishment Clause have forbidden, are those involvements of religious with secular institutions which (a) serve the essentially religious activities of religious institutions; (b) employ the organs of government for essentially religious purposes; or (c) use essentially religious means to serve governmental ends, where secular means would suffice. When the secular and religious institutions become involved in such a manner, there inhere in the relationship precisely those dangers — as much to church as to state — which the Framers feared would subvert religious liberty and the strength of a system of secular government. On the other hand, there may be myriad forms of involvements of government with religion which do not import such dangers and therefore should not, in my judgment, be deemed to violate the Establishment Clause.[61]

The key question, in this view, is how the Court should distinguish the "myriad forms of involvements of government with religion" that do not run the risk of "subvert[ing] religious liberty and the strength of a system of secular government" from those that do.

Because my operative assumption is that it would be illegitimate for any grantee or contractor to use government resources for anything other than a legitimate use, we need not concern ourselves here with Justice Brennan's second concern: an attempt to "employ the organs of

---

60. See generally William D. Anderson, Jr., "Religious Groups in the Educational Marketplace: Applying the Establishment Clause to School Privatization Programs," *Georgia Law Journal* 82 (1994): 1869.

61. *Abington School District v. Schempp*, 374 U.S. at 294-95 (1963).

government for essentially religious purposes." His approach would, however, require the exclusion of religious associations whenever the Court finds that participation of a religious association would either "serve the essentially religious activities of religious institutions; . . . or . . . use essentially religious means to serve governmental ends, where secular means would suffice."

So I raise my earlier question again: Does the First Amendment require the government to discriminate between and among community-based associations that contribute to the common good by providing otherwise legitimate goods or services? In Justice Brennan's view, the answer is "yes" to the extent that either the services they deliver or the means they use to deliver them are "essentially religious."

Such an approach highlights the inherently problematic nature of the Court's own vision of the First Amendment. In *Palko v. Connecticut,* Justice Cardozo described freedom of speech, thought, and religion as rights belonging to a class of liberty interests so fundamental that justice would "perish" were they not protected.[62] The liberty issue really involved in *Palko* — protection against double jeopardy — was, by contrast, not so fundamental. We do not know why Justice Cardozo felt this way about the double jeopardy clause, but, as Mary Ann Glendon and Raul Yanes have observed, the justice "did not suggest any more sophisticated [a] ranking [for his category of rights that are "fundamental"] than 'in' and 'out,' nor did he offer an exhaustive catalogue of the rights that ought to be 'in.' "[63]

Although both freedom of religion and freedom of speech are fundamental in the Court's view, we learn from the writings of Justices Cardozo, Holmes, Brandies, and Stone that freedom of speech is "the matrix, the indispensable condition of nearly every other form of freedom."[64] Despite their importance, however, these rights are not solidly rooted in clearly articulated concepts of human dignity and the common good. The Court's First Amendment jurisprudence is purely pragmatic.

Described by the commentators and treatise writers as functional, the Court's jurisprudence of the speech-and-press clause does not pro-

62. *Palko v. Connecticut,* 302 U.S. 319, 326 (1937).
63. Glendon and Yanes, "Structural Free Exercise," *Michigan Law Review* 90 (1991): 477, 479.
64. 302 U.S. 319, 327 (1937).

tect free speech and press because a person or citizen has an idea to share or an insight to communicate, or even because the First Amendment says that speech and press are to be protected. In the Court's view, freedom of speech and press are "implicit in the concept of ordered liberty" because those freedoms play an important role in the democratic experiment. Anything that does not contribute to the common good, or that does so to a more attenuated degree, can be regulated on the basis of its content!

The entire corpus of rules governing First Amendment interests — political and commercial speech, obscenity, political campaign contributions, and religious speech, to name only a few — bear witness to judicial involvement in precisely the kind of content-based and viewpoint-based discrimination that would be forbidden if it were to be practiced by Congress, a state legislature, the president, or a state or territorial governor. In an oft-quoted statement, the late Justice Frank Murphy described utterances that are "lewd and obscene" as constituting "no essential part of any exposition of ideas, and . . . of such slight social value as a step to truth that any benefit that may be derived from them is clearly outweighed by the social interest in order and morality."[65]

Justice Murphy's observation may be true, but it is beside the point. The determinative factor in the Court's approach to the question is neither the common good nor, to use the Court's words, "the social interest in order and morality." For Justice Murphy at least, the primary consideration was whether or not the speech or press to be regulated is an "essential part of any exposition of ideas" or "a step to truth." The construct is functional, and the result, pragmatic.

And what of religion? To the framers it was "The First Freedom"; to the Court, the incorporated First Amendment's religion clause is a grant of power to the judiciary to follow the admonition of John Locke and "distinguish exactly the business of civil government from that of religion and to settle the just bounds that lie between the one and the other."[66] It is therefore not surprising that rules under the speech-and-press clause appear, at least in theory, to be firm and robust, even while there is now nearly complete unanimity among commentators and

---

65. *Chaplinsky v. New Hampshire*, 315 U.S. 568, 572 (1942).
66. Locke, *A Letter Concerning Toleration*, quoted by J. T. Noonan, Jr., in *The Believer and the Powers That Are* (New York: Macmillan, 1987), p. 80.

judges that the law of religious liberty is in a state of doctrinal disarray.[67] The law of the establishment clause has been aptly described by the Court itself as a "blurred, indistinct and variable barrier depending on all the circumstances of a particular relationship."[68] The words of the late Justice Joseph P. Bradley, writing in *The Late Corporation of the Church of Jesus Christ of Latter Day Saints v. United States*,[69] underscores the minimalist quality of the Court's concern for free exercise: "The State," he wrote, "has a perfect right to prohibit . . . all . . . open offenses against the enlightened sentiment of mankind, notwithstanding the pretense of religious conviction by which they may be advocated and practiced."[70]

Conclusion

The promise of the equal treatment principle will remain unrealized without a robust conception of religious liberty to back it up. As I write these words, there is a political consensus that a more robust understanding of religious liberty is needed, but there is precious little evidence that it is shared by more than a few members of the Supreme Court.

Judicial conservatives, like Justice Antonin Scalia, are of the view that legislatures can and should be trusted to make laws that accommodate religious belief and practice.[71] Judges, by contrast, are not to be trusted.[72] Strict separationists, like Justices John Paul Stevens and Ruth Bader Ginsburg, read the due process clause of the Fourteenth Amendment as a device that empowers the Court to "distinguish exactly the business of civil government from that of religion and to settle the just

67. In *Murray v. City of Austin, Texas*, 947 F.2d 147, 163 (5th Cir., 1991), Judge Goldberg observed that "anyone reading Establishment Clause precedent — the cases on non-purposeful symbolic government support for religion — cannot help but be struck by the confusion that reigns in this area."

68. *Lynch v. Donnelly*, 465 U.S. 668, 104 S. Ct. 1355, 1362 (1984), quoting *Lemon v. Kurtzman*, 403 U.S. 602, 614 (1971).

69. 136 U.S. 1 (1890).

70. 136 U.S. at 50.

71. *Employment Division v. Smith*, 494 U.S. at 902.

72. *Texas Monthly v. Bullock*, 489 U.S. at 45.

bounds that lie between the one and the other."[73] In their view, it is legislatures that are not to be trusted.[74]

As a result, it is safe to predict that even if the Court accepts in principle the concept of equal treatment, an organization that desires to maintain its essentially religious character will have problems when it comes time to apply for a contract or a grant. Bureaucrats will balk because they will be afraid of lawsuits, and legislatures will be called in to pass equal access legislation.

At that point, the battle will be joined. And it will come down to this: Does the First Amendment require a nonprofit organization to be religiously "neutral" (that is, secular) as an essential precondition for becoming a partner in the community's joint endeavors? My view is that the answer is "no." The dominant view, by contrast, is well-stated by Professor Metzger in the context of university education: an organization that is "essentially religious" cannot be "neutral" with respect to ultimate truth claims. Under the strict separationist approach, only those whose ideological views are religiously "neutral" need apply. A better example of why the framers of the Constitution insisted that the Constitution contain *both* a no religious test clause and an establishment clause could not be imagined.

73. Locke, *A Letter Concerning Toleration*, quoted by Noonan in *The Believer and the Powers That Are*, p. 80.

74. See Robert A. Destro, " 'By What Right?': The Sources and Limits of Federal Court and Congressional Jurisdiction over Matters 'Touching Religion,' " *Indiana Law Review* 29 (1996): 1.

CHAPTER 6

Equal Treatment: A Christian Separationist Perspective

DEREK H. DAVIS

In this chapter, Derek Davis argues that equal treatment is insufficient as a theory for interpreting the religion clauses of the First Amendment because it equates religious speech with other forms of protected secular speech and thereby undermines religion's special constitutional status. He also contends that this approach robs the establishment clause of its power to restrict government support of religion, which is necessary to preserve both the separation of church and state and religious liberty. Derek Davis is the director of the J. M. Dawson Institute of Church-State Studies at Baylor University and editor of the Journal of Church and State.

Until recently, the Supreme Court's analysis of religion cases typically began with a review to see if either the establishment clause or the free exercise clause of the First Amendment was implicated under the facts of the case. Only after the Court concluded its analysis and was assured that the religion clauses had not been violated did it proceed to determine whether other constitutional protections might have been breached. This approach by the Court recognized the pre-eminent position our Constitution grants the American people's right to follow freely their conscience in the private practice of religion, and the concurrent right to be free from government coercion in matters of faith.

136

A recent series of opinions by the Court has signaled a departure from this historic pattern of analysis. In these cases, the Court seemed satisfied to equate religious speech with other forms of secular speech, so that it adjudicated the cases strictly pursuant to a free-speech analysis. This approach emphasized that religious speech is not in a privileged position vis-à-vis political, philosophical, or other forms of speech, leading the Court to justify its decisions according to an "equal treatment" or "nondiscrimination" principle. Concurrently, some members of the United States Congress have introduced various versions of a constitutional amendment, any of which, if adopted, would endorse this approach as a viable means to forbid discrimination of any kind based on the religious beliefs of an individual or a group.

Many Christians herald the Court's recent decisions and the proposed amendments as a major victory, believing that the "equal treatment" of religious speech and secular speech necessarily constitutes greater religious liberty. But this trend actually raises serious concerns for those Christians dedicated to the concept of the separation of church and state as the surest guarantor of religious liberty. While Christians might rejoice over the most recent results of the equal treatment approach, they should be aware of the possible implications and perhaps inevitable negative impact that equal treatment may have on the status of religion in America, a status that has primacy due to the nation's longstanding commitment to the separation of church and state.

A New Paradigm — The Equal Treatment Approach

The Supreme Court's equal treatment approach in religious speech cases began with the 1981 case of *Widmar v. Vincent*.[1] The Court determined that a state university could not refuse to allow Christian Bible-study groups to use campus facilities when the school extended the same privilege to nonreligious groups. The university's discrimination against the study groups based upon the religious content of their speech violated the students' right to free speech.

The Widmar case became the legal basis for the 1984 Equal Access Act, which grants to students of both religious and nonreligious clubs

1. 450 U.S. 909 (1981).

"equal access" to school facilities for meetings before or after school. Religious meetings are required to be student-initiated and student-led. The constitutionality of the Act was upheld in 1990 in *Westside v. Mergens*.[2] The Supreme Court appropriately held that it was reasonable to require that all student groups, regardless of their religious nature, be granted equal access to school facilities, since there is little, if any, government advocacy of religion, and no realistic perception that government is endorsing religion, when religious groups use the school facilities. In her plurality opinion in *Mergens*, Justice Sandra Day O'Connor commented, "There is a crucial difference between government speech endorsing religion, which the Establishment Clause forbids, and private speech endorsing religion, which the Free Speech and Free Exercise Clauses protect."[3] As a supplement, not as a precursor, to its free-speech analysis, the Court determined that the use of the public facilities by religious groups would not violate the establishment clause.

Other issues traditionally analyzed under the establishment clause have begun to be decided primarily as free-speech cases, following the *Widmar* and *Mergens* precedents. For example, typically it was under the establishment clause that the Court examined the constitutionality of placing religious symbols (crèches, menorahs, crosses, Stars of David, etc.) on government property, holding that it is permissible to display such symbols only in concert with secular symbols or objects so that they do not convey a message of governmental endorsement of religion.[4] Recently, however, the Supreme Court has begun to consider these symbols primarily as forms of protected free speech rather than specifically religious speech, and therefore has allowed their display on government property on the theory that all forms of speech in public forums, including religious speech, should be protected. (The lower courts have begun to follow the Supreme Court's lead.)

For example, in June 1995, the Court in *Capitol Square Review and Advisory Board v. Pinette*[5] held that the free-speech clause required the city of Columbus, Ohio, to allow the display of a Ku Klux Klan Latin

2. 496 U.S. 226 (1990).
3. 496 U.S. at 250.
4. See, for example, *Lynch v. Donnelly*, 465 U.S. 668 (1994); and *County of Allegheny v. Pittsburgh A.C.L.U.*, 492 U.S. 573 (1989).
5. 115 S. Ct. 2440 (1995).

cross in its capitol square along with a Christmas tree and a menorah. The Court affirmed the appellate court's ruling that "speakers with a religious message are entitled no less access to public forums than that afforded speakers whose message is secular and otherwise nonreligious."[6] The seven Supreme Court justices affirming the free-speech analysis nevertheless disagreed over the extent to which the establishment clause could operate to limit the "equal treatment" of religious and nonreligious speech. Justices Scalia, Thomas, and Kennedy and Chief Justice Rehnquist proposed a standard whereby the establishment clause could rarely be invoked; Justices O'Connor, Souter, and Breyer proposed that there should always be an establishment clause analysis of a ruling to determine whether the government had endorsed religion. As the two dissenters, Justices Stevens and Ginsburg proposed that a violation of the endorsement standard of the establishment clause necessarily always occurs when any religious symbol is placed on public property, even by private parties. But even with the disagreement, the majority of the Court proposed elevating the free speech clause to such an extent that it would nearly always "trump" establishment-clause analysis — a clear reversal of the Court's prior approaches, in which establishment clause concerns took precedence.

Essentially the same "equal treatment" or nondiscrimination principle operative in *Widmar, Mergens,* and *Pinette* was used by the majority of the Court in deciding the case of *Rosenberger v. University of Virginia,*[7] in which the justices reviewed the university's refusal to fund the printing of *Wide Awake,* the publication of a student religious group. In a five-to-four vote, the Court held that the religious character of a student publication was immaterial; because the university was funding other kinds of private student speech, it was also required to fund *Wide Awake.* Four separate opinions were written in *Rosenberger:* Justice Kennedy wrote for the five-person majority (which included Chief Justice Rehnquist and Justices O'Connor, Scalia, and Thomas); Justices O'Connor and Thomas each wrote concurring opinions; and Justice Souter wrote for the four dissenting justices (himself and Justices Stevens, Ginsburg, and Breyer). The opinions reveal deep divisions within the Court regarding how to decide religion cases.

6. 30 F.3d 675 (6th Cir., 1994) at 679.
7. 115 S. Ct. 2510 (1995).

Justice Kennedy's majority opinion — accepting the argument that the case falls under the free speech clause rather than the religion clauses of the First Amendment — held that the university's refusal to fund the printing of *Wide Awake* discriminated against the group in question because of its viewpoint. According to this analysis, the religious speech in *Wide Awake* is on a par with all other types of speech. In fact, in their brief to the Court, the petitioners equated the constitutional position of *Wide Awake*'s Christian message with "a gay rights, racialist, or anti-war point of view." Justice Thomas, in a concurring opinion, focused not on the content of the speech but on the constitutional position of the speakers. Since the First Amendment requires neutrality in the matter of religion, "religious adherents" should be treated the same as all others in the public forum. Justice O'Connor's concurring opinion emphasized that the political equality between religious and nonreligious speakers demanded by the Constitution required that governmental entities not favor any political group over another.

Clearly, the majority writers regarded religious speech as the same as any other type of speech advocating a point of view, not as speech receiving special constitutional stature. Because it was determined to treat all types of speech equally, the majority never subjected *Wide Awake*'s message and the university's activity in paying for its printing to an establishment-clause test; the religious content of the student newspaper was irrelevant to the question of whether the university could, or even must, fund the publication. Only Justice Souter, in his dissenting opinion, considered *Wide Awake*'s religious message to be special, necessitating special review under the establishment clause. He was concerned that the publication went beyond providing "student news, information, opinion, entertainment, or academic communication."[8] He quoted from the publication itself to make his point; *Wide Awake* said that its aim was to "challenge Christians to live, in word and deed, according to the faith they proclaim and . . . to consider what a personal relationship with Jesus Christ means."[9] He warned that "the Court is ordering an instrumentality of the State to support religious evangelism with direct funding. This is a flat violation of the Establishment Clause."[10]

8. 115 S. Ct. at 2535.
9. 115 S. Ct. at 2534.
10. 115 S. Ct. at 2547.

The Christian student group won the funding for the printing of its publication, but at the price of having its religious message reduced to the commonality of every other form of human speech. To insist on equal treatment for religious speech, the petitioners were willing to give up the special status that religion is otherwise granted under the Constitution. The Court bought the petitioners' argument, which is a disturbing development indeed. If protected religious speech is simply free speech, then why, we might ask, do we need the religion clauses of the First Amendment? Those who drafted the Bill of Rights were, of course, concerned to protect the free exercise of religion. They took special pains to do so by separating the free exercise clause from the free speech clause, which should indicate the differences they saw between "religion" and "speech." They also took care to juxtapose the free exercise clause with an establishment clause that would act as a restraint on religion to prevent its power from becoming too closely identified with state activity. This was not something they did for other forms of protected speech. In other words, the Founding Fathers believed that religious speech is different from mere speech, and they could scarcely have done more to make the point.

The *Rosenberger* decision denies the power of religion by approving state subsidization for the preaching of the gospel. By not denying religion its place in a marketplace of ideas, the Court denies the special place held by religion in our constitutional framework. Private exercise of religion must be protected, to be sure, but only when it is unaided by government funds. The Founding Fathers, because of their appreciation of the coercive effects of religion when joined with political power, intended the establishment clause to act as a special restraint on religion. If "preaching the word," the stated purpose of *Wide Awake*, is only speech, it is outside the restraints of the establishment clause. But "preaching the word" is not mere speech; it is religious speech and must, therefore, suffer the inconvenience of full protection only when disassociated from the power of government.

Widmar, Mergens, Pinette, Rosenberger, and similar cases are difficult because they deal with the *private* exercise of religion in *public* settings. The easy cases deal with *private* expressions in *private* settings (e.g., church attendance), which are clearly protected by the free-exercise clause, and *public* advocacy of religion in *public* settings (e.g., teacher-led prayer in public schools), which is clearly prohibited by the estab-

141

lishment clause. But *private* religious expression in *public* settings might or might not be protected, depending on whether the religious activity is the result of state advancement, sponsorship, or endorsement. A feeble appreciation of the importance and value of the establishment clause lies at the heart of the "equal treatment" concept. While the Supreme Court, as seen in *Pinette*, continues to acknowledge that the establishment clause has *some* degree of application in religious speech cases, the devaluation of the establishment clause can be seen particularly in various proposals that have been made to amend the Constitution to remove virtually all of the jurisdiction of that clause.

Legislative Proposals to Amend the Constitution

In the final weeks of November 1995, Congressmen Henry Hyde (R-Ill.) and Ernest Istook (R-Okla.) introduced before the U.S. House of Representatives their respective versions of a constitutional amendment, either of which, if adopted, would drastically alter the meaning of the First Amendment's religion clauses. A month later, Senator Orrin Hatch (R-Utah) joined forces with Congressman Hyde and introduced Hyde's measure in the Senate. Believing that a congressional battle over these rival versions would be self-defeating, Congressman Dick Armey (R-Tex.) marshaled forces and crafted a joint House-Senate resolution that sought to combine the best features of both proposals. He introduced his resolution on 16 July 1996, and the House Judiciary Committee held hearings on the proposed amendment shortly thereafter. Then, early in 1997, pro-amendment forces collaborated once again, producing what they believed was the most tightly worded, carefully drawn-up proposal yet to be offered. Congressman Istook introduced the measure on 8 May with 106 Republican and 10 Democratic co-sponsors. Hearings were held on 22 July by the House Judiciary Committee on the Constitution.[11] As of

---

11. For an analysis of the 1995 proposals, see Derek H. Davis, "A Commentary on the Proposed Religious Liberties/Equality Amendment," *Journal of Church and State* 38 (Winter 1996): 5. For comments on an earlier version of a religious equality amendment, see Derek H. Davis, "Assessing the Proposed Religious Equality Amendment," *Journal of Church and State* 37 (Summer 1995): 493. For the testimony offered at the 22 July 1997 hearing, including that of the author, see http://www.house.gov/judiciary/2.htm.

the date of this writing, a House vote on the proposal was still forthcoming, but even some of the measure's most vigorous supporters were skeptical of it garnering the necessary two-thirds vote in both chambers of Congress for it to be referred to the states. Thus, the amendment proposal has an uncertain future, but even if it is defeated, there is every likelihood that a similar proposal will be reintroduced in the near future.

Supporters claim that an amendment is needed to protect religious expression in public settings (especially the public schools) and to guard against a perceived growing trend toward religious discrimination by the nation's courts, public officials, and society in general. The amendments proposed in 1995, 1996, and 1997 would expand the courts' equal treatment approach to such an extent that the First Amendment's religion clauses would be virtually stripped of their power. If enacted, any of these four attempts to amend the First Amendment's jurisdiction over religion's place in public America would seriously jeopardize religion's special constitutional status.

The first proposed amendment — the Hyde-Hatch proposal,[12] which supporters called the "Religious Equality Amendment" — read as follows:

Preamble: Proposing an amendment to the Constitution of the United States in order to secure the inalienable right of the people to acknowledge, worship, and serve their Creator, according to the dictates of conscience.

Text: Neither the United States nor any state shall deny benefits to or otherwise discriminate against any private person or groups on account of religious expression, belief, or identity; nor shall the prohibition on laws respecting an establishment of religion be construed to require such discrimination.

Congressman Istook's earliest proposal, which supporters called the "Religious Liberties Amendment," read as follows:

12. Congressman Henry Hyde (R-Ill.) introduced before the U.S. House of Representatives his version of the constitutional amendment, which included a preamble. Senator Orrin Hatch (R-Utah) joined with Hyde and introduced Hyde's measure in the Senate, with the only difference being the omission of the preamble.

Preamble: To secure the people's right to acknowledge God according to the dictates of conscience.

Text: Nothing in this Constitution shall prohibit acknowledgments of the religious heritage, beliefs, or traditions of the people, or prohibit student-sponsored prayer in public schools. Neither the United States nor any state shall compose any official prayer or compel joining in prayer, or discriminate against religious expression or belief.

Congressman Armey's proposal, usually called the "Religious Freedom Amendment," read as follows:

Preamble: Proposing an amendment to the Constitution of the United States to further protect religious freedom, including the right of students in public schools to pray without government sponsorship or compulsion, by clarifying the proper construction of any prohibition on laws respecting an establishment of religion.

Text: In order to secure the right of the people to acknowledge and serve God according to the dictates of conscience, neither the United States nor any State shall deny any person equal access to a benefit, or otherwise discriminate against any person, on account of religious belief, expression, or exercise. This amendment does not authorize government to coerce or inhibit religious belief, expression, or exercise.

Congressman Istook's 1997 proposal, also called the "Religious Freedom Amendment," read as follows:

To secure the people's right to acknowledge God according to the dictates of conscience: The people's right to pray and to recognize their religious beliefs, heritage or traditions on public property, including schools, shall not be infringed. The government shall not require any person to join in prayer or other religious activity, initiate or designate school prayers, discriminate against religion, or deny equal access to a benefit on account of religion.

Even a casual reading reveals the vagueness and ambiguity of these four proposals. Ambiguities are usually inherent in constitutional language, given this nation's commendable tradition of writing constitutional provisions in broad, general language, then entrusting interpretation and application to the courts and the other branches of government. But overly broad provisions like these fall below an acceptable level of generality. In these circumstances, the hopelessly vague language utilized in each proposal will only tend to confuse rather than clarify the jurisprudence attending the intersections of law and religion in America.

But there is more than a problem of form here; the content of these proposals should alarm any Christian dedicated to the proposition of religious liberty. If for whatever reason these proposals fail to be adopted, then, given today's climate of suspicion and the overreaction among some of the more conservative members of the Christian community, other proposals just like these are likely to arise. It is therefore appropriate to analyze the potential effect of these proposals on the American doctrine of separation of church and state as traditionally understood.

Nondiscrimination Provisions

All four amendments specifically forbid "discrimination" against any individual or entity on the basis of religious expression of belief. These statements appear innocuous and even laudatory, since it is the goal of our system of religious freedom that no person or group face discrimination on religious grounds. Surely religious persons and organizations should not be singled out for discriminatory treatment. But in maintaining the separation of church and state, the Supreme Court has traditionally recognized that under certain circumstances, the government must "discriminate" against religious individuals or organizations by forbidding expressions that are tantamount to government endorsement of religion.

To avert this effect of the establishment clause and void over two hundred years of religion-clause jurisprudence, these relatively innocent-sounding proposals seek to sanction religious practices in public forums, practices the legality of which either has been denied or is disputed under current court decisions. The Hyde-Hatch version makes such acts legal under the free exercise clause by emasculating the establishment clause.

145

The free exercise clause essentially would trump any potential application of the establishment clause. It is difficult to see what jurisdiction, if any, would remain to the establishment clause other than forbidding an official act of establishment of a government-sponsored religion, or the express preference of one religion over another. Any concern over "excessive entanglement" of church and state would be a thing of the past. The Armey and Istook versions operate much like the Hyde-Hatch version. They expressly seek to legalize certain practices that have been found to violate the establishment clause, as well as to protect other unspecified free-exercise practices in a "catch-all" fashion.

Additionally, the Hyde-Hatch and Armey proposals, and arguably the Istook proposals also, move beyond free-exercise issues and require government to give "equal treatment" to religious activities by funding them in the same way that it funds secular activities. The Hyde-Hatch and Armey proposals, and probably the Istook proposals as well, extend the discrimination principle in a way that would open the public purse to all churches and religious organizations across America, including religious schools. These proposals, in other words, unabashedly seek to revolutionize church-state relations in America by permitting governments to fund religious activities in the same way that they fund secular activities. Thus, if a state government funds public education, it would also be permitted to fund religious education. If a city gives funds to a civic organization to run a homeless shelter, it would have to make funds available to religious organizations undertaking the same activity. Actually, there would be no limits on the range of activities for which churches could receive government funds. It would appear that churches could, for example, receive Small Business Administration loans to operate any of the kinds of businesses that private citizens might receive loans for, from oil and gas exploration to computer sales.

There are several serious problems attending a framework of non-discriminatory distribution of benefits. First, every distribution of tax-payer dollars to a church, synagogue, mosque, or other religious organization is a violation of the religious liberty of taxpayers who would find objectionable the propagation of the form of religious belief represented by the recipient. In the words of Thomas Jefferson, "to compel a man

13. Jefferson, "Statute for Religious Freedom," in *The Papers of Thomas Jefferson*, ed. Julian P. Boyd (Princeton, N.J.: Princeton University Press, 1950), 2: 545.

to furnish contributions of money for the propagation of opinions which he disbelieves and abhors is sinful and tyrannical."[13]

Second, a nondiscriminatory program should be expected to operate in a genuinely nondiscriminatory way. Since there are now approximately two thousand identifiable religions and sects in this nation, it would be impossible to distribute government monies fairly and equitably among them all. Instead, governments at all levels would be forced to make hard choices about which faith groups would receive public money, which would necessarily result in weighing the utility of certain religious programs. Inevitably, those with the most financial resources and political clout would get the largest share of the pie; smaller, less popular faith-groups would be forced to the periphery in the new climate of destructive competition among American communities of faith.

Third, those faith groups receiving public dollars would justifiably be subjected to government audits and monitoring. This would lead to excessive entanglements between religion and government and an unhealthy dependence of religion upon government. Making religion the servant of government would likely inaugurate the decline of religion's current role as the nation's "prophetic voice" and conscience against ill-advised governmental policies. Religion with its hand out can never fulfill its prophetic role in society.

All four proposals prove the point that many Americans still fail to understand that religion is better off without government money. It should be made clear, of course, that current law enables religious organizations to receive government funds for the operation of certain social programs, but only if those funds are not commingled with other funds or used to advance a religious message. This allows churches and other religious groups to become partners with government in administering welfare programs, but without losing their autonomy as they pursue their other spiritual goals. Under the amendment proposals, however, the limitation on proselytization and religious advancement would disappear, and lead to denying the religious liberty of American citizens whose receipt of benefits might be conditioned upon their willingness to first hear a religious message. What is so wrong with the current system of requiring religions to rely upon their supporters —

14. Quoted from *The Works of Benjamin Franklin,* ed. Jared Sparks (Chicago: MacCoun, 1882), 8: 505.

and ultimately, upon God — for sustenance? Benjamin Franklin's counsel is surely appropriate here: "When a Religion is good I conceive that it will support itself; and when it cannot support itself, and God does not care to support it, so that its Professors are obliged to call for the help of the Civil Power, 'tis a sign, I apprehend, of its being a bad one!"[14]

It is ironic but nonetheless true that passage of an amendment to allow for nondiscriminatory benefits to religion will destroy over time the hallowed and sacred character of religion in America. Religion remains robust in America precisely because it has remained independent of government support and regulation. Americans are willing to support their religious institutions because government does not do it for them. A new era of government benefits to religion will kill the voluntary spirit that sustains the vibrancy and dynamism of American religion. If we are willing to take a lesson from our European friends, we will know that government aid and support is a wolf in sheep's clothing. Today, many Europeans look upon religion as just another government program. Attendance in most European churches is abysmal. The people have lost, to a very large degree, the will to support their own religious institutions because government does it for them. It would be a disappointment indeed if in the United States of America, where religion is alive and robust, we would choose to adopt funding practices common in Europe, where religion is essentially moribund.

Effects of Proposed Amendments

Unmistakably, these four proposals and any others of their ilk launch full-scale assaults not only upon the majority of the Supreme Court's church-state decisions of the last fifty years, but also upon the First Amendment's religion clauses as originally framed by the Founding Fathers. If any of these proposals were to pass, the scenario is predictable. Cases like *Pinette* probably would never reach the courts. Indeed, *Pinette*-like results would be automatic. While religious symbols on public property are not to be discouraged in all cases, the Hyde-Hatch amendment, or one like it, would eliminate any possibility that religious symbols on public property constitute religious establishments. It would be clear that all religious speech is to be treated no differently from secular speech, and once government review boards like the one in

Columbus, Ohio, adopted a public forum policy, they would have no authority to deny to any organization the right to display its symbols. Religious symbols and ideological messages of all kinds, for better or worse, would become prominent in public parks and on courthouse lawns. In fact, this is precisely what happened in Columbus. Once the District Court approved of the KKK's right to display its cross, religious groups (mostly Christian churches) sought and received permits to display their own symbols. Apparently some members of the religious community attempted to mute the effect of the KKK cross with numerous displays of their own.

The passage of an amendment like the ones proposed would alter the treatment of religious speech in other public forums as well. For example, in litigation involving the right of public-school students to engage in religious expression, it has become fashionable for students' attorneys to argue that all religious expression is protected by the free speech clause rather than the free exercise clause. A case in point is *Harris v. Joint School District No. 241,*[15] a 1992 case challenging the right of a high-school senior class in Idaho to choose one of its members to say a prayer at commencement ceremonies. On its face, this kind of student-led, student-initiated prayer, built upon the sensible principles of *Widmar v. Vincent* and the Equal Access Act, hardly seems to offend the free speech clause. In fact, in 1992, the Fifth Circuit Court of Appeals in *Jones v. Clear Creek Independent School District*[16] held on almost identical facts that such an arrangement in a Texas high school in no way violated the First Amendment. The *Jones* court found the prayer to be protected under the free speech and free exercise clauses, and not in violation of the establishment clause, since the prayer had the secular purpose of solemnizing the occasion, did not advance or endorse religion, and did not create an excessive entanglement between religion and government. The *Harris* court, however, ruled differently. The court first held that the prayer was not protected by the free speech clause because the commencement ceremony was not an "open" or "public" forum. The court found it significant that only a student chosen by the majority of the senior class was allowed to speak and pray; no matter what religious message a minority of students may have wished to convey,

15. 41 F.3d 447 (9th Cir., 1994).
16. 977 F.2d 963 (5th Cir., 1992).

the graduation forum was closed to them. Accordingly, there was no open or public-forum framework here, the framework upon which *Widmar, Mergens,* and the Equal Access Act depended.

The *Harris* court also did an extensive establishment-clause analysis, finding that the graduation ceremony was ultimately a school-controlled, school-sponsored event. Thus, the ceremony amounted to an endorsement of the proceedings, including the religious elements. On appeal, the decision was affirmed by the Ninth Circuit Court of Appeals. "School officials," wrote Justice Charles E. Wiggins, "cannot divest themselves of constitutional responsibility by allowing the students to make crucial decisions."[17] He added, quoting *West Virginia v. Barnette* (1943), that the "very purpose of a Bill of Rights was to withdraw certain subjects from the vicissitudes of political controversy, to place them beyond the reach of majorities and officials and to establish them as legal principles to be applied by the courts."[18] Unfortunately, the Supreme Court later vacated the lower courts' judgments for mootness. (The student-plaintiff had graduated.)

Had the Hyde-Hatch proposal been the law when the Harris case was decided, the courts would have been stripped of their ability to make an establishment-clause analysis. The Hyde-Hatch proposal ignores the delicate balance among the various First Amendment freedoms that only the courts are equipped to preserve. If the Armey or either of the Istook proposals had been the law when the Harris case was decided, an establishment analysis would have been permitted, but the case's outcome would have been virtually the same as if there had been no establishment analysis allowed, since all of the proposals suggest that "prayer" must always be allowed, no matter the context or its effect on objecting students.

Clearly, the passage of any of these proposals would accomplish no less than the complete demolition of Jefferson's celebrated "wall of separation between church and state." While the Supreme Court's recent trend toward an equal treatment approach is of serious concern to those who support the Supreme Court's commitment to church-state separation, proposals to amend the Constitution and remove any possibility of Supreme Court interpolation are intolerable.

17. 41 F.3d 447 (9th Cir., 1994) at 455.
18. 41 F.3d 447 at 455.

American Christianity's Historic Commitment to Separation of Church and State

All of the recent proposals to amend the Constitution contain nondiscrimination provisions which attempt to ensure that public religious expressions will receive the same treatment as public secular expressions. In other words, the proposals seek to ensure that courts may not discriminate against religious speech in public forums where philosophic or political speech is permitted. As noted earlier, the Supreme Court already has made significant strides toward this end, but constitutional amendments like those recently proposed would require results similar to those of *Widmar, Pinette,* and *Rosenberger,* without any need to analyze the possible impediment raised by the establishment clause. On the surface, the recent cases decided under equal-treatment analysis have resulted in victories for religious freedom. However, many religious advocates view the recent decisions as dangerous to the religious freedom which our forebears fought so hard to preserve.

The modern idea of the separation of church and state resulted from the religious pluralism that was an outgrowth of the Reformation and the accompanying recognition that religion is perhaps more a matter of private conscience than public concern. The atrocities of the Middle Ages and the Reformation in which hundreds of thousands died in inquisitions, witch-hunts, and religious wars were thought to be the result of government having too much authority in matters of religion. The evolution of individual rights, which began in earnest in the fourteenth century, led human government, in the West at least, to abandon its previous role of requiring all people to conform to a common faith in favor of a new role of protecting individual rights, including the free exercise of religion.

During the founding of America, Christian leaders labored zealously to secure religious freedom via the founding documents, believing that religious liberty is necessary to enact the biblical doctrine of the individual's freedom of conscience. God's creation of human beings in his own image endowed each individual with dignity as a free moral agent. Faith in God is the individual's free act of responding to his creator, and the freedom and independence of that act must not be compromised by any outside influence or coercion. Religious liberty removes the state from any coercive position. The Founding Fathers believed that the separation of church and state offered the best protection for the individual, for the state, and for the church. This separation also served to recognize the inherent difference between the spheres of influence of church and state — the spiritual and the secular.

Roger Williams, founder of the colony of Rhode Island and the first Baptist church in America in 1638, argued from Scripture for religious liberty and the separation of church and state. Williams believed that the state is not religious or Christian, but a man-made civil institution and therefore without authority to proscribe conscience or legislate regarding religious matters. Williams saw that church and state must remain separate for the state to be the state and the church to be the church. It was, in fact, Williams who coined the analogy of a "wall" separating church and state, an idea that was later used by Thomas Jefferson. Williams warned that a system of interrelation between church and state would "[open] a gap in the hedge, or wall of separation, between the garden of the church and the wilderness of the world."[19] Williams's wall exists to protect the sanctity of the church from the encroachment of the secular government.

Later, Isaac Backus, a pastor, evangelist, historian, and ardent apostle of religious liberty, aggressively campaigned throughout the colonies for church-state separation. Like Williams, he believed in the God-given freedom of human conscience. Backus wrote, "Religion is a concern between God and the soul with which no human authority can intermeddle."[20] Backus appeared before the Continental Congress in 1774 and the Constitutional Convention in 1787 to advocate religious liberty for all American citizens. A third leader, John Leland, influenced Thomas Jefferson and James Madison with his views on freedom of conscience and the moral necessity of disestablishment throughout the colonies. Leland noted that the union of church and state, so charac-

---

19. Williams, *Mr. Cotton's Letter . . . Answered,* reprinted in *The Complete Writings of Roger Williams,* 7 vols. (New York: Russell & Russell, Inc., 1963), 1: 392. Among the many good books detailing the life and work of Williams are *Roger Williams and His Contribution to the American Tradition* by Perry Miller (New York: Bobbs-Merrill, 1953); *Roger Williams and Religious Freedom: A Controversy in New and Old England* by Irwin H. Polishook (Englewood Cliffs, N.J.: Prentice Hall, 1967); and *Liberty of Conscience: Roger Williams in America* by Edwin S. Gaustad (Grand Rapids: William B. Eerdmans, 1991).

20. Quoted by William G. McLoughlin in *Isaac Backus and the American Pietistic Tradition* (Boston: Little, Brown, 1967), p. 131.

teristic of other societies throughout history, resulted in the corruption of both.[21]

Many early Americans were concerned by the Constitution's failure to make reference to God. But this was neither an inadvertent omission nor an attempt to subjugate religion's place within the new government. It was the Founders' unmistakable intention to create a neutral state that would be without authority in religious matters. Their decision to omit God's name in the Constitution had to do with their belief that the power to frame a new government derived not immediately from heaven but from the American people. Moreover, the failure to specify a particular deity within the founding documents was intended to acknowledge the religious plurality that already existed within the young country, and to allow all Americans the right to believe and act upon their own religious convictions, as dictated by conscience. The decision to create not a religious state but rather, in modern terms, a secular, neutral, or liberal state had nothing to do with a desire to impede religion but everything to do with a desire to vitalize it in all of its variety, something that could be achieved only by requiring church and state to remain separate and distinct.

America was the first nation to construct a constitutional framework that officially sanctioned the separation of church and state. It was a noble experiment in the founding era and remains so today. The experiment was undertaken by the Framers in the hope that it would enable America to escape the persecutions and religious wars that had characterized the Christian West since the emperor Theodosius had made Christianity the Roman Empire's official religion in A.D. 380. The First Amendment's religion clauses have proved to be, in the words of the great Catholic theologian John Courtney Murray, "Articles of Peace."[22] Religion of all persuasions is accorded a greater respect in the United States than in any other civilized society.

From America's earliest days, many religious leaders have strongly advocated the separation of church and state — both for the protection

21. See generally Lyman Butterfield, *Elder John Leland, Jeffersonian Itinerant* (Worcester, Mass.: American Antiquaries on Society, 1953). See also Don M. Fearheiley, *The John Leland Story* (Nashville, Tenn.: Broadman Press, 1964).

22. Murray, *We Hold These Truths: Catholic Reflections on the American Proposition* (New York: Sheed & Ward, 1960), p. 45.

of religion itself and for the protection of human conscience in religious matters. The result has been a formal national commitment to the twin pillars of freedom: religious liberty and the separation of church and state — what eminent religious historian Sanford Cobb rightly referred to earlier this century as "America's greatest gift to civilization and to the world."[23] Only when the individual freedom of conscience is upheld can all citizens be allowed to respond to God — in their own way or not at all, but free from any coercive powers of the state. Any movement to diminish the separation between the state and religion can only diminish every citizen's freedom of self-determination.

Equal Treatment's Potential Erosion of the Separation of Church and State

The concept of equal treatment — treating all religious expression the same as other forms of speech — sounds alluringly democratic, pluralistic, and fair. To the Christian who, rightly or wrongly, feels increasingly marginalized within American society and disenfranchised by the Supreme Court's many rulings that keep religious exercise out of the public sphere, exercise of the concept may seem like a return to "better" days when Christianity enjoyed an undisputed nationwide hegemony and de facto establishment. But in fact, it may signal the triumph of the postmodern relativist mind, in which every statement is of equal value to any other.[24] If equal treatment prevails, one's religious beliefs would be protected equally and at the same level as one's right to attend a particular university, live in a certain neighborhood, or express a particular political opinion. In short, one's religious faith would be on a par with every other worldview and life belief. Americans of every religious belief and no religious belief should carefully consider whether this is a desirable result.

In the recent equal-treatment cases, religious speech has been placed on equal footing with all speech, thereby removing the traditional additional analysis to determine whether a reasonable observer would infer

23. Cobb, *The Rise of Religious Liberty in America: A History* (New York: Macmillan, 1902), p. 2.
24. See the thoughtful article by Winnifred Fullers Sullivan, "The Difference Religion Makes: Reflections on *Rosenberger*," *Christian Century*, 13 March 1996, p. 294.

154

EQUAL TREATMENT: A CHRISTIAN SEPARATIONIST PERSPECTIVE

a message of endorsement by the government. Some of the proposed constitutional amendments advocated in the name of equal treatment go so far as to prohibit the Supreme Court from ever invoking the establishment clause. In the name of religious zeal, proponents of these amendments would tear down almost every vestige of church-state separation. That would certainly spell disaster for the elevated and protected status now enjoyed by religion.

Contrary to popular mischaracterization by many religious people, especially the more politically conservative, the Supreme Court's historic decisions concerning religion in the public square, including the public schools, have never sought to establish irreligion in America, but rather have sought to protect the right of all to freely exercise their own religion, free from government coercion or interference. The best guarantee of the free exercise of religion has been the requirement that the government and its property remain neutral regarding religion, thereby preventing any advancement or endorsement of any kind of religious doctrine. And by keeping the government out of every aspect of religion's business, Americans have ensured the sanctity of their religious practices. As Justice O'Connor noted in her concurring opinion in *County of Allegheny v. Pittsburgh A.C.L.U.,* "We live in a pluralistic society. Our citizens come from diverse religious traditions, or adhere to no particular religious beliefs at all. If government is to be neutral in matters of religion, rather than showing either favoritism or disapproval towards citizens based on their personal religious choices, government cannot endorse the religious practices and beliefs of some citizens without sending a clear message to non-adherents that they are outsiders or less than full members of the political community."[25]

At the same time, as religious speech and practice are reduced to the level of any secular speech and practice, American churches lose their protection from governmental encroachment. The situation will worsen if equal treatment is broadened to allow government funding of religious activities and institutions. The Framers of the Constitution, who named religion as the *first* freedom in the First Amendment, intended that religion be treated differently, *unequally,* when it comes to government entitlements. Since the founding of this country, the Constitution has been understood to prohibit the advancement or endorsement of religion.

25. 492 U.S. at 627.

Churches, mosques, synagogues, and other houses of worship have always been required to be self-sustaining, not because they were to be the objects of discrimination but because their mission and influence were thought to be so vital to American life that the regulation and control which would inevitably follow the grant of government benefits was to be avoided at all costs. But if religious expression is no more protected than political opinion, and if religious practice is no more sacrosanct than social club membership, no valid reason remains for exempting churches and religious organizations from tax requirements or government regulations. Every exemption extending to religion arises from the belief that the churches, synagogues, and mosques, as houses of faith, are fundamentally different from a business or a club. If there is nothing special about our religious speech and practices, then perhaps churches should be forbidden to discriminate in whom they hire for their staff or whom they decide to ordain. Perhaps the content of what is taught in religious day schools should be regulated to match the curriculum being taught in public schools. Equal treatment could become the Pandora's box that drives government regulation and government interference every bit as much in the sanctuary as it does in other places in society.

Equal treatment also means the equal treatment of all ideologies as well as every type of religious faith. The public square indeed will be clothed and populated, not only with religious expressions of every type but also with every identifiable belief system. The crèche on the courthouse lawn may well be completely obscured by the swastika, the flaming white cross, or any other ideological symbols a group may wish to display publicly. When the wall of separation crumbles, government property will degenerate into a billboard advertising all types of beliefs and ideas, religious and nonreligious. The fear will be not that our government endorses the Christian, Jewish, Buddhist, or Islamic faith, but that it will be required to endorse all viewpoints. The secular state will become hopelessly entangled with every known and yet unknown belief a person could espouse.

Conclusion

Equality is a hallmark of American democracy, but it should not rule in every case. The Framers, recognizing the special place of religion in our lives, provided both special protection for religion and important limitations on government support of religion. At times our system of separation of church and state results in limitations on the public expression of our religious faith. At times it results in unintended discrimination against religious individuals and organizations. Certainly the Supreme Court's analysis of religious issues sometimes has been confused and even overly restrictive. And many times the confusion caused by the Court's decisions has trickled down to public officials below, who have then misunderstood and misapplied the fine distinctions drawn by the Court. The separation of church and state, as a grand experiment in human history, is still in a state of infancy. It is to be expected that problems and difficulties within the separation framework will arise from time to time. But in spite of some missteps, the American system of separation of church and state remains the most brilliant conception of religious freedom ever conceived. Overhauls to the system — and the equal treatment concept represents a major overhaul — should be avoided.

In the end, all Americans must recognize that, in a democratic framework that values religion in all its diversity, it is the *private* expression of religion in *private* spheres that is the heart of religion and that must be protected at all costs. Compromises that respect religious diversity must be made when religion enters our shared *public* institutions. The equal treatment principle denies the need for any such compromise and actually endorses a form of tyranny by the majority. The religion clauses as they have come to be interpreted and applied over two hundred years of history demand such compromises, denying to government the right to favor the religion of any American citizen over others. We would do well to remember the words of James Madison: "The religion then of every man must be left to the conviction and conscience of every man. . . . In matters of Religion, no man's right is abridged by the institution of Civil Society and . . . [R]eligion is wholly exempt from its cognizance."[26]

26. Madison, "Memorial and Remonstrance," in *The Founders' Constitution*, ed. Philip B. Kurland and Ralph Lerner (Chicago: University of Chicago Press, 1987), 5: 82.

CHAPTER 7

American Jews and the Equal Treatment Principle

GREGG IVERS

In this chapter, Gregg Ivers reviews the role played by Jewish organizations in the development of the Supreme Court's establishment-clause jurisprudence, and outlines the reasons why American Jews resist embracing an equal treatment approach to church-state issues. Equal treatment, he argues, is based on the misguided assumption that the Court can create a neutral legal principle that would treat equally all persons and institutions seeking government aid. He contends that this kind of neutrality is not possible, and that equal treatment would be used to advantage the theology of the majority religion, Christianity. Ivers concludes that the Jewish community has benefited from the Court's no-aid-to-religion approach to establishment clause issues. Gregg Ivers is associate professor of political science at American University.

Since their entrance into the arena of church-state conflict some five decades ago, American Jews and the considerable number of organizations that represent their interests in law and public affairs have, almost without exception, clung steadfastly to a position often referred to by students of constitutional law as "absolutist" or "strict separationist" in nature. Whether the question has involved state-supported religious practices in public schools, governmental financial assistance to parochial institutions, religious displays on public property, or any one of several other church-state issues, the dominant position of organized American Jewry has been that the establishment clause prohibits the government from giving even the slightest appearance that church and state are symbolically, much less substantively, linked in word and deed. Indeed, as modern church-state law passes the half-century mark, with its roots established in the foundational case of *Everson v. Board of Education* (1947),[1] little has changed to move American Jews away from their belief that religious freedom is best secured when church and state remain properly distinct from each other.

For the better part of this fifty-year period, the absolutist position on the establishment clause articulated by the major Jewish organizations, along with the American Civil Liberties Union and, to a somewhat lesser extent, mainline Protestant agencies such as the Baptist Joint Committee on Public Affairs and the National Council of Churches, served as the dominant strain in the Supreme Court's church-state jurisprudence. From the late 1940s through the early 1980s, the Court struck down a series of state and federal programs that either supported or gave the impression of supporting one religious denomination over another, that preferred religious over nonreligious societal interests, or that offered financial support for parochial education.[2] While the absolutist, no-aid approach, even at its high-water mark, never commanded a unanimous Court, there was a consistent, if transient, ma-

---

1. 330 U.S. 1 (1947).

2. See, for example, *Aguilar v. Felton,* 473 U.S. 402 (1985) (striking down government funding for remedial education in religious schools); *Wolman v. Walter,* 433 U.S. 229 (1977) (striking down assistance to religious schools for off-campus "field trips"); *Lemon v. Kurtzman,* 403 U.S. 602 (1971) (striking down a comprehensive government aid package to parochial schools); *Wallace v. Jaffree,* 472 U.S. 38 (1985) (holding unconstitutional a "moment-of-silence" statute that included time for prayer); *Abington v. Schempp,* 374 U.S. 203 (1963) (striking down Bible reading and recitation in public schools); *Engel v. Vitale,* 370 U.S. 421 (1962) (holding unconstitutional the recitation of state-composed prayers in public schools); *Torcaso v. Watkins,* 367 U.S. 488 (1961) (holding unconstitutional state law requiring the taking of a religious oath to hold public office); *McCollum v. Board of Education,* 333 U.S. 203 (1948) (holding unconstitutional a released-time program for religious instruction in public schools); and *U.S. v. Seeger,* 380 U.S. 163 (1965) (holding that conscientious objectors to military service were not required to believe in God).

jority during this period that heeded the dicta set out in Justice Black's *Everson* opinion, in which he wrote that "no tax in any amount, large or small, can be levied to support any religious activities or institutions, whatever they may be called, or what form they may adopt to teach or practice religion."[3] Borrowing Thomas Jefferson's famous metaphor, Justice Black wrote that the "wall of separation between church and state . . . must be kept high and impregnable."[4] From *Everson* forward, the Court on occasion would carve out a constitutional exception to its otherwise firmly separationist position on the meaning and application of the establishment clause. These occasional turns were sometimes peculiar in their constitutional logic.[5] Still, at the time, they were thought to be a benign threat to the Court's settled church-state jurisprudence on weightier matters such as school prayer and the provision of government aid to religious schools.

As Professors Monsma and Soper point out in the introduction to this volume, the late 1980s and thus far the 1990s have been a period in which the Court has slowly but surely moved away from the separationist impulses that once guided its establishment clause jurisprudence and toward an approach that it calls "equal treatment." Monsma and Soper define the equal treatment approach as one which "holds that limited forms of governmental accommodation and assistance to religious groups and their activities — even financial assistance — do not violate the establishment clause as long as that assistance is offered equally to all religious groups and to religious and nonreligious groups on the same basis." If Monsma and Soper are correct in calling the Court's new line of reasoning a "clear departure" from its no-aid, strict separationist past, then an establishment clause jurisprudence with equal treatment as its animating principle will have substantial and nonbeneficial effects on the church-state interests of the American Jewish community.

In this chapter, I will address three major questions. First, what role

3. *Everson v. Board of Education,* 330 U.S. at 15.

4. 330 U.S. at 12, 18.

5. See, for example, *Lynch v. Donnelly,* 465 U.S. 668 (1984) (holding that religious displays on public land do not violate the establishment clause because of the "secular context"); and *Marsh v. Chambers,* 463 U.S. 783 (1983) (upholding legislative prayers as constitutional because of their traditional acceptance).

did the major American Jewish organizations have in the development of the Court's post-*Everson* church-state jurisprudence? Second, why have American Jews resisted previous invitations to embrace a more accommodationist establishment clause? Third, will the equal treatment principle benefit the interests of American Jews, who are destined to remain a permanent religious minority in what is an overwhelmingly Christian society?

American Jews and the Establishment Clause

Since *Everson,* American Jews and the organizations that represent their interests have been at the forefront of organized efforts to influence the church-state jurisprudence of the Supreme Court. Through the sponsorship of test-case litigation, the submission of amicus curiae (friend-of-the-court) briefs, intervention as third parties, and extra-judicial efforts to influence constitutional doctrine, the major American Jewish organizations have played a historic role in this century's development of church-state law and public policy. Soon after their arrival in significant numbers in their new homeland, American Jews recognized that their minority status would require nontraditional routes of group advocacy if they hoped to abolish the frequent de jure presence of pan-Christian values in American civic culture and public institutions. Indeed, organized Jewish interests were among the first to understand litigation as an effective method to instigate constitutional reform, whether such action challenged religious practices in public schools or state-mandated programs to assist parochial institutions.[6]

But prior to *Everson* and, more generally, the pre–World War II era, the major national agencies that carry out most Jewish public-affairs advocacy — the American Jewish Committee (AJCommittee), founded in 1906; the American Jewish Congress (AJCongress), founded in 1918; and the Anti-Defamation League of B'nai B'rith (ADL), founded in 1913 — had almost no influence in American law and politics. Even after the great wave of Jewish immigration to the United States that began in the late 1800s and the subsequent establishment of a strong communal

6. Gregg Ivers, *To Build a Wall: American Jews and the Separation of Church and State* (Charlottesville, Va.: University Press Virginia, 1995), pp. 1-6.

presence, American Jews "simply did not think of themselves as a community of citizens who could or should make heavy demands on their government, who could or should assert themselves in a politically organized fashion to achieve goals of critical importance to them."[7] On public affairs and politics in general, but on church-state issues in particular, the major Jewish organizations kept a low profile because of their concern that any concerted action to challenge what they viewed as constitutionally suspect religious practices would result in an anti-Semitic backlash and raise questions about their "American-ness." Instead, organized American Jewry relied upon the social relations approach, which consisted of public education and public relations efforts, interfaith negotiations to enlist the support of sympathetic Christian churches and leaders, and the creation of "multicultural" education programs in public schools that included instructional materials on the theological, cultural, and historical components of Judaism.[8]

Over time, however, the AJCommittee, the AJCongress, and the ADL realized that multicultural education and faith in the willingness of Christians to divest the public schools of sectarian influences would never win Jews their rightful place as equals in the scheme of American religious and cultural pluralism. Cognizant of the limitations of the social relations approach, the major Jewish organizations soon began to emphasize litigation and legislation as the tools with which to effect legal and constitutional change. The legal reform model has since guided in substantial part the organized efforts of American Jews to influence the law of church and state. While community relations and education remain an important part of their work in the church-state field, it has been through law and litigation that American Jews have won their most significant constitutional victories. Until *Everson* and, one year later, *McCollum v. Board of Education* (1948), law and education, as forces for constitutional change, were viewed as exclusive of one another, with law "almost always . . . given an inferior role."[9] But tumultuous events, both abroad (the Holocaust being perhaps the most extreme example) and at home (as in the cases of continued discrimination against Jews in all

7. Theodore Mann, "The Courts," *Present Tense,* January-February 1985, pp. 25-28.
8. Ivers, *To Build a Wall,* pp. 75-83.
9. Will Maslow, "The Use of Law in the Struggle for Equality," *Social Research* 22 (1955): 297-314.

facets of American life), encouraged Jewish organizations to pursue a direct action strategy through law and litigation, rather than remain dependent on indirect appeals to the Christian conscience, as the core of their campaign to turn the promises of the establishment clause into a reality.

Evidence of the rapid changes within the organizational structure that represented American Jewry quickly surfaced on two fronts. The first consisted of a sweeping campaign initiated by the AJCongress, soon joined by the AJCommittee and the ADL, to attack the anti-Jewish discrimination practiced by colleges, universities, and professional schools, in real estate and the rental housing market, and in private-sector employment. Second, and far more controversial among Jews, was the decision of the AJCongress in 1945 to form the Commission on Law and Social Action (CLSA) in order to concentrate its attention on church-state separation issues. The upshot of this decision was to place law and litigation, and by extension the courts, at the center of its systematic efforts to promote policy change in this area. This decision created shock waves that were felt throughout the upper reaches of the AJCommittee and the ADL, both of which were committed to education and goodwill campaigns as the best means of educating America about Jewish concerns and interests. The AJCommittee and the ADL did not share the AJCongress's degree of commitment to the efficacy of litigation as an instrument to achieve social change. But after much internal deliberation, and faced with the need to keep pace with their organizational rival, the AJCommittee and the ADL responded to the bold stroke of the AJCongress by forming litigation capacities of their own, although with nowhere near the same scope and sophistication. Innovation in establishment-clause law over the next constitutional generation would bear the stamp of the organizational force of the AJCongress and the individual imprint of its chief lawyer during that time, Leo Pfeffer.[10]

When Pfeffer joined the AJCongress in 1945 as a junior staff lawyer, he did so without any special training or expertise in church-state law, nor with any idea that he would lead a litigation campaign over the next generation that would rewrite the core jurisprudential principles of the establishment clause. Alexander Pekelis and Will Maslow, who co-directed the CLSA of the AJCongress until Pekelis's death in a plane

10. See, generally, Ivers, *To Build a Wall.*

163

crash in 1946, had long been interested in the issue of released time for religious instruction in the public schools. They had also begun to research a constitutional basis upon which to challenge such practices. But Pekelis and Maslow were also determined to involve the CLSA in the other pressing civil rights and liberties issues of the day, which, beyond the immediate concerns of the Jewish community, included support for the NAACP's campaign in the federal courts to dismantle legal segregation. Thus, for no other reason than convenience, responsibility for developing a constitutional and policy position on released time fell to Pfeffer, who later confessed in an autobiographical essay that he received his start by simply being in the right place at the right time.[11]

However serendipitous the initiation of Pfeffer's career path may have been, there was nothing accidental about the impact that he had on the constitutional development of church-state law over the next four decades. Political scientist Samuel Krislov has commented that Pfeffer is sui generis in the annals of modern constitutional litigation, for no other lawyer has exercised such complete intellectual dominance over a chosen area of law for so extensive a period — as an author, scholar, public citizen, and, above all, legal advocate who harnessed his multiple and formidable talents into a single force capable of satisfying all that an institution needs for a successful constitutional reform movement.[12] Pfeffer's emergence as such a powerful singular force would not have been possible without the commitment of his first and longest employer, the AJCongress, to his constitutional vision. When Pfeffer arrived, an organizational model built around an agenda of law-based reform was in place, a model that had already won praise from academic commentators as both visionary and promising.[13]

But it was Pfeffer, more than any other lawyer among an extraordinarily talented staff, who pushed the CLSA into the litigative maelstrom of the church-state arena. Moreover, he did so with the insistence that the establishment clause be understood to reflect an absolutist view of

11. Ivers, *To Build a Wall*, pp. 70-71.
12. Krislov, "Alternatives to Separation of Church and State in Countries Outside the United States," in *Religion and State: Essays in Honor of Leo Pfeffer,* ed. James E. Wood, Jr. (Waco, Tex.: Baylor University Press), pp. 421-40.
13. Yale Comment, "Private Attorneys-General in the Fight for Civil Liberties," *Yale Law Journal* 58 (1949): 574-98.

the separation between church and state. This vision, one that reflected no compromise on religious practices in public schools, government aid to parochial institutions, religious requirements to engage in public service or to obtain conscientious objector status from military service, later became so steeped in the Court's post-*Everson* church-state jurisprudence that almost all of Pfeffer's critics rarely fail to castigate him as the person responsible for the lost meaning of the establishment clause.[14] Even Pfeffer's institutional and individual allies were sometimes put off by his unyielding absolutism, as was the case when the AJCongress refused to allow him to file an amicus brief in support of revoking the tax-exempt status of religious property.[15]

It would be difficult to overstate the influence of Pfeffer and the AJCongress on establishment clause law during the critical period from *McCollum* through Pfeffer's last truly great victory, *Lemon v. Kurtzman*, the 1971 parochial-aid decision that, despite some minor departures, all but shut off the spigot of government funds that once flowed to religious schools. But it would be unfair to ignore the influence that the other major Jewish organizations have had on church-state relations as well. While the AJCommittee and the ADL initially resisted the path upon which Pfeffer had chosen to place the interests of the American Jewish community, they had all but endorsed the absolutist, no-aid approach by the time the Court, in 1962 and 1963, decided the landmark school prayer cases of *Engel v. Vitale* and *Abington v. Schempp*, respectively. There remained behind-the-scenes clashes among the three organizations, some of which were philosophical and ideological in nature. What remained of the problems between the AJCongress on the one hand and the AJCommittee and the ADL on the other were generated in substantial part by Pfeffer's heavy-handed manner of dealing with others in the separationist community, individual and organizational, Jewish and non-Jewish alike, whom he viewed as inferior in skill and intellect. By this time, the ends were less objectionable than the personal manner in which Pfeffer sought to achieve them.

14. See especially Robert L. Cord, *Separation of Church and State: Historical Fact and Current Fiction* (New York: Lambeth Press, 1982); Daniel L. Dreisbach, *Real Threat or Mere Shadow: Religious Liberty and the First Amendment* (Westchester, Ill.: Crossway Books, 1987); and Richard John Neuhaus, *The Naked Public Square* (Grand Rapids: Wm. B. Eerdmans, 1984).

15. *Walz v. Tax Commission,* 397 U.S. 664 (1970). This dispute is recounted in Ivers, *To Build a Wall,* pp. 165-69.

Pfeffer's personal qualities aside, most American Jewish organizations acknowledged that Pfeffer's work in shaping public opinion — through the courts and the legislatures as well as through his books, articles, and public appearances — had been responsible for the transformative constitutional principles articulated in *Engel* and *Schempp*. So much were the principles of those cases, as well as their real-world effects, consistent with views of the American Jewish community that one prominent Jewish leader wrote to Pfeffer after these decisions, commenting that "for the Jewish community," *Engel* and *Schempp* were "equal in importance to the desegregation decision [*Brown v. Board of Education*] of 1954. I believe that we now have the most potent weapon which we have ever possessed to really clean up the religion in the public schools problem. You have indeed become a great hero."[16] Whether Pfeffer remains a hero to the American Jewish community in the current moment is less important than how well his constitutional vision remains intact, three decades after the school prayer cases were decided, over twenty years since the Lemon case, and almost ten years since he last appeared as a counsel of record before the Supreme Court.[17] For all the internal disagreements within the organized American Jewish community over strategy, tactics, and substantive constitutional arguments, the major Jewish organizations (excluding those with Orthodox affiliations) have sided with the government in an establishment clause case less frequently than any other religious group since 1947. In fact, you can count on one hand the number of times non-Orthodox Jewish organizations have endorsed government support for religious objectives.[18]

16. Quoted by Ivers in *To Build a Wall*, pp. 144-45.
17. *Bowen v. Kendrick*, 487 U.S. 589 (1988).
18. Gregg Ivers, "Religious Organizations as Constitutional Litigants," *Polity* 25 (1992): 243-66. Those cases are *Thornton v. Caldor*, 472 U.S. 703 (1985), in which the AJCongress and the ADL argued in favor of a state law requiring employers to give days off to Sabbath observers; *Witters v. Washington*, 474 U.S. 481 (1986), in which the AJCongress and the AJCommittee supported government aid that allowed a handicapped student to attend divinity school (the ADL entered a brief in opposition to the program); *Lamb's Chapel v. Center Moriches Union Free School District*, 113 S. Ct. 2141 (1993), in which the AJCongress and the AJCommittee supported the plaintiff's claim to "equal access" for nonstudent religious speakers in public schools as a free speech right (the ADL did not); and, most recently, *Zobrest v. Catalina Foothills School District*, 509 U.S. 1 (1993), in which the AJCongress and the AJCommittee, differing from the ADL, filed a brief in support of a government program assisting handicapped students

Today the AJCongress, the AJCommittee, and the ADL, as well as other Jewish organizations within their constitutional orbit, are less likely to describe their church-state philosophies as "absolutist" or "strict separationist" in nature, but instead as rooted in principles of "neutrality," a term that sounds less threatening and antagonistic. Nevertheless, their ultimate objective is not much different than it was during Pfeffer's heyday: to restrain government in the affairs of religion and to prevent religion from seeking or receiving government support for its practices or educational system. While there have been some disagreements about the threat posed by certain government programs involving benefits to religion, the non-Orthodox organized American Jewish community is still united in its belief that the religious and political equality of American Jews remains intertwined with a strong — or, dare I say it, absolutist — establishment clause. As Professors Soper and Monsma point out, the Court has announced, under the guise of "equal treatment" of religion, its more willing embrace of religious speakers on public land or in public schools, and of government subsidies for individuals or groups to engage in religious education or activity within a secular context. As I will argue in the remainder of this chapter, what the Court calls equal treatment for religion is really nothing more than a rhetorical device in defense of a formal legal mechanism whose objective is to secure a more rightful place for religion — politically powerful, majoritarian religion — in American public life. Such a position has never been good for the interests of American Jews as civic and political equals. And, no matter how benignly the Court phrases its challenge to the separation principle, that is not about to change.

The False Promise of Neutrality

In contrast to what supporters of the equal treatment principle argue, the constitutional premise that underlies it is anything but neutral. Before I explain why neutrality and equal treatment cannot be reconciled with one another, and thus cannot operate as a constitutive prin-

---

with the costs of their education, whether received in a public or a private school. Data on group participation in the cases decided after the 1991-92 Supreme Court term was compiled by the author.

ciple in the Court's establishment-clause jurisprudence, or, for that matter, its constitutional jurisprudence in general, be it free speech, equal protection, or anything else, I will first turn to the problem of neutrality itself. Granted, neutrality and equal treatment are attractive principles around which to organize a jurisprudence of church-state relations. What I will argue is that, in the purest sense, neutrality in the application of general or particular legal principles is impossible, if for no other reason than that the rules which are the subject of judicial review reflect partisan choices themselves.[19] The notion that an adjudicative mechanism such as equal treatment is possible under some utopian vision of the First Amendment is fallacious as well, since the courts do not now recognize, nor have they ever recognized, all religious practices as deserving of constitutional protection.[20] These reasons range from the persuasive, as in the case of child endangerment or human sacrifice, to the questionable, as in the case of consensual polygamy or the use of non-narcotic drugs in religious ritual. Whatever views one might hold on any or all of the above practices, placing them outside the protection of the Constitution reflects a conscious choice. There might be good reasons for that choice, but there is nothing neutral about it. As I will explain, assigning value to and thus granting protection to certain religious practices but not to others eliminates outright the possibility of a legal jurisprudence rooted in neutrality.

Neutrality, as envisioned by constitutional scholars supportive of its application in constitutional jurisprudence, assumes impartiality; impartiality, in turn, suggests a commitment to the equal treatment of persons, ideas, beliefs, and so forth. For example, subjecting all persons,

19. For a sophisticated argument on the difficulties of recognizing and enforcing neutrality in constitutional law, see Cass R. Sunstein, *The Partial Constitution* (Cambridge, Mass.: Harvard University Press, 1993).

20. See, for example, *Employment of Division of Oregon v. Smith*, 110 S. Ct. 1595 (1990) (holding that ritual use of peyote did not qualify as an exemption from criminal law); *O'Lone v. Shabazz*, 482 U.S. 342 (1987) (upholding restrictions on prisoners' religious rights as necessary for penal security); *Bowen v. Roy*, 476 U.S. 693 (1986) (holding that government is not obligated to exempt adherents of American Indian faiths from social security regulations); *Goldman v. Weinberger*, 475 U.S. 503 (1985) (ruling that the Air Force regulation banning individuals from wearing non-issued headwear while in uniform included religious coverings); and *Reynolds v. U.S.*, 98 U.S. 145 (1878) (upholding the criminalization of polygamy, even if polygamy is required as an article of religious faith).

institutions, or organizations to the same rules reflects neutrality on the part of the agent responsible for applying or enforcing those rules. There is something almost transcendent about such a principle because it appears to work in so many different contexts. On the golf course, "par" applies to everyone, and thus everyone has a benchmark against which to measure his or her skill. For admission to law school, the LSAT provides a sorting mechanism that tests aptitude without prejudice and thus allows the best students to come forward, regardless of their prior training, the rigor of their undergraduate curriculum, or accidents of birth. If a legal principle requires the government to remain impartial toward religion, as proponents of neutrality argue, then religion is the recipient of nothing more than equal treatment. Equal treatment, with neutrality as its core principle, provides a legal mechanism that precludes hostility toward religion by bringing religious speech into the pantheon of protected First Amendment values. Rather than discriminate against religious speech *because* it is religious speech, a jurisprudence of equal treatment affords such speech the same rights as all other expression — nothing more, but nothing less either.

In truth, there is nothing neutral about the rules and their enforcement in any of the above scenarios. Par reflects the score an expert golfer ought to achieve based on his or her cumulative score on eighteen holes; it does not take into consideration whether the course conditions are good or bad, whether the holes require powerful drives off the tee or putting finesse, whether you are playing a course for the first time or the fiftieth, whether you are eight or eighty years old, whether you play a lot or a little, and whether you can afford better equipment, private lessons, and lots of practice, or can afford only used clubs, no lessons, and occasional practice. Moreover, golf-course architects have in mind certain kinds of players when they design courses. Not all players are expected to perform well on all golf courses. An architect purposely gears a certain course to particular strengths and weaknesses. Golfers who possess those strengths but not the weaknesses will score better than others not as fortunate. On a different day, on a different golf course, different fortunes will rise and fall. How else does one explain the common refrain of golfers struggling through an endless round that "the course just wasn't set up for my game"? The rules and conditions of golf might appear to have equal application, but they do not and cannot because players bring different levels of skill to the game, in part because some of them enjoy the considerable advantages of money and leisure time that allow them to improve their game.

As much as educators and professional academics would love to have the LSAT or any other standardized test reflect the true aptitude of a student to study law, medicine, or political science, thus relieving them of the arduous task of selecting the most qualified of a generally competent pool of students for admission into their schools, most know that standardized test scores reflect where the student received his or her previous education, whether the student was able to afford an expensive review course that focuses solely on how to *take* that particular standardized test, and his or her life experiences. Still, there is something irresistible about trotting out the average SAT or LSAT scores of an entering class for all to see, especially when those scores fall into the high end of the percentile range. (This is done, of course, with no regard for the feelings of the graduating seniors, who compare as sloth against the new regime of the best and the brightest.) The worth of the scores as predictors of academic and professional success are less important than the status attached to them. The SAT, the LSAT, or any of the other standardized tests are not the least bit objective. But admissions counselors consider them the most impartial of the available choices with which to discern aptitude because at least all students get asked the same questions. That does not, however, make these tests neutral in their conception and administration.

Whatever the theoretical attraction of the equal treatment principle, equal treatment for religious speech or religious activity under the First Amendment is likewise impossible because, to begin with, not all expression or conduct, whether linked to the speech or religion clauses, receives constitutional protection. Certain speech or expression, no matter how reprehensible to the consensual norms of society, may still be of value to some, or even a significant minority. Even so, if enough people, representative of a powerful societal interest, decide that certain expression is beyond the acceptable constitutional boundaries of a society steeped in the culture of protection for unpopular viewpoints, then legislatures are within their rightful power to proscribe such expression. True, government must satisfy a "compelling interest" when it chooses to prohibit expression based on its content. And, in all fairness, the compelling-interest standard is a difficult one to meet; and time has shown that government is largely without authority to squelch unpopular points of view *because* they are unpopular. Still, states, localities, school boards, and even Congress have legislated to proscribe certain kinds of expression because of content in a fashion the Supreme Court has found acceptable.[21] This categorization of protected speech, which also includes subcategories of more and less protected expression, has developed despite the Court's common invocation of Justice Oliver Wendell Holmes's "marketplace of ideas" metaphor to describe its First Amendment jurisprudence.[22] Our acceptance of the "marketplace" metaphor to explain an optimal free-speech standard perpetuates the myth that a formal legal mechanism can impartially regulate what enters the lexicon of societal values. Expression is there for people who want it, no matter how despicable the expression might be, because the people, not government, regulate speech. The truth is somewhat more complex.

I break no new ground when I point out that expression which is obscene or libelous, threatens national security, or poses a "clear and present" danger has market value. So does cocaine. Government restricts that drug's access to the legal marketplace, as it does proscribed categories of expression. And it might have perfect reasons for doing so, reasons that are "compelling" in nature. But in no sense are we to describe the government's behavior in restricting the marketplace for drugs and speech as neutral, impartial, or reflective of an equal treatment ideal. Criminalizing cocaine but not alcohol, marijuana but not nicotine, may reflect sound, rational principles related to public policy, but these decisions have to do with politics as well as with health because it is the political process through which such regulations must pass.

A jurisprudence that allows for some regulation of speech or expression that carries grave societal risk might well promote a rational public-policy objective. I have tried to argue here, within the space constraints here, that equal treatment is not an adjudicative mechanism

21. See, for example, *Osbourne v. Ohio*, 495 U.S. 103 (1990) (child pornography); *Roth v. U.S.*, 354 U.S. 476 (1957) (categorical ban on obscenity); *New York Times v. Sullivan*, 376 U.S. 254 (1964) (libel); *Brandenburg v. Ohio*, 395 U.S. 444 (1969) (speech associated with "imminent lawlessness"); *Chaplinsky v. New Hampshire*, 315 U.S. 568 (1942) (fighting words); and *Schenck v. U.S.*, 249 U.S. 47 (1919) (clear and present danger).

22. See *Abrams v. U.S.*, 250 U.S. 616, 630 (1919): "The best test of truth is the power of the thought to get itself accepted in the competition of the market, and that truth is the only ground upon which their wishes safely can be carried out."

which stands apart from political and social choices, and that courts are incapable of creating a jurisprudence that treats equally all persons or institutions who seek refuge under the First Amendment. Such a proposition collapses under the weight of its own illogic. This does not mean that the Court is without the imagination and intellectual resources to develop a jurisprudence that tries to promote fairness, respect, and tolerance for religion and that would allow it to flourish independent of government support and sustenance within the paradigm of liberal legal jurisprudence. Nonetheless, equal treatment, as I will argue in the final section of this chapter, is not the answer.

Equal Treatment, Absolutism, and the Jewish Community

American Jews, along with the religious and secular agencies that represent them in law and public affairs, are no strangers to the practice of minoritarian politics. Despite their economic affluence and their social assimilation into the fabric of American life, Jews have remained acutely conscious of their minority status in the American religious and cultural milieu and the limitations that this status has placed on their power to influence the majoritarian institutions of government. During their formative period, the AJCommittee, the AJCongress, and the ADL, the most powerful of these organizations, came to understand that their best prospect for abolishing state-sponsored religious preferences and reconstituting the law of church and state lay not in hoping for precursory action by the elected branches of government but in pursuing a constitutional mandate from the courts. Perhaps the best summation of the religious and political protection that an absolutist position on church and state offered the American Jewish community was expressed by David Petegorsky, the executive director of the AJCongress during the 1940s, the period in which the major Jewish organizations were first testing the litigation waters:

> We are acutely conscious of the fact that few issues present more serious problems to the Jewish community in terms of its relationship to the non-Jewish world. Opposition to any or all of these [religious] practices carries with it the dangers of being falsely accused of indifference or hostility to the dissemination of religious faith and teaching. We submit, however, that Jews have always been,

and will always be, far better advised to take their position on the basis of fundamental principle rather than of temporary or immediate considerations of expediency. The attitude of the non-Jewish community towards Jews is only one of the many factors determining the status and security of the Jewish community. A far more important factor affecting that status is the strength and health of the democratic system under which we live. In opposing any impairment of the separation of church and state, we stand firmly on sound and tested democratic principle.[23]

Little has changed during the past fifty years to convince the overwhelming majority of the American Jewish community that it stands to benefit from a cooperative relationship between government and religion. Now as much as ever, American Jews oppose tax subsidies and other forms of government aid for parochial schools and policies supportive of increased place for religious activities in the public schools. The mobilization of the organized Jewish community, along with an ecumenical coalition of allied organizations, to block the introduction of a religious equality amendment by the 104th Congress has been swift and impressive. Jews not only have remained consistent in their attitudes toward church-state issues, but have opposed such government accommodation of religious practices and education in greater numbers than any other religious group or denomination.[24] Perhaps non-Jews are perplexed by the intensity with which the Jewish community has embraced Jefferson's metaphorical wall of separation between church and state and its persistent demand that it be understood to limit, almost without exception, government involvement with religion. Anti-Semitism as a force in the social, political, and economic lives of most American Jews continues to wane. Moreover, as Jews prepare to celebrate the hundredth anniversary of their arrival in mass numbers in America, the American Jewish community is more politically and economically secure than ever before.[25] So what accounts for Jewish discomfort with a more passive establishment clause?

23. Petegorsky, quoted by Ivers in *To Build a Wall*, p. 73.

24. Phi Delta Kappa/Gallup Poll 77 (September 1995): 441.

25. The most persuasive analysis of contemporary anti-Semitism and its impact, or lack thereof, on contemporary Jewish America is found in Leonard Dinnerstein's *Anti-Semitism in America* (New York: Oxford University Press, 1994), pp. 228-44.

Two things explain Jewish support for a government without power to intervene in or support private religious beliefs. One is that Jews, a religious minority, have never fared well in the theologies of Christian religions. Christian theology, Catholic and Protestant, in America and in Europe, has cast Jews as thieves, liars, predators, murderers, and, above all, those responsible for the crucifixion of Jesus Christ. For decades, Catholic parochial schools used textbooks that routinely placed Jews in villainous roles. Protestant churches, in their religious education programs, did much the same. Leonard Dinnerstein has pointed out that the Catholic Church has made great strides in bringing about changes in Christian attitudes toward the Jews, from the Second Vatican Council's issuance of a statement "exonerating" the Jews for Christ's death, to a complete review of textbooks used in Catholic schools to detect anti-Jewish sentiments and portrayals. Churches, scholars, and other agencies within the Protestant community have followed suit. But Dinnerstein also notes that much of this effort on the part of Christians to renounce and repair their anti-Semitic past has come only within the last twenty years.[26] For Jews, a Constitution that prohibits a partnership between government and religion also eliminates the possibility that government power can be used to endorse or support the theology of the religious majority, Christianity, which still in the eyes of many Jews — and, in all fairness, many Christians as well — has much for which to account.

The second, and far less abstract, reason that Jews distrust efforts to weaken the establishment clause is that they believe it would lessen their status as equals in American political and religious culture. Jews have prospered in the United States as nowhere before because the government, sometimes against its desire, has been restrained by the Supreme Court from supporting the religious and political objectives of majoritarian religion. Indeed, a common complaint by supporters of greater government accommodation of religion is that the absolutist approach to church-state relations promotes a civic environment in which the forces of "irreligion" are preferred over those of religion. In this view, jurisprudence of equal treatment, the latest manifestation of the accommodationist argument, represents a long overdue correction of the core principles behind the establishment clause and inaugurates a period of

26. Dinnerstein, *Anti-Semitism in America*, pp. 237-42.

healing of our civic culture. In its most recent establishment-clause decision, *Rosenberger v. University of Virginia* (1995), the Court ruled that the university's failure to fund a religious magazine when it was funding other, nonreligious publications smacked of hostility toward religious speech and thus violated the free speech clause.[27] In response, supporters of the equal treatment principle argue that the Court is doing nothing more than freeing religion from the oppressive discrimination of church-state absolutism. However, for the Jewish organizations that supported the University of Virginia's policy of prohibiting the use of student activity fees for "religious activity . . . that primarily promotes or manifests a particular belief in or about a deity or an ultimate reality,"[28] *Rosenberger* was not about free speech but about the unlawful transfer of public funds for core religious activities of private individuals and groups. That rule applied to Jews as much as it did to the evangelical Christians who were the plaintiffs in *Rosenberger*. If, as the Court's majority opinion claims, *Rosenberger* was about eligibility in a government program that is neutral toward religion, why did the Jewish organizations that participated as amici see it as a funding case, as the four dissenters did, and not, as the majority did, a case about equal access for religious speech? Is this an example of "irreligion" run amok?

Jewish organizations represented in *Rosenberger* did not see it as an equal-access case because there was nothing neutral about the request of Wide Awake Productions, the student group that filed the lawsuit, to receive government funds to support its stated purpose to "challenge Christians to live, in word and deed, according to the faith they proclaim and to encourage students to consider what a personal relationship with Jesus Christ means."[29] Wide Awake's purpose is to spread the Christian faith, a mission that falls squarely within its constitutional rights. What is questionable is whether the government has an obligation to fund that mission simply because it has chosen to fund other student activities. The Court likened the issues in *Rosenberger* to those of its previous equal-access cases involving the rights of student and nonstudent religious organizations to use the public schools if secular organizations had such privileges. But those cases were about the rights of private

27. 115 S. Ct. 2510 (1995).
28. 115 S. Ct. at 2513.
29. 115 S. Ct. at 2534.

speakers to use a forum designated for public discourse, not about whether the schools were required to *fund* the activities of those organizations. The *Rosenberger* Court held that there was no difference between allowing an organization to use an open classroom building and funding the proselytizing of Wide Awake through the publication of its magazine. The Court, in allowing the use of public funds to support Wide Awake's mission, concluded that "any benefit to religion is incidental to the government's provision of secular services for secular purposes on a religion-neutral basis." Because school payments would go directly to the printer that published Wide Awake's magazine, the government's hands were free of unconstitutional taint.[30]

Rosenberger thus opens the door for student religious clubs, at least at the university level, to receive public funds for core religious activities, a holding nowhere found in the Court's previous line of establishment clause cases dealing with equal access or parochial aid.[31] For most American Jews, *Rosenberger* is problematic on two fronts. First, it means that Jews will be called upon to support religious activities with their tax dollars, a specter against which James Madison warned in his *Memorial and Remonstrance Against Religious Assessments* when he wrote that "the same authority which can force a citizen to contribute three pence only of his property for the support of any one establishment, may force him to conform to any other establishment in all cases." Second, *Rosenberger* elevates to a whole new level the problem of political divisiveness that previous Courts recognized was exacerbated by government support for religious mission.[32] Even in previous equal-access cases such as *Widmar v. Vincent*,[33] *Board of Westside Community Schools v. Mergens*,[34] and *Lamb's Chapel v. Center Moriches Union Free School District*,[35] the Court encouraged the adaptation of strong guidelines by school districts to ensure that a coercive environment did not develop that would offend the rights of religious minorities. *Rosenberger* cannot reassure Jewish students on our nation's college campuses, where, in the case of public universities, they fail in every case to make up a majority population. An effort to have

30. 115 S. Ct. at 2523-24.
31. 115 S. Ct. at 2533-51 (Justice Souter, dissenting).
32. *Lemon v. Kurtzman,* 413 U.S. at 613-16.
33. 454 U.S. 263 (1981).
34. 496 U.S. 226 (1990).
35. 113 U.S. 2141 (1993).

the equal treatment principle of *Rosenberger* enforced in the nation's public secondary schools portends even more trouble, since the parochial nature of such environments makes principled resistance to state-sponsored religious activities more difficult for religious minorities.

Equal treatment poses little attraction for American Jews because it demonstrates little concern for the counter-majoritarian check on the power of religious majorities to curry government favor. An absolutist, or no-aid, approach to church-state relations offers religious minorities protection that cannot be found under a more permissive establishment clause. An absolutist approach does not have its moral anchor in hostility toward religion, but rather seeks to promote the vision that all individuals, regardless of their denominational or religious affiliation, remain free from the unequal burden and sense of isolation that government preferences for organized religion impose on those who are not its beneficiaries. Moreover, equal treatment poses a threat to the interests of majoritarian religion as well. If the government is required to remain neutral toward religion and not advantage or disadvantage it in any particular manner, then the preferred treatment afforded to religion under the current interpretation of the establishment and free exercise clauses, such as its exemption from compliance with federal civil-rights statutes and other generally applicable laws, may be ripe for review as well.[36] Few advocates of equal treatment would argue for the wholesale abolition of special protection for religion on the grounds that religious individuals and institutions should not have more rights than their secular counterparts. Justice Scalia argued precisely that point in his opinion for the Court in *Employment Division of Oregon v. Smith* (1990), which resulted in the formation of an unprecedented 45-member coalition (that counted among its members the ACLU, the AJCongress, the Christian fundamentalist group Concerned Women for America, and the National Association of Evangelicals); the group successfully persuaded Congress to overturn that opinion through statute.[37] Equal treatment, then, is fine when it advantages religion, but not when it places religion at a disadvantage.

36. See, for example, *Frazee v. Illinois Department of Employment Security,* 109 S. Ct. 1514 (1989); *Corporation of the Presiding Bishops v. Amos,* 483 U.S. 327 (1987); and *Wisconsin v. Yoder,* 406 U.S. 205 (1972).

37. See the Religious Freedom Restoration Act of 1993.

Conclusion

In sum, American Jews do not stand to benefit from an establishment clause with equal treatment as its animating principle. Because equal treatment as an adjudicative mechanism fails to meet its own standard — that of neutrality — and because it cannot stand apart from the social and political values that serve as its foundation, it will never apply to all groups in an impartial way. American Jewish organizations have long been front and center in the struggle for religious equality under the Constitution. Their success has been due in part to the persuasive power of their argument: that civil peace and religious equality bloomed in a constitutional setting where religion and government were prohibited from forming a temporal or permanent partnership. That argument seems lost on the current Court, which seems determined to enforce an unworkable and illogical rule whose effect will be to restore the symbolic and financial support sought by segments of Christian America. Religious minorities, including American Jews, will find themselves returning to fight battles thought to have been won long ago.

CHAPTER 8

"Equal" Treatment?
A Liberal Separationist View

ROGERS M. SMITH

In this chapter, Rogers Smith acknowledges that equal treatment is an appropriate principle for the Supreme Court to adopt in deciding church-state issues. He argues, however, that equal treatment must apply to establishment and free-exercise cases to insure that there are no special protections for religious viewpoints that are not available to secular ones. Contrary to most advocates of equal treatment, Smith contends that secular perspectives, not religious ones, are at greatest risk of being disadvantaged in American culture and law. Rogers M. Smith is professor of political science at Yale University.

Demands for better treatment of religion in American law and life have mounted visibly in the 1990s. In 1993, Yale law professor Stephen Carter published the acclaimed book *The Culture of Disbelief*, in which he argued that "American law and politics trivialize religious devotion." Carter maintained that, although the American public overwhelmingly professes religious beliefs and religiosity has been resurgent in recent years, American judicial, political, and intellectual elites understand the relationship of church and state in ways that reduce faith in God to a "hobby" rather than recognize it as a respectable dimension of

179

public discourse.[1] Also in 1993, congressional leaders as diverse as Orrin Hatch and Edward Kennedy joined in sponsoring the Religious Freedom Restoration Act, a law designed to compel the judiciary to protect the free exercise of religion more strictly than it had been willing to do in the 1990 decision of *Department of Human Resources of Oregon v. Smith*.[2]

The statute had an "establishment clause" predecessor in the Equal Access Act of 1984, which countered some contrary judicial rulings by requiring secondary schools that received federal funds and provided a "limited open forum" for meetings to make their facilities equally available to both religious and nonreligious student groups. The Christian Coalition has since made the passage of a broader "religious equality" constitutional amendment the first item of its proposed "Contract with the American Family," and in 1996 House Majority Leader Dick Armey joined Representative Henry Hyde in proposing a version of that amendment which would insure all persons "equal access" to governmental benefits regardless of their religious beliefs. Although those proposals have not yet prevailed, the Supreme Court has moved decisively in a similar direction: in 1995, a majority of the justices permitted state funding for an explicitly evangelistic student paper in *Rosenberger v. The Rector and Visitors of the University of Virginia*.[3]

Separationist liberals like myself tell ourselves that we value equal respect, tolerance, and a considerable diversity of viewpoints. How, then, can we possibly object to efforts to insure that public institutions do not discriminate against religious believers, but instead protect their freedoms while offering public services to them on the same basis as

---

1. Carter, *The Culture of Disbelief: How American Law and Politics Trivialize Religious Devotion* (New York: Basic Books, 1993), pp. 3-11, 21-22, 45.

2. *Congressional Record*, vol. 139, #30, 103rd Cong., 1st Sess., S 2822; *Employment, Division, Department of Human Resources v. Smith*, 494 U.S. 872 (1990). The Religious Freedom Restoration Act was enacted as Public Law 103-41 on November 16, 1993. The Supreme Court declared it unconstitutional in *City of Boerne v. Flores*, 117 S. Ct. 2157 (1997).

3. Gerald Gunther, *Constitutional Law*, 12th ed. (Westbury, N.Y.: The Foundation Press, 1991), p. 1530 (discussing the Equal Access Act of 1984, 28 U.S.C. sec. 4071); Bruce Nolan, "Rewritten First Amendment Divides Religious Organizations," *The Times-Picayune*, 2 Sept. 1996, p. A1; *Ronald W. Rosenberger et al. v. The Rector and Visitors of the University of Virginia*, 115 S. Ct. 2510 (1995).

everyone else? In some respects we cannot: I will not argue here against "equal treatment." Nonetheless, I will discomfit many advocates of equal treatment policies by insisting on two implications of that principle.

First, "equal treatment" must apply not only to "establishment" but also to "free exercise" cases: there should be no special protections for religious perspectives over and above those provided for claims of secular moral conscience. Otherwise, the Constitution as a whole will clearly provide not "equal treatment" but preferential treatment for religious over against nonreligious views, reinforcing discriminatory practices that have prevailed through most of U.S. history. My call for *fully* equal treatment does not mean that rights of religious conscience cannot be placed in a "preferred position," as in the Religious Freedom Restoration Act. It does mean, however, that rights of secular conscientious belief should be given equal preferred standing. That fact will inevitably limit the circumstances in which governments can afford to defer to such consciences. The shared "preferred position" status of religious and secular consciences may mean that religious claims will not prevail as often as they would if they held that position alone.

Second, even as we aim at "equal treatment" in establishment clause cases, we must acknowledge that there are some circumstances in which it is chimerical. Many policies will inevitably favor either majority religious perspectives, minority religions, or nonreligious views, and the losers will contend plausibly that they are being treated unequally. In such circumstances, I submit, a genuine concern for equal treatment will often require governments to be especially protective of those views that are disfavored by the great majority of the people. It is unpopular views that are most at risk of being denied equal respect through some hard or soft form of the "tyranny of the majority," correctly identified as the great danger of republican institutions in the eyes of framers like James Madison and (later) Alexis de Tocqueville.

And though the category of "unpopular views" includes some unconventional religious beliefs, the outlooks that are most at risk of being denied genuine public respect in the United States today, as throughout our history, especially include beliefs that are overtly critical of much conventional religiosity. Secular philosophy and science have long prompted highly plausible doubts about the claims of divine revelation and miraculous occurrences that form part of most traditional religious doctrines. Yet, even though much public discourse in the U.S. is cast in

181

secular terms, and even though views that implicitly dispute traditional religious claims are often advanced, the explicit challenges that secular perspectives imply to such doctrines are rarely uttered, much less elaborated. Instead, public statements praising religion are ubiquitous. Even if many seem platitudinous, as Stephen Carter charges, it is not and never has been possible for an American political leader to question conventional religious beliefs without reaping widespread charges of intolerance and immorality that are likely to sweep the speaker out of public life. Whatever we make of the repeated appeals to God in presidential speeches, for example, we will search there in vain for comments opposing religious faith. It is simply not acceptable in American public life to say that the religious beliefs of one's opponents are false and wrong, even if one deeply believes that to be the case, and even if pernicious causes are gaining credibility from their (sincere) presentation as such religious commitments. Instead, any hint that views opposed to prevailing religions might gain overt political primacy triggers powerful opposition, as the Religious Freedom Restoration Act and the 1984 Equal Access Act show.

I believe that the issue of "equal treatment" must thus be analyzed by first recognizing that Stephen Carter's book won widespread applause precisely because it had the facts almost exactly backward.[4] Far from being publicly marginalized, religious views are so popular that openly championing piety, as Professor Carter did, is bound to win praise. Far from threatening to be hegemonic, views overtly hostile to conventional religions are so publicly unacceptable that a book urging such hostility could not possibly gain a similarly favorable reception. Now as ever, it is secular outlooks explicitly opposed to basic religious beliefs that come closest to being silenced in contemporary public discussions. Hence these, along with genuinely unconventional religious viewpoints, are the ones that courts must be most concerned to safeguard.

Moreover, if courts do not do so, it is likely that contemporary calls for "equal treatment" of religion in establishment clause cases, com-

4. Carter is largely correct that overtly religious arguments are not common currency in elite intellectual centers like the Yale Law School, although even discounting Carter himself, they are far from absent there. He is wrong, however, to suggest that such arguments are unacceptable in American political discourse. They are sometimes controversial, but, as noted below, it would privilege religion inappropriately to treat criticisms as improper.

bined with "special protection" for religion in free exercise cases, will not end up advancing "equality" in any sense. They will instead help compound the advantages already enjoyed by the religious viewpoints that are most widely shared and most politically potent in the United States. Today, those viewpoints are evangelical forms of traditionalist, sometimes anti-rationalistic religions. Not surprisingly, it is proponents of these outlooks like the Christian Coalition and their political allies like House Majority Leader Armey that have been pushing hardest for statutory and constitutional changes that they know will benefit them far more than most other Americans — and they have been succeeding in their efforts. To ignore those facts is to ignore the actual political and moral significance of the current controversies.

The Embattled Project of Reasonable Religion

To grasp that significance, we must go beyond recent court cases and narrow discussions of abstract principles to the broader realities of the historical place of religion in American life. Michael McConnell, among others, has argued persuasively that the peculiar structure of church-state relations in the United States arose from a variety of perspectives that included "evangelical" strains of Protestantism, which McConnell links ultimately with the free exercise views of James Madison, as well as more "secular liberal" Enlightenment views, which McConnell identifies with John Locke and Thomas Jefferson. And it was, he correctly contends, the more conventionally Protestant Madisonian viewpoint that came closest to capturing the thrust of the diverse ideas on religion that prevailed in the founding era. Americans established separation of church and state first in some states, then at the national level, and later in all the states out of the belief that their preferred religions and religion in general would then best flourish. Most did not do so out of any desire to erode or transform traditional forms of religiosity, as many Enlightenment thinkers sought to do.[5] More secular Enlightenment outlooks like Jefferson's were instead embraced only by a tiny minority of Americans from the earliest years of

5. McConnell, "The Origins and Historical Understanding of Free Exercise of Religion," *Harvard Law Review* 103 (1990): 1437-55.

the nation, and his type of rationalistic religiosity has never gained many more followers. Yet perspectives on religion like Jefferson's deserve consideration, because due to their enduring unpopularity, we have yet to realize the enrichment of human understanding that they might provide.

Enlightenment writers like Locke, Immanuel Kant, and (later) Jefferson all embarked on a radical but highly defensible project: they sought to revise inherited religious doctrines so that all elements of the magical, the supernatural, and the physically impossible or historically false would be purged from them. That project was embodied in now little-read volumes like Locke's *The Reasonableness of Christianity*, Kant's *Religion Within the Limits of Reason Alone*, and Jefferson's *Bible*, which retold the life of Jesus by stressing biblical moral teachings and entirely eliminating all references to miracles. It is not surprising that today, while the Declaration's reference to a "Creator" is often invoked, this other work of Jefferson's is rarely mentioned. The ideal toward which it and these other works pointed was one in which "religions" would not resemble the systems of belief based ultimately on faith in revelations and miracles that still predominate today. Instead, "religions" would be what John Dewey later argued they should be: sets of essentially moral beliefs tested on the anvil of reason, perhaps attached to what were acknowledged to be merely speculative beliefs about the ultimate nature of the cosmos and its creation. Science and reason, not revelation, were to decide what could properly be deemed knowledge, and no notions contrary to them could henceforth claim the title of truth.[6]

Although such views were most openly defended by Enlightenment radicals like Thomas Paine, probably no one was more attached to them than Jefferson. As late as 1822, he hoped that public education would eventually eradicate all irrational religiosity or "fanaticism." Prior to that, he predicted, the same end would be served by the progress of the most anti-supernatural, rationalistic religion available, Unitarianism, which

6. Locke, *The Reasonableness of Christianity* (Stanford, Calif.: Stanford University Press, 1958); Kant, *Religion Within the Limits of Reason Alone* (New York: Harper Torchbooks, 1960); Jefferson, *The Jefferson Bible* (Greenwich, Conn.: Fawcett Publications, 1961); Dewey, *Reconstruction in Philosophy* (Boston: Beacon Press, 1957), pp. 210-13. (It is probably no coincidence that these modern editions of works on rationalistic religion appeared during the relatively brief modern reform period that produced the school prayer decisions.)

he expected "ere long" to be "the religion of the majority from north to south."[7]

Jefferson was, however, wildly wrong. The nation was then well along in its Second Great Awakening, which fueled Unitarian growth far less than that of "evangelical Protestant churches," which "reached their high point of cultural influence" in those years, in the judgment of religious historian Sydney Ahlstrom. In the 1830s, Alexis de Tocqueville argued that human fears of "annihilation" and longings for "immortality" meant that "faith is the only permanent state of mankind," so that any temporary predominance of secular viewpoints would be an "intellectual aberration." As he was well aware, whatever the influence of secular Enlightenment doctrines on the American founding, the subsequent record of American life was bearing him out. During the nineteenth century, U.S. policies and institutions came to express ever more fully the evangelical Protestant outlooks that had already predominated at the nation's start.[8] A regime of formal separation and extensive informal accommodation of religion became pervasive, and under it church affiliation rose. Roger Finke and Rodney Stark estimate that only 17 percent of Americans belonged to churches in 1776 (although that pattern probably stemmed from a variety of frontier conditions rather than any general lack of religiosity), and they report that this percentage rose to 37 percent by 1860, reached 53 percent by 1916, and then rose to over 60 percent, where it remains today. According to Ahlstrom, "the ideology of the Protestant establishment" dominated American life to a greater or lesser extent throughout these years, at least until the 1960s. Only then, he suggested in 1972, did "the age of the WASP" appear to be coming to an end.[9]

7. Indeed, he predicted that "there is not a *young man* now living in the United States who will not die an Unitarian" (Thomas Jefferson to Dr. Thomas Cooper, 2 Nov. 1822, in Jefferson, *Writings*, ed. Merrill Peterson [New York: Library of America, 1984], p. 1464). See also McConnell, "The Origins and Historical Understanding of Free Exercise of Religion," p. 1450.

8. Ahlstrom, *A Religious History of the American People* (New Haven: Yale University Press, 1972), p. 387; Tocqueville, *Democracy in America*, ed. J. P. Mayer (Garden City, N.Y.: Doubleday, 1969), pp. 295-97.

9. Finke and Stark, *The Churching of America, 1776-1990: Winners and Losers in Our Religious Economy* (New Brunswick, N.J.: Rutgers University Press, 1993), pp. 1, 16, 31-39; Ahlstrom, *A Religious History of the American People*, p. 1079.

Indeed, until the landmark school-prayer decisions of the early 1960s, American governments treated Christianity, and especially Protestant Christianity, as in many respects the official religion of the land. Its tenets structured the curriculum of the public schools in which Jefferson had placed his hopes. Its symbols and mottoes regularly appeared in documents, on monuments, on holidays, and in various practices, from dollar bills to Thanksgiving proclamations to the rituals by which most legislatures and the Supreme Court still open their sessions. Fidelity to this recognizably Christian "civil religion" was frequently espoused in political rhetoric like the greatest speech of nineteenth-century America, Lincoln's Second Inaugural, which argued that Americans on both sides of the Civil War "read the same Bible and pray to the same God," and which interpreted the war as "the providence of God." In his influential *Commentaries on the Constitution,* Supreme Court Justice Joseph Story argued that it was "the especial duty of government to foster and encourage" Christianity "among all the citizens and subjects." The Court itself later dismissed Mormon claims for polygamy as rejected by "all civilized and Christian countries," an approach that made traditional Christianity the measure of legitimate religiosity. It is true that despite this overt favoritism of Christianity, other religious viewpoints were broadly tolerated in nineteenth-century America; but, as the Mormon decisions indicate, tolerance ceased if religions departed too greatly from dominant Protestant norms. The most divergent religions present on the continent were those of the native tribes, and repeatedly U.S. leaders announced as an explicit aim of public policy the conversion of all native peoples to Christianity, a goal to be achieved by tactics that combined persuasion and force.[10]

Contrary not only to Jefferson's expectations in 1822 but to Ahlstrom's anticipations 150 years later, the beliefs of most Americans

10. The quotations from Lincoln's address can be found in *The Writings of Abraham Lincoln,* vol. 7, ed. A. B. Lapsley (New York: Lamb Publishing Company, 1906), p. 330. Joseph Story is cited by Richard E. Morgan in *The Supreme Court and Religion* (New York: Free Press, 1972), p. 38. Polygamy is denigrated in *Davis v. Beason,* 133 U.S. 333 (1890). On the Protestant character of public schools, see, for example, Carl F. Kaestle, *Pillars of the Republic: Common Schools and American Society, 1780-1880* (New York: Hill & Wang, 1983). On U.S. policies toward Native American religions, see, for example, Ronald Wright, *Stolen Continents: The Americas Through Indian Eyes Since 1492* (Boston: Houghton Mifflin, 1992).

have not greatly altered in late twentieth-century America. Most Americans still seem to be comfortable with a "permanent state" of religiosity. In 1994, 96 percent of Americans still expressed belief in "God or a universal spirit," a figure unchanged since the 1940s, and 88 percent labeled religion "very important" or "important" in their lives. Moreover, their religiosity was overwhelmingly not of the rationalistic Enlightenment variety. Ninety percent of Americans reported that they believed in heaven, 79 percent believed in miracles, 73 percent believed in hell, and 65 percent believed in the devil, with the last figure having risen significantly in recent years. Younger "baby boomers," born between 1956 and 1965, were more likely to believe in the devil, and to regard religion and science as in conflict, than were older "boomers," born between 1946 and 1955, though both groups were well above 50 percent on both questions. Around two-thirds of all Americans belonged to a church or synagogue, a level higher than at most times in U.S. history. Almost nine out of ten thought that the nation "was founded upon biblical principles" and had a special divine "destiny," and that these facts should be taught in public schools.[11]

It is true that, whereas in the late 1960s Protestants and Catholics still collectively made up 92 percent of Americans expressing religious preferences, by 1993 they were only 82 percent, though they still made up 91 percent of churchgoers. It is also true that forty years ago, 75 percent of Americans called religion "very important" in their lives, while today the figure is only 60 percent. In some ways, then, American religiosity has grown more diverse and a bit less salient. Those changes do not, however, represent any greater success for more rationalistic views of religion. The denominations that have been growing in the last quarter century are ones that offer comparatively traditional forms of Christianity. From 1970 to 1995, for example, the Southern Baptist Convention grew from 11.3 to 15.4 million members; the National Baptist Convention, U.S.A., went from 5.5 million to 8.2 million adherents; and the Roman Catholic Church grew from 47.9 to 59 million

11. *Opinions '90: Extracts from Public Opinion Surveys and Polls Conducted by Business, Government, Professional and News Organizations,* ed. Chris J. Miko and Edward Weilant (Detroit: Gale Research, 1991), p. 469; George Gallup, Jr., *The Gallup Poll: Public Opinion 1995* (Wilmington: Scholarly Resources, 1996), pp. 8-9, 12, 16-20; Peter Steinfels, "Beliefs," *New York Times,* 2 Nov. 1996, p. 29.

members. Those three denominations alone accounted for almost a third of all Americans, and there are many other smaller but also growing traditionalist churches. In contrast, the more theologically liberal United Church of Christ declined from 2 million to 1.5 million members over the last twenty-five years; Stephen Carter's Episcopal Church dropped from 3.4 million members to 2.5 million; the two main Presbyterian churches went from 4.2 million to just under 4 million; and Jefferson's cherished Unitarians faded from 282,000 to numbers so low that they are no longer reported by the U.S. Census Bureau. In total, less than 5 percent of Americans belong to these sorts of (generally) more theologically liberal Protestant churches. And many members of the surging traditionalist religions appear to be at least as strongly motivated by their beliefs as most religious adherents in the past, if their willingness to translate religious commitments into political and social activism is any measure. Politically and religiously conservative groups like the Christian Coalition and the fast-rising Promise Keepers movement boast large budgets of $25 million and $115 million, respectively. In contrast, the most prominent "secular humanist" association, the American Atheists group, has a membership that is dwarfed even by the Unitarians, and its annual budget is $500,000. In short, organizations explicitly espousing secular views on religious matters or even inclining toward more rationalistic theologies are small and on the decline in the U.S. today, whereas groups evangelistically advancing traditional religious beliefs are huge, on the rise, and much closer to the religious outlook of the great majority of Americans.[12]

Those statistics, moreover, actually understate the plight of rationalistic views of religion today. Ahlstrom was probably correct to argue that American religiosity reached a historic turning point in the 1960s, even though it was not quite the one he perceived. Until that time, proponents of more liberal, modernistic theological perspectives that sought to bring American religiosity "into the world of modern science,

---

12. Gallup, *The Gallup Poll: Public Opinion 1995*, pp. 16-20; Bureau of the Census, Statistical Abstract of the United States, 90th ed. (Washington: U.S. Department of Commerce, 1970), pp. 41-42, and Bureau of the Census, 115th ed. (1995), pp. 68-69; Joe Canason, Alfred Ross, and Lee Cokovinas, "The Promise Keepers Are Coming: The Third Wave of the Religious Right," *The Nation*, 7 Oct. 1996, p. 11; Jim Jones, "O'Hair Still Speaking for Separate Church, State," *Fresno Bee*, 3 June 1995, sec. C, p. 7.

scholarship," and "philosophy" could often ally themselves with adherents of more conservative theological outlooks on many social reform issues. From the antebellum antislavery crusade to turn-of-the century causes like temperance, missionary work, public schooling, and urban reform, on to the civil rights movement of the 1950s, theological liberals could often join with more religiously conservative figures to support social change, as did antislavery leader Theodore Dwight Weld with many antebellum northern Methodists, Social Gospel advocate Washington Gladden with the Gilded Age evangelist Dwight Moody, and Martin Luther King, Jr., with the more traditional civil rights leader Ralph Abernathy. But in the wake of the civil rights movement, many theological liberals came to see some of their own former causes as further dimensions of the system of WASP supremacy that civil rights advocates had opposed so inspirationally. Rather than instruments of civilization, a Christianity-infused curriculum and compulsory school prayers now seemed repressive toward other spiritual outlooks. Rather than bulwarks of morality, "blue" laws banning contraception, abortion, and unconventional sexuality seemed expressions of Puritanism and patriarchal subordination of women. Rather than conformity to God's will, ardently nationalistic American patriotism seemed a rationale for violent imperialism. Adherents of these political positions often embraced more radical theological perspectives calling for "demystification" of claims for the Bible as God's word and of promises of miraculous eternal life through conversion. And in the wake of the triumphs of the civil rights movement, these adherents had some success during the 1960s and early 1970s in winning Supreme Court decisions disallowing mandatory school prayer and many forms of aid to religious education, establishing rights to contraception and abortion, and protecting anti-war dissent such as flag burning, among other liberal rulings.[13]

As a result, not only did theological liberalism come to be seen as radically opposed to the religious tenets many conservative believers

13. Ahlstrom, *A Religious History of the American People*, pp. 652, 743, 779, 797, 1076, 1080, 1082, 1084-94; *Engel v. Vitale*, 370 U.S. 421 (1962); *Abington School District v. Schempp*, 374 U.S. 203 (1963); *Epperson v. Arkansas*, 393 U.S. 97 (1968); *Lemon v. Kurtzman*, 403 U.S. 602 (1971); *Griswold v. Connecticut*, 381 U.S. 481 (1965); *Roe v. Wade*, 410 U.S. 113 (1973); *Street v. New York*, 394 U.S. 576 (1969); *Spence v. Washington*, 418 U.S. 405 (1974).

found most sustaining; it also came to be more strongly associated than ever before with political causes that many Americans regarded as profoundly unsettling and immoral, rather than religiously sanctified. The outcome has been not the further spread of secularization that Ahlstrom anticipated in 1972, but rather the more Tocquevillean scenario documented above: the resurgence of more traditional forms of religious belief, now often politicized into efforts to reverse many of the liberal judicial doctrines and social policies of the 1960s and early 1970s. To be sure, this development is not wholly new. Many of the reforms advocated by theological liberals from abolition onward were controversial in their time and fueled conservative reactions. But today, advocates of social reform are probably less able than ever before in U.S. history to build coalitions via religious appeals that can move theological conservatives as well as liberals. In their modern forms, both theologically and politically liberal positions have become more anti-traditionalist than any of their predecessors, and they have come to seem profoundly anti-religious and unacceptable to growing numbers of Americans. True, most Americans are not ready to turn back the clock in all regards. But many are anxious to do so in some important respects, and relatively few are eager to push the discussed changes further. Hence it is that the never-popular cause of rendering religion more compatible with reason, whatever the cost to traditional beliefs, is suffering so severely in today's climate that it rarely musters the strength to venture out openly into the political arena.

The Implications for Principles of "Equal Treatment"

I mean to make no secret of the fact that, as a liberal who believes that many of the political and intellectual changes of the 1960s deserve to be extended, not reversed, I regard the current state of affairs as morally regrettable. Let me nonetheless note the important points on which I share common ground with many traditionalist believers. In keeping with the concerns for truth and intellectual honesty that are central to Enlightenment rationalism, I accept that, though I can offer reasons and evidence to support my views, I cannot claim to know for certain that they are true. I also cannot rule out the possibility, faint though it seems to me, that conservative religious beliefs I reject are in fact correct; and

190

I concede that in many ways they do good in the world. In any case, I accept that Tocqueville may be right, and that humanity may not be capable of moving much beyond widespread adherence to traditional religious beliefs, whatever my own hopes might be. Hence I cannot deny that, in principle, these outlooks deserve to be treated by governments with no less respect than my own.

Indeed, the first way in which I am likely to part company with many proponents of "equal treatment" is by insisting on that principle more consistently. Like Justice Sandra Day O'Connor, I believe that equal treatment is an appropriate approach for analyzing not only the First Amendment's ban on establishments of religion but its religious free-exercise clause, along with the religious test clause of Article IV, clause 3, and the Fourteenth Amendment's equal protection clause as applied to religion.[14] Not all agree. In the same essay cited earlier, Michael McConnell argues that although the "historical evidence is limited and on some points mixed," on balance the free exercise clause can and should be read as granting judicially enforceable protections to the conscientious conduct of religious believers that are not accorded to adherents of secular moral perspectives.[15]

The historical evidence certainly is mixed, and McConnell over-states the support it gives to his view. He contends that the "central point" on which the dominant Madisonian perspective on religious free exercise "differs from Locke, Jefferson, and other Enlightenment figures" is that Madison believed, in the founder's own words, that duties to humanity's "Creator" were "precedent both in order of time and degree of obligation, to the claims of Civil Society." Hence, McConnell concludes that for Madison "the dictates of religious faith must take precedence over the laws of the state," contrary to the claims of Enlightenment adherents.[16]

This contrast is, however, overdrawn. As McConnell later notes without comment, Locke in fact argued something very similar, con-

14. See O'Connor's concurrence with the result in *Board of Education of Kiryas Joel Village School District v. Grumet*, 114 S. Ct. 2481 (1994).

15. McConnell, "The Origins and Historical Understanding of Free Exercise of Religion," pp. 1511-12, 1515-17.

16. McConnell, "The Origins and Historical Understanding of Free Exercise of Religion," p. 1453.

tending that everyone "should do what he in his conscience is persuaded to be acceptable to the Almighty" because "Obedience is due in the first place to God, and afterwards to the laws." Locke therefore counseled against laws that needlessly restricted religious practices. He nonetheless did insist that actions which were "not lawful in the ordinary course of life" due to legitimate regulatory reasons could not be made legal by the claim that they were done "in the worship of God." If believers felt compelled to do things properly forbidden by law, they should "undergo the punishment" in the spirit of conscientious civil disobedience. Again, however, it is not clear that Madison differed on these points. He argued that the "equality which ought to be the basis of every law" would be violated if some claims of religious conscience were given "peculiar exemptions" and "extraordinary privileges" not available to those "whose minds have not yet yielded to the evidence" that convinced such believers. Madison was not explicit on whether this position meant no special exemptions for religious beliefs as opposed to claims of secular moral conscience, or only no special privileges for some religions against others. His emphasis, however, was on assuring that those "whose opinions in Religion" did not conform to "those of the Legislative authority" were not thereby degraded "from the equal rank of Citizens." Taken literally, that position would require equal protection for nonbelievers. And Madison steadfastly denied that the truly religious were entitled to "pre-eminencies over their fellow citizens." Hence it is far from clear that he thought the priority of obligations to God justified special religious exemptions from otherwise valid laws, any more than Locke did.[17]

In any case, it should be clear that the "equality" of civic standing that Madison espoused would be greatly endangered today if judicial rulings and legislative statutes adopted an "equal treatment" approach to establishment clause issues while upholding McConnell's "special religious privilege" approach to free exercise claims. Such a regime would permit politically and culturally powerful religious groups to receive every form of public assistance available to secular ones, while

17. Locke, *A Letter Concerning Toleration* (Indianapolis: Bobbs-Merrill, 1955), pp. 39, 47-48; James Madison, "Freedom of Conscience: Memorial and Remonstrance," in *The Mind of the Founder*, ed. Marvin Meyers (Indianapolis: Bobbs-Merrill, 1973), pp. 10-11, 13; McConnell, "The Origins and Historical Understanding of Free Exercise of Religion," p. 1497.

also permitting those religious groups to escape the rare legislated obligations that ran contrary to their beliefs. Nonbelievers in modern America, who already know themselves to be a minority, would thus in all likelihood find the public arena ever more filled with publicly assisted religious adherents, and they would be aware that the government was officially committed to deferring to those believers in some circumstances where nonbelievers would have to obey. Under such circumstances, it is hard to think that nonbelieving citizens would perceive themselves and their views as respected by their government just as much as those of the faithful, because they would not be.[18]

Accordingly, the only approach that is genuinely compatible with equal treatment, equal protection, and equal respect for all citizens is treating claims of religious and secular moral consciences the same. Fully recognizing the historical, philosophical, and moral force of claims for deference to sincere conscientious beliefs and practices whenever possible, I would place all such claims in a "preferred position" as defined by modern constitutional doctrines: governmental infringements upon such conscientious claims would be sustainable in court only if it were shown that they were necessary for compelling governmental interests. I concede, however, that extending "preferred position" protection to secular as well as religious consciences might have significant consequences for the results courts reach via that test. When a legal requirement such as national military service is opposed only by a small number of religious adherents, the state interest at stake may not seem so compelling, or at least a means like universal conscription may not seem so necessary. But if the population entitled to make conscientious claims against governmental policies is enlarged to include all those advancing morally conscientious beliefs, religious and nonreligious, judges might properly conclude that granting the exemption would be too destructive

18. It may be objected that the Court has in the past interpreted statutory exemptions for religious believers by defining "religion" so broadly that few if any claims of secular moral conscience would be excluded. I agree with Stephen Carter and others, however, that such a broad definition of religion (which the Court has not adopted in its readings of the free exercise clause) renders the term opaque and useless. Even more importantly, such maneuvers fall short of full and explicit recognition of the equal claims of secular moral consciences. See, for example, *United States v. Seeger*, 380 U.S. 163 (1965); *Welsh v. United States*, 398 U.S. 33 (1970); Carter, *The Culture of Disbelief*, pp. 17-18.

of governmental purposes. The upshot might be something like the approach Locke recommended: laws would usually be upheld in court, and conscientious objectors would have only the option of civil disobedience, accompanied by acceptance of suitable punishments. That result may often be unsatisfying, but if the alternative is to grant religious believers special privileges that deny others the "equal rank of Citizens," I believe the more egalitarian standard is to be preferred.

The same sensitivity to concerns for equal civic standing and for the realities of the power of religiosity in American life should, I believe, guide interpretations of the establishment clause. With the proponents of "equal treatment," I therefore accept that, insofar as judicial rulings and public policies attempt to disfavor religious beliefs, practices, or organizations simply because they are religious, and insofar as laws or customs try to prevent religious viewpoints from being articulated in public life, they are undesirable and wrong. I oppose the view, put forth most magisterially by John Rawls, that we should ask citizens not to employ controversial religious arguments in the processes of "public reason" that should characterize political debates.[19] I agree with the Supreme Court that a law must have a "secular purpose" *as well as* religious ones if it is not to run afoul of the establishment clause, but that it remains perfectly proper for believers to advance religious rationales along with secular ones for their preferred policies.[20] Jefferson was wrong to suggest that there should be a solid "wall" between church and state, between religious consciences and public arguments. The establishment clause should instead be understood as setting up a dam between religion and politics. That dam should be designed to regulate the flow of predominant religious perspectives into the fields of public life in order to prevent those fields from being submerged under a flood of religiosity; but it should not be used to prevent them from being irrigated by whatever vital elements religious viewpoints may provide.

Here again, however, the principle of equal treatment ought to be consistently applied. If religious arguments are offered in the public sphere, then we should accept that it is entirely appropriate to subject

19. Rawls, *Political Liberalism* (New York: Columbia University Press, 1993), pp. 212-22, 240-54.

20. The modern "secular purpose" doctrine is frequently attributed to *Abington School District v. Schempp*, 374 U.S. 203 (1963).

them to searching, even scathing criticisms. That point seems obvious; yet many who urge greater receptivity to religious arguments in the public realm appear to regard such criticism as offensive and wrong. In *The Culture of Disbelief*, for instance, in the very first example Stephen Carter gives of improper hostility toward religion, he complains that after "a national magazine devoted its cover story to an investigation of prayer," it subsequently published a single letter from a "disgruntled reader" who wanted to know "why so much space had been dedicated to such nonsense." Carter insists that, despite the undeniable statistical rarity of his views, this writer was politically and culturally "in the American mainstream," and that "for Americans to take their religions seriously" is thus to "risk assignment to the lunatic fringe."[21]

Leaving aside the fact that his own announcements of his religious seriousness have somehow escaped this fate, Carter's argument here comes close to suggesting that public discourse is unfair if even a single letter writer feels entitled to call religious perspectives "nonsense" and urge less attention to them. But it is perfectly possible that many religious beliefs are nonsense. If we reinforce already widespread beliefs that it is impolite or even impermissible to say so publicly, then we will be according religious claims not equality but rather a privileged position in public discourse that no other viewpoints receive.

Indeed, I believe they enjoy such a position already: the occasional calls to keep religious arguments out of political arenas are, I suspect, often misguided efforts to evade the unpalatable task of publicly criticizing the content of theological claims. Nonetheless, with the Enlightenment thinkers I continue to believe that it is possible we might all learn from discussing religious beliefs seriously, which must include discussing them critically. Fully recognizing the divisive potential of doing so, then, I believe we would be better off in the long run with a public arena where religious claims could not only be put forth but also challenged.

Going beyond public practices to constitutional interpretation, I believe that Justice O'Connor's Madison-like concern to make sure that all citizens are accorded equal status by government has produced the most promising position in contemporary establishment-clause jurisprudence and the best articulation of an "equal treatment" approach.

21. Carter, *The Culture of Disbelief*, p. 4.

Since the mid-1980s, she has been developing what she terms an "endorsement" test for establishment cases. It aims to prevent governments from either endorsing or disapproving any and all religions, in order to insure that no one is denied equal standing in the political community because of his or her viewpoint on religion.[22] With certain exceptions discussed below, that general approach seems to me sound; and I also agree with the manner in which O'Connor applied it in the recent *Rosenberger* decision, the ruling that has most sparked current discussions of the principle of equal treatment. Because the University of Virginia was funding nonreligious student publications as well as one religious paper, and because the university accompanied all its funding with explicit disavowals of the various publications' viewpoints, the equal access to such funding sought by the evangelical student publication *Wide Awake: A Christian Perspective* was not only constitutionally permitted but required. Justice David Souter's eloquent dissent in *Rosenberger* correctly observed that bans on public funds for "the direct subsidization of preaching the word" form a central current of establishment clause jurisprudence; but many forms of indirect aid with the same financial impact have long been quite properly upheld. The directness of any financial aid is important only because it can foster the appearance if not the reality of governmental favoritism toward one or all religions, the concern of the "endorsement" test. And since the financial support in this case could not reasonably be construed as such an endorsement, it should not have been disallowed.[23]

Nonetheless, I believe there is abundant cause for concern about the recent legislative and judicial trends toward provision of more public funds to religious schools and religious student groups. Those trends must be viewed in light of the larger historical pattern of American public education, which shows that the nation's schools have generally favored religious over nonreligious perspectives, and in light of current polling data, which show that most Americans still believe schools should do so. Moreover, many of today's religious conservatives and

22. O'Connor first defined her "endorsement" approach in her concurring opinion in *Lynch v. Donnelly,* 465 U.S. 668 (1984). She linked it with an emphasis on "equal treatment" in her concurrence with the result in *Board of Education of Kiryas Joel Village School District v. Grumet,* 114 S. Ct. 2481 (1994).

23. *Rosenberger v. The Rector and Visitors of the University of Virginia,* 115 S. Ct. 2510 (1995).

proponents of aid to parochial schools openly believe that American education should restore this preference for religiosity, generally defined in terms of the versions most prevalent in the contemporary United States. Hence today many forms of governmental assistance to religious schools and groups may easily by interpreted by most citizens as renewed governmental endorsement of the superiority of conventional religious viewpoints, especially in communities where the denominations receiving aid already command the allegiance of much of the local populace. The endorsement test will fail to provide equal treatment if it is not applied with close attention to the empirical realities of how governmental funding of religious educational bodies is being understood and experienced by those affected. If judges find that a particular type of aid is commonly interpreted as representing an official preference for religious viewpoints, it must be disallowed, even if the aid is titularly available on an equal basis to all groups.

Furthermore, some recent decisions make me more worried than *Rosenberger* does about whether O'Connor and her fellow justices are applying her "endorsement" approach in ways sufficiently sensitive to the real-world context of U.S. governmental actions. That context, again, is one in which public avowals of traditionalist religious beliefs are ubiquitous and popular, while public criticism of religion is muted and disdained. Accordingly, I disagree with the Supreme Court's decision in *Lynch v. Donnelly*; I would judge that when a city owns and erects a nativity scene in a park, the inevitable widespread inference is that Christian viewpoints remain publicly favored in America. Adding the symbolism of other religions only broadens the public endorsement of religion against purely secular moral views.[24] It is true that under current rulings, private groups critical of traditional religions could erect counter-displays if they so desired. But in a massively pious nation, secular groups will frequently lack the resources to match the efforts of religious believers in many locales; and when the government is openly funding popular religious viewpoints, secularists are likely to experience well-founded fears that they are severely disadvantaging themselves before public officials and their fellow citizens if they express what they conscientiously believe. Such fears and disadvantages are hallmarks of second-class citizenship.

24. *Lynch v. Donnelly*, 465 U.S. 668 (1984).

Attention to the realities of how citizens are situated in the United States also raises concerns about a yet more controversial "equal treatment" ruling. In 1995, the Supreme Court decided that the Constitution required the city of Cleveland to allow the Ku Klux Klan to erect a cross in a public park facing the state capitol.[25] Taken in the abstract, that result was indeed demanded by the equal treatment principle. Heinous as they are, the views of many Klansmen are genuinely though unconventionally religious, and if public spaces are to be made generally available for groups to express their views, there is no way these perspectives can be excluded.

Yet if no more is done, I question whether the consequences of permitting such displays amount to genuine "equal treatment." In a society that remains pervasively structured by the legacies of legal systems of white supremacy that were justified in religious terms through most of their history, I fear this permission inevitably signals to all Americans that the government is instead once again condoning such inegalitarian views, rather than adhering to the rejection of racism that is supposed to be public policy in the United States today. What else is an African-American likely to think when she or he sees a Klan cross boldly displayed at the center of a city's government? Even if that cross is opposed by, for example, an NAACP display, the impression that the government is turning a helpfully blind eye toward efforts to reassert white supremacy, as it has so often in the past, is not likely to be dispelled.

Under such circumstances, I believe the "no endorsement" standard requires that Klan symbols be accompanied not just by governmental disclaimers, which are also likely to be ineffectual, but by explicit governmental repudiations of their historic meaning. It is true that posting such statements would single out certain religious views for official public criticism, an apparent violation of O'Connor's "endorsement" standard. The views that would be thus criticized, however, embody and advocate denials of the equal protection guarantees enshrined in the nation's constitutional and statutory laws. It can hardly be wrong for the government to state its support for its own policies. Moreover, if it fails to do so in this context, its silence is not likely to signal its commitment to "equal treatment" so much as its renewed

25. *Capitol Square Review Board v. Pinette,* 115 S. Ct. 2440 (1995).

willingness to retreat from genuinely recognizing all Americans as equal citizens.

Let me acknowledge, however, that my readings of what the government is likely to be seen as "endorsing" in these difficult cases are disputable and may be wrong. As a social scientist who is not a lawyer, I believe that it might even be desirable for courts to begin to use some actual empirical evidence of how different governmental actions involving religion are understood in the pertinent American communities, rather than relying simply on judicial intuitions of what reasonable people might construe as "endorsements" of religion. Existing data make me think such research would vindicate the claims I am making here, but it might undercut them. Even if it did not, such evidence admittedly has great limitations as well, and judgments about when government was inappropriately "endorsing" some or all religions would remain difficult.

But at a minimum, I want to insist that all judicial and legislative efforts to apply the standard of "equal treatment" must be concerned to insure that, in the United States as it exists today, governmental policies do not really amount to what they have been through most of our past: arrangements designed to accommodate powerful religious perspectives rather than to accord all viewpoints on religion genuinely equal respect. The fact that law is currently being changed in many ways to comply with positions put forth by groups that include many who believe that religion should be specially privileged in American life is thus deeply disturbing; and I believe courts must not be blind to the aims and likely beneficiaries of the positions they are being asked to adopt. If my view of the implications of "equal treatment" were followed, I do not know whether long-eclipsed efforts to pursue more fully reasonable forms of religiosity would fare any better than at present, and I do not know if Americans would be better off if they did. But I believe that the United States would then be undertaking a highly desirable experiment of genuinely according equal treatment to both religious and nonreligious perspectives, an experiment that today, as throughout our past, remains at best an unredeemed promissory note of the American commitment to enlightened, egalitarian constitutional self-governance.

199

The Implications of
Equal Treatment

In this book, eight authors have presented eight perspectives on equal treatment as a basic point of departure for thinking about religious freedom for all and, more specifically, for interpreting the establishment clause of the First Amendment. In so doing, they have presented much information about and varied perspectives on the equal treatment concept. On certain points they agree. All are fully committed to the widest possible freedom of religion for all; none advocates a Christian nation or some other form of theocracy.

Yet the perspectives presented in the foregoing chapters reveal deep and persistent differences among the authors. They have given us compelling countervailing arguments about the utility of equal treatment as an approach to interpreting the establishment clause and more generally about the proper relationship between the institutions of church and state in the United States. On the issue of whether equal treatment holds promise of moving the United States closer to full religious freedom for all and a genuine religious neutrality by government, we see the clearest differences of opinion between the first five authors on the one hand and the last three authors on the other. There are also more subtle and probably more important differences in terms of the assumptions and frameworks on the basis of which the eight authors are operating.

In this concluding chapter, we will first review the main contentions presented by the eight authors on the legal and public-policy implications of equal treatment. Given these insights, we will then propose some tentative conclusions about how we believe the Supreme Court and policy makers can use equal treatment to advance the religious rights of all American citizens in a pluralistic society.

The Case for Equal Treatment

A basic point of agreement for those who support equal treatment is that the Supreme Court has disadvantaged religious groups in various ways with its strict separationist reading of the establishment clause. The establishment clause implies that the government must be neutral concerning religion. But strict separationism equates that neutrality with the government withdrawing all support for religion, and sees the establishment clause as mandating the withdrawal of that support. This excludes direct state funding for religious elementary and secondary schools and for the religious activities of faith-based social services agencies, as well as state support for religious speech on public land or in public schools. Under this interpretation of the clause, however, the state may aid secular speech and provide benefits to secular activities and organizations without violating the principle of governmental neutrality, since strict separationists presume that secular viewpoints are neutral toward religion.

According to the proponents of equal treatment, this rendering of the establishment clause is misguided because secularism is anything but neutral. It is a worldview, an ideological perspective that is often-times hostile to organized religion. As a consequence, strict separationism has resulted not in state neutrality toward religion but in discrimination against it and state support for secular viewpoints. Michael McConnell points out that under strict separationist doctrine, the courts have denied access to public spaces to students who wish to engage in religious speech or expression, but they have allowed students desiring to engage in anti-religious speech to use those spaces. Charles Glenn contends that the effect of strict separationism has been a denial of public funds to religious schools and a limitation on the right of parents to choose an appropriate education for their children. James Skillen and Robert Destro assert that the Court's doctrine forces religious nonprofit

201

organizations to assume a secular identity if they want to receive government aid, but does not similarly challenge the autonomy of secularly based organizations. In each instance, strict church-state separation disadvantages religion.

A second argument posed by those who support equal treatment is that under strict separationism, the Court has adopted a liberal Enlightenment understanding of religion that views faith primarily as a private matter of individual choice. With this understanding, the liberal state can be both secular and neutral toward religion so long as it protects individual rights, including the free exercise of religion. Since the Constitution protects the expression of religion in the private sphere, it doesn't seem all that significant, from a strict separationist perspective, if the state discriminates against the public expression of religion.

As several of these authors have noted, however, religion is as much a public matter as it is a private one. The religious service organizations and educational activities in which churches are actively involved are natural public expressions of faith. Therefore, defining religion as purely a private matter and protecting only individual religious rights is insufficient, because that denies the public manifestation of faith and devalues the role of religious mediating institutions. This issue has become particularly relevant with the expansion of the comprehensive administrative state into areas traditionally left to local and religious control. Because the state increasingly has a hand in more and more areas of education, health care, and social services, the "private" realm where religion is free to act with neither the help nor the hindrance of government is shrinking, and the "public" realm where government is free to support secular activities and programs, but not religious ones, is expanding.

Finally, those authors who endorse an equal treatment principle argue that strict separationism has restricted the religious liberty rights of people of faith. As Carl Esbeck notes, the point of strict separationism was to vitalize religion, not to impede it, by freeing churches from the corrupting influences of the state. According to strict separationists, church schools and social-service agencies are better off without government aid, which would necessarily come with a series of regulations that would restrict the autonomy of religious groups and threaten religious liberty. The rejoinder to this view is that strict separationism, far from

202

advancing religious liberty, restricts it because it handicaps people of faith when they seek to live out their faith in public settings. The absence of state funding for religious schools, for example, limits the religious liberty rights of parents who would like a religious education for their children but cannot afford it. Their freedom to follow the dictates of conscience is constrained. A more robust form of religious freedom would be one in which the state took positive measures aimed at protecting and promoting the right of religious believers to act on the basis of their faith in public ways.

Equal treatment is seen as a remedy to the shortcomings of strict separationism because it is considered to be more genuinely neutral among religions and between religious and secular points of view, because it protects religious groups in public as well as in private life, and because it advances religious liberty. It is important to note that the authors in this book who support equal treatment believe that the Supreme Court did not go nearly far enough in the *Pinette* and *Rosenberger* decisions of 1995 to strike down a strict separationist reading of the establishment clause. There is a consensus among these contributors that those Court decisions are of limited utility because of their narrowness.

What is significant about these cases is that the Supreme Court equated religious speech with other forms of secular speech on the grounds that religious views are no more ideologically biased than secular ones. Rather than discriminate against religious speech because it is religious, the Court recognized that such speech deserves the same rights as all other kinds of expression. As many of the authors point out, a jurisprudence based upon equal treatment should logically lead the Court to abandon the claim that the state can best achieve neutrality toward religion by the government's withdrawing all support for religion. The state is truly neutral only if it is evenhanded in its treatment of religious and secular systems of belief.

According to its advocates, equal treatment would return the Supreme Court to the original understanding of the First Amendment religion clauses, which call for equality of treatment among all persons. The result would be support for a pluralistic political culture that would create a level playing field for a myriad of secular and religious entities. The implications of equal treatment would be profound for religious nonprofit organizations and schools. Under equal treatment, the state would no longer deny benefits to groups solely on the basis of their religious viewpoints, but would be obligated to accommodate and support education and social services provided in a religious setting, if it was accommodating and supporting similar programs provided in secular settings. Religious groups could no longer be denied benefits that their secularly based counterparts were receiving. According to the advocates of equal treatment, this would advance religious liberty rights for those persons whose faith calls them to live out their beliefs in public as well as private settings.

The Case against Equal Treatment

The three chapters in this book that challenge equal treatment combine liberal arguments in favor of church-state separation with claims about the unintended and possibly negative effects of equal treatment for religious individuals and groups. Each of the authors contends that religion has benefited from the Supreme Court's doctrine of strict church-state separation. Derek Davis argues that American religion is robust because the Court's policy of church-state separation has enabled churches to remain free of government funding and regulation. He claims that the support to religion that equal treatment makes possible would rob churches of the voluntary spirit that has sustained them over time, and would threaten the liberty of religious groups that would need to comply with restrictive government regulations. He concludes that it is ironic that some religionists in America wish to replicate an accommodationist church-state policy that is common in European countries where religious life is moribund.

Gregg Ivers and Rogers Smith note that religious majorities in America have historically used accommodationist arrangements to curry government favor and to discriminate against religious and secular minorities. They connect arguments in favor of equal treatment with a social and political climate that they claim favors, rather than discriminates against, Christian views. Given this assumption, they fear that all groups, both secular and religious, would not be treated with equal impartiality but that socially and politically powerful religious groups would receive special treatment.

Ivers further contends that church-state separation provides a

204

countercheck on the power of religious majorities and has enabled Jews, along with other religious minorities, to prosper in the United States. Smith concludes that unless policy makers and the Court carefully and consistently monitor the application of equal treatment, the result is likely to be discrimination against secular views that have always been unpopular in America and that command neither the political resources nor the social prominence to counter the religious views of the majority.

The other main point on which these authors agree is that if the Supreme Court applies an equal treatment analysis to establishment clause cases, where strict church-state separationism arguably disadvantages religionists, the Court should also apply this principle to free-exercise-clause cases, where separationism has advantaged religious believers. The effects of a consistent equal treatment approach to church-state issues would not, however, redound to the benefit of religious individuals and groups. Davis points out that the Court's determination to treat all speech equally would remove the special constitutional status that religious belief currently enjoys. Religious individuals and institutions would no longer be in a preferred position relative to their nonreligious counterparts. The result of equal treatment, therefore, would be legal challenges to the special protection that the law currently provides to religionists.

Smith agrees that an equal treatment analysis is the preferred path for the Court to take in future religion clause cases, but he ironically concludes that because of its egalitarian thrust, equal treatment would limit, not increase, the situations in which the state would allow religious exemptions from otherwise binding laws and regulations. The reason for this is simple: with two thousand identifiable religions and an indeterminate number of secular systems of belief in America, it would be too costly and destructive to the government purpose to grant so many legal exemptions. A similar argument could be made about the inability of the government to provide financial benefits to all these systems of belief. Given this limitation, the Court would either favor politically powerful religious groups, and thereby degrade the ideological views of other systems of belief, or grant "religious" exemptions equally and substantially limit the situations in which they would be allowed. The former result would fail to satisfy the dictates of equal treatment, while the latter should concern the lover of religious liberty.

205

Equal Treatment and Religious Liberty

In our view, the chapters in this book demonstrate that the principle of equal treatment has the potential to increase the religious freedom of all Americans, but that the concept needs refining in order to address some of the problems that several of the authors have raised. We believe that equal treatment is a means to an end, and that end or goal is substantive governmental neutrality among all religions and between religious and secular systems of belief. This neutrality is defined by the government's minimizing, to quote Douglas Laycock (as we did in Chapter 1), "the extent to which [it] either encourages or discourages religious belief or disbelief, practice or nonpractice, observance or non-observance."[1] Government policies should make it neither harder nor easier to follow the dictates of conscience; they should neither burden nor favor persons or groups whose consciences have been shaped by a particular faith tradition or by a secular belief structure. We are convinced that this type of government neutrality can be better attained with equal treatment than with strict separationism.

Equal treatment rightly appreciates that the relationship of religiously based and secularly based systems of belief to the First Amendment should be essentially the same. Both religious and secular belief structures constitute worldviews that are, as we noted in Chapter 1, competing for adherents in today's society. As sociologist James Davison Hunter has demonstrated, the most significant religious divide today is no longer between Catholic and Protestant or Christian and Jew, but between traditional religionists of various traditions and secularly minded persons.[2] Government should be neutral in the contest between religionists and secularists. Strict separationism, by contrast, discriminates against religious views because it allows the government to favor secular speech and to provide funding for a variety of secularly based social-service agencies and schools, but excludes their religiously based counterparts. This is not religious neutrality.

The decision of one of the lower courts in the Rosenberger case is

1. Laycock, "Formal, Substantive, and Disaggregated Neutrality toward Religion," *DePaul Law Review* 39 (1990): 1001.
2. See Hunter, *Culture Wars: The Struggle to Define America* (New York: Basic Books, 1991).

instructive. This is the case that dealt with the University of Virginia's policy of funding a wide range of student publications, but refusing to fund religious publications, including one called *Wide Awake*. At one point, the decision of the federal Court of Appeals for the Fourth Circuit stated that the University of Virginia's proscribing the funding of religious organizations "thus creates an uneven playing field on which the advantage is tilted towards CIOs [student organizations] engaged in wholly secular modes of expression."[3] The court went on to hold that *Wide Awake*'s "receipt of government benefits [had been made dependent] upon their foregoing constitutionally protected religious expression."[4] Yet that same court went on to hold that this uneven playing field which discriminated against religion was required by the strict separationist interpretations of the establishment clause currently held by the Supreme Court. It therefore upheld the constitutionality of the university's not funding the religiously based student publications, even though it was funding a wide range of secular publications.

However, we are convinced that equal treatment, with neutrality as its central goal, would increase religious freedom for all Americans. In establishment clause cases, the doctrine implicitly acknowledges that religion not only is a matter of private faith but has public aspects as well. This is a basic fact about which Robert Bellah and his associates have written in *Habits of the Heart*: "Yet religion, and certainly biblical religion, is concerned with the whole of life — with social, economic, and political matters as well as with private and personal ones. Not only has biblical language continued to be part of American public and political discourse, the churches have continuously exerted influence on public life right up to the present time."[5] Religious leaders as diverse as Martin Luther King, Jr., and Pope John Paul II have given testimony by their words and lives to the public facet of religion. The Supreme Court needs to recognize and accommodate this basic fact. The expansion of the comprehensive administrative state in recent decades has involved

---

3. *Rosenberger v. Rector*, Court of Appeals for the Fourth Circuit, 18 F. 3rd 281 (1994).

4. *Rosenberger v. Rector*, Court of Appeals for the Fourth Circuit, 18 F. 3rd 281 (1994).

5. Bellah et al., *Habits of the Heart: Individualism and Commitment in American Life* (New York: Harper & Row, 1986), p. 220.

the government in the provision of social services that private religious agencies also provide. It violates the principle of substantive neutrality for the government to finance secular schools and social-service agencies and to refuse to finance similarly situated, parallel religious organizations on account of their religious character. Governmental neutrality demands that the diverse religious and secular communities that make up a nation have a right to live out their beliefs in the context of freedom, with those beliefs being neither favored nor burdened by the state.

This book has concentrated upon equal treatment as it relates to establishment clause issues, since this is the context in which it has emerged in Supreme Court rulings, but several authors have also raised free exercise concerns. Thus some comments on equal treatment and the free exercise of religion are in order. One concern that has been raised is this: If equal treatment is to be the norm in establishment clause cases, should it not also be the norm in free-exercise-clause cases? It has been claimed that this would result in the loss of the special protections that the free exercise clause now gives religion. In free-exercise-clause cases, substantive neutrality demands that the government should not make either religious or secular beliefs and practices illegal or pass laws of general application that negatively affect certain religious groups unless there is a compelling public interest for doing so.[6] To do so would disadvantage or place burdens on those faiths that would be affected by such laws. It is wrong, however, to see the free exercise clause — even when fully developed and applied — as giving religious adherents certain advantages or privileges that others are denied. Rather, it should be seen as leveling the playing field, as assuring that government is not making it either easier or harder to follow the dictates of one's religion. It thereby is rooted in the neutrality or equal treatment principle.

Under fully developed free-exercise protections, the person who, for example, refuses to work Saturday because that is his golfing day would not be eligible for unemployment benefits; but the person who refuses to work Saturday because that is his religion's holy day would be eligible. The difference between the two is that the golfer's free exercise of reli-

6. The Religious Freedom Restoration Act is a good example of Congress attempting to enact into law this sort of governmental neutrality. See Public Law 103-41 (103d Congress).

gion is not being interfered with in any way. And that is the issue. The Sabbatarian may prefer to play golf on Sunday or Monday, but could be required to work on those days on pain of losing his unemployment benefits. As golfers the two are being treated equally — their favorite golfing day may be interfered with by the demands of an employer with no government financial compensation. As religious persons they are also being treated equally — if the dictates of their religion are interfered with by an employer, they are both eligible for government financial compensation. For the Sabbatarian, that may relate to not working on Saturday; for someone else it may take some other form. For the totally nonreligious person who has a well-defined secular belief system that operates as the functional equivalent of religion in his or her life, the same sort of government protections should apply to that person's dictates of conscience.

Thus the free exercise clause really does not give religious persons certain advantages that no one else enjoys. It is rooted in neutrality and equal treatment; it assures that the government will not make it either easier or more difficult for anyone to live out his or her deepest beliefs. Government is thereby treating persons equally in equal circumstances. It is neutral on matters of faith.

A second concern is that following the equal treatment principle would cause an increase in the number of groups and individuals who would claim a religious exemption from a law or government regulation. Rogers Smith makes this point in his essay, and it is well taken. Smith emphasizes that one of the issues the Court must address as it moves toward an equal treatment doctrine is how to define what constitutes a religious or secular worldview that is deserving of the Court's protection. But this issue is not unique to an equal treatment approach to religious liberty. Whenever religion is specified as a protected human activity, or whenever, for that matter, religious activity is held to be strictly separated from other nonreligious human endeavors, religion must be defined. Law continually involves making distinctions and establishing categories, and there is always the possibility of difficult, borderline cases. But that ought not to serve as a basis for rejecting the legitimacy of making distinctions and establishing categories.

A third significant concern is that equal treatment and the public funding of religious groups it would allow might provide the opportunity for socially and politically powerful groups to win state aid, but would disadvantage weaker religious and secular minorities that lack those resources. This has happened all too often in the past. However, this kind of discriminatory treatment would be possible only if the Court abandoned the neutrality principle that stands at the heart of equal treatment. If certain large groups received a disproportionate amount of state support and recognition, or if small, weak groups were disadvantaged by certain rulings, that would clearly be unequal treatment, and legal remedies would be in order. Equal treatment does not call for a no-holds-barred political struggle for governmental favors, with a winner-take-all outcome. Rather, equal treatment says that religious groups may not be discriminated against *because of* their religious nature.[7] Thus, if government policies would favor one religious group over another, or would generally favor either religious groups over secular or secular groups over religious, there would be legal remedies available independent of political clout. Thus the more likely outcome of equal treatment is that its beneficiaries would be both religious and secular minorities who have a strong desire to provide social services within their own faith tradition, but who currently have few opportunities to express their faith in this way. There is evidence to support this supposition: the experience of other countries that have these kinds of funding arrangements for religious schools and agencies suggests that it is not inevitable that public policy would favor religious majorities. Australia and the Netherlands are two examples of countries that have seen the development of a pluralistic political culture in which the education and social-service programs of a myriad religious organizations are financed equally by the state, including those of minority Muslim and Hindu groups.[8]

We are thoroughly convinced that there are theoretical and, increasingly, practical problems with strict separationism that are constricting religious freedom in the United States. Equal treatment holds the prom-

7. Under equal treatment, religiously based service organizations could, of course, be discriminated against on bases other than religion, as long as there was a rational, reasonable basis for such discrimination. Government could, for example, stipulate that only organizations of a certain size could receive a certain benefit (thereby eliminating some religious organizations), if size was relevant to achieving the goals of the program providing the benefits.

8. See Stephen V. Monsma and J. Christopher Soper, *The Challenge of Pluralism: Church and State in Five Democracies* (Lanham, Md.: Rowman & Littlefield, 1997).

ise of being a better approach. Yet the concerns raised by the critics of equal treatment are legitimate and worthy of careful consideration. As equal treatment evolves — if indeed it does continue to evolve — it is important that its advocates, ourselves included, listen carefully to the voices of the critics; it is no less important that the critics listen to the voices of those who see the discriminatory effects of strict separationism. A genuine governmental neutrality on matters of religion may emerge out of the conversation between the advocates and the critics of equal treatment. If so, greater religious freedom for all will be the final result. It is our hope that this book will contribute to that conversation.